95 Prostheses

95 Prostheses

Appendages and Musings
for the Body of Christ in Transition

Frank G. Honeycutt

CASCADE *Books* • Eugene, Oregon

95 PROSTHESES

Appendages and Musings for the Body of Christ in Transition

Copyright © 2018 Frank G. Honeycutt. All rights reserved. Except for brief quotations in critical publications or reviews, no part of this book may be reproduced in any manner without prior written permission from the publisher. Write: Permissions, Wipf and Stock Publishers, 199 W. 8th Ave., Suite 3, Eugene, OR 97401.

Cascade Books
An Imprint of Wipf and Stock Publishers
199 W. 8th Ave., Suite 3
Eugene, OR 97401

www.wipfandstock.com

PAPERBACK ISBN: 978-1-5326-0539-0
HARDCOVER ISBN: 978-1-5326-0541-3
EBOOK ISBN: 978-1-5326-0540-6

Cataloguing-in-Publication data:

Names: Honeycutt, Frank G.

Title: 95 prostheses : appendages and musings for the body of Christ in transition / Frank G. Honeycutt.

Description: Eugene, OR: Cascade Books, 2018 | Includes bibliographical references and index.

Identifiers: ISBN 978-1-5326-0539-0 (paperback) | ISBN 978-1-5326-0541-3 (hardcover) | ISBN 978-1-5326-0540-6 (ebook)

Subjects: LCSH: 1. Theology. | 2. Church Year. | I. Title. | subject

Classification: BR85 .H55 2018 (print) | BR85 (ebook)

Manufactured in the U.S.A.　　　　　　　　　　　　　　DECEMBER 21, 2017

In memory of Frances Hudson Christmas

1929—2012

Contents

Preface ix

I. ADVENT/CHRISTMAS

Introduction to the Season 1

1. Jesus the Safecracker 5
2. Ready and Waiting 9
3. The Odd Gift of Endings 13
4. The Ax at the Root 16
5. Fire and Soap 20
6. The One 25
7. Mom of God 30
8. Jesus, Son of Joseph 34
9. God Con Carne 38
10. Unacceptable 41

II. EPIPHANY

Introduction to the Season 45

1. King Herod's Fear 48
2. Drenched in Divine Delight 51
3. Walk on By 55
4. Sex and Saint Paul 59
5. Tonic for Demonic 63
6. Furious with Jesus 67
7. Jesus Gets Ticked 71
8. Spring Training 75
9. Analysis Paralysis 80
10. Passing on the Mantle 85

III. LENT

Introduction to the Season 89

1. Dust and Return 93
2. Water and Struggle 97
3. Nocturnal Midwifery 101
4. Coercion Aversion 105
5. Bad News, Front Page 109
6. Snakebitten 114
7. Baptism in Seven Scenes 119
8. Bound in the Boneyard 124
9. Save Now 128
10. Giving Tree 132

IV. EASTER

Introduction to the Season 137

1. Scar Show 142
2. Elliptical Easter 147
3. Trapper of Air Revisited 151
4. The Gotcha God 155
5. Get Up, Gazelles 159
6. You Know the Way 163
7. A Life Laid Down 168
8. Holy Detour 171
9. Step by Step 175
10. Keeper of the Keys 180

V. PENTECOST

Introduction to the Season 185

1. Something on the Edge 191
2. God at Rest 195
3. Storm Dozing 199
4. Trusting in a Lie 203
5. Delayed Weed-Whacking 208
6. Persuasive Love 213
7. Hang on Tightly 217
8. The Entitled 221
9. Night Nemesis 225
10. Man in the Middle 230

Bibliography 235

Preface

MARTIN LUTHER (1483–1546) WAS obsessed with the Bible and in love with his Lord revealed therein. *Time* magazine named Luther "Man of the Millennium" for myriad accomplishments in the sixteenth century that shaped theology, language, hymnody, art, and so many things now taken for granted in Christianity across the world—all fueled by his high regard for Holy Scripture. This book is released in conjunction with the 500th anniversary of his posting of the now-famous 95 Theses in October of 1517 in Wittenberg, Germany.

I've chosen the whimsical title, *95 Prostheses*, partly because my own body is propped up gratefully with two prosthetic devices, and partly because the church (the body of Christ) is at a juncture where old Bible stories known by Luther need recasting and reframing with a generation of people for whom biblical narrative is foreign and even downright weird. Theologian Karl Barth (1886–1968) was prescient when he wrote about "the strange new world within the Bible," for the church's book is indeed both strange *and* new for adult converts seriously perusing its often odd pages for the first time.

The book is arranged around the classic themes of the church year and best read with a Bible nearby and with a pace that matches the steady, unfolding wisdom of the seasons. Authentic faith requires unhurried percolation. Each section of the book will include a general introduction followed by ten essays based upon Bible stories familiar to that season and chosen with new Christians, study groups, and Christian formation teams in mind. Each essay concludes with questions or exercises inviting deeper reflection and understanding. May these cyclical seasonal rhythms lead you into deeper discipleship and a joyful following of the man who changed Luther to change the world: Jesus the Christ.

I. ADVENT/CHRISTMAS

Introduction to the Season[1]

BETWEEN OUR HOUSE ON Woodland Way Road and the nearby middle school is a small stream whose name I do not know. It flows under the road through a large culvert and empties into a small pool, rising and falling with the rain. I always stop and look in the pool on daily walks, shielding eyes from the setting sun reflecting off the water.

I'm looking for fish. My wife says I'm crazy. On the way to the store the other day, she slowed down and called to me, a hunched figure on the side of the road squinting into the pool: "There's no fish in that creek, you lovable nut job!"

Obsessed with fish from a young age, the hatchery was the first place I wanted to go while visiting grandparents in the mountains of North Carolina; we'd hardly unpacked before heading into Pisgah Forest to watch the contained and squirming schools. I had this idea as a child, passing a body of water in the car on vacation trips, that I could toss a baited hook out the back window, and with enough line and a little patience would reel in a whopper upon reaching our destination. I was always out early at the beach as a little boy, wading into the surf with my hand-line and a pocketful of bait shrimp, and once caught a good-sized pompano in the waves, just inches from my kneecap.

Recently, on a warm day after a rain shower, I was peering into the pool on Woodland Way and saw three small fish, each maybe two inches long. My wife says I'm lying. And I do confess to lying to her on occasion

---

1. Portions of this introduction first appeared in Honeycutt, "Keeping Watch."

just to keep things interesting. Nothing important—small, innocent, sensational fibs that hook her like a bluegill. But that day on Woodland Way they were there, in my pool: three small fish.

*

The story (Luke 2:8–20) says they "lived in the fields," keeping watch. I suspect that was some kind of life—actually living in fields, making your home there with an evening fire taking the place of your basic indoor Kenmore on a much wider range that seemed even bigger at night. They took care of the flock. That was their job, day in and day out. They slept out on a hillside protecting fluffy fur for an absent owner. I doubt it paid a whole lot.

Some Bible scholars say that many shepherds were ex-cons who'd spent time in jail—which is to say they lied professionally (rather than recreationally, like me). They kept watch and developed an eye for odd movements and an ear for strange sounds. Some of the shepherds were probably pretty salty characters (Jeff Bridges as "The Dude" from *The Big Lebowski* comes to mind), old seasoned men prone to mild fabrication around a roaring fire. They watched over the flock with alert senses honed by suspicion born from experience. They kept watch. It was their whole life, this watching. If the angels had appeared to princes with indoor heat, then maybe Jesus would've had better Christmas digs that holy night. But the angels came to watchers. The angels came to guys who watched the stars and listened to the song of crickets. The angels came to folk who lived in fields with their antennae already up.

In a pastoral ministry spanning four decades, I've met all kinds of interesting people in a variety of interesting settings—some with lots of faith and others with hardly any at all. It's not my job to judge others based on the intensity of their faith, although some think it is (or should be). One of my dearest friends is the most committed atheist you'll ever hope to meet. His forty-year friendship has helped me realize that doubt and skepticism can be allies to faith. It's sometimes hard to maintain faith in a world such as ours, but I think it's also hard to maintain unbelief in anything at all. It's hard to explain away the existence of leopards and coyotes and trout and mitochondria and the color purple as purely accidental and random. Theists have their own set of befuddling challenges, but so do atheists.

They kept watch. Those three words are not a bad summary of the first two seasons of the church year. The words are incredibly important for true believers and others who aren't so sure. The life of faith is sort of like looking for fish where none are really expected. You won't always get what you're looking for. And you won't always find the answer you're seeking. But you keep watching, on tiptoe, ready for revelation.

A young scientist named Manu Prakash teaches at Stanford and grew up in India. Prakash is an advocate of what he calls "frugal science," an attempt to make the wonders of science more accessible to poor people across the world. He invented something called the Foldscope, an actual microscope that can be mailed in a flat nine-by-twelve-inch envelope and costs very little to make. Upon arrival, one uses several simple origami-style folds and voila, a handy microscope emerges that can be used in the field. Manu Prakash has a passion for helping people see the marvels of life all around them; a passion, you might say, for keeping watch.

The angels came to shepherds with their antennae up and senses sharpened. They were outside in a field. And they heard and saw some wonderful news: God's promises taking on flesh and blood.

"The Word became flesh and lived among us" (John 1:14). The Greek word for "lived" in this verse literally means "to live in a tent." Here's a pretty close paraphrase: "God became human and *camped* among us." The word hearkens back to the ancient tabernacle (the portable abode for God) that accompanied the people of Israel wherever they went. Christmas is the celebration of an ongoing camping trip where Jesus chooses to pitch his tent right next to ours. He drives in his stakes, kindles a little fire, strings up a hammock, and lives among us. When we move, he moves—sharing our lot, our flesh, with his unfading glory. The gift of incarnation, from an ecological perspective, is that God's light fills our world; specific, nameable places. It's the message Isaiah heard one morning from other angels in the temple at the time of his calling: "Holy, holy, holy is the Lord of hosts; the whole earth is full of his glory" (Isa 6:3).

*

"And suddenly there was with the angel a multitude of the heavenly host, praising God" (Luke 2:13) and bringing peace. One striking word for me here is "suddenly." They were keeping watch, like all other nights, and then *suddenly*.

There is a directional flow in Luke's version of the Christmas story. There is a "back-and-forth" geographical ranging between heaven and earth. It was true when Jacob used a stone for a pillow, on another night centuries before, in another field; he saw a ladder of angels (Gen 28:10–22) with traffic moving in both directions. And it's true in the shepherds' field. The angels were there, and then they were not there, returning to heaven. God's glory does indeed fill this earth, but keen watchfulness might be the most important spiritual discipline for latter-day shepherds to develop in order to discern the traffic.

A couple of springs ago I was on the Blue Ridge Parkway for several days with a bicycling companion. One morning we broke camp and the fog was so thick, pea soup, that it probably wasn't a very smart thing to be out in it on a bicycle. My friend, Kent, twenty yards ahead of me, would disappear and reappear, in and out of the cloud. It was a weird feeling—ghostly, almost as if he were passing through a door into another world with other people appearing and receding. I have a photo of another friend standing in the fog on the Appalachian Trail in Georgia, a friend now dead almost two decades. I look at the picture, through the mist, and time vanishes. We're on the trail together again and I halfway expect him to speak.

*

I've not seen those three fish again since I saw them in that culvert pool. But I keep looking and watching every day—not because I know they're really there, but maybe because Advent watchfulness is even more important than verification in the life of faith. We live in the fields of a wonderful world. God reveals luminous truth and light, back-and-forth, up and down; angelic traffic.

"To you is born this day…"

Any day, really.

1. Jesus the Safecracker

"If the owner of the house had known in what part of the night the thief was coming, he would have stayed awake and would not have let his house be broken into" (Matthew 24:43).

SOMETIMES I WONDER WHAT it will be like to live the last day of my life. Ever think about the circumstances of your death? I've had cancer twice in my life—radiation treatments, surgery; the best health care possible and all is fine today. I suppose I'm a candidate to ponder these vexing questions more than many. Would you want to know the details and date if that were possible? Why or why not?

I remember reading an article several years ago where the author (a historian) said a curious thing. He said that in the Middle Ages the death of choice was cancer. If you were going to die, cancer was the preferred route back then. That sounds very strange to modern ears that dread the "C"-word more than most any other. But in the Middle Ages one could die pretty quickly from ailments ranging from the plague to a spear chucked through your head in battle. Cancer gave people time—time to get your affairs in order; time to settle debts; time to pass on wisdom and gather children to your bedside for conversation and prayer.

In this so-called "information age" where so many things seem to be knowable and describable, it's refreshing in a way that some mysteries are beyond our reach. We are not in control of our debut into this world, or our exit from it. Even Jesus didn't know everything. "About that day and hour no one knows, neither the angels of heaven, nor the Son, but only the Father" (Matt 24:36). He is speaking here of the end of time, of course—his own return, rather than anyone's individual mortality. But the issues are related. Jesus was not some divine know-it-all in this regard. Even Jesus had limits to his knowledge.

But that did not keep him from giving specific advice about the unknown. He likens his return to the days of Noah when people were going about their own business—marrying, starting families, drinking toasts to the good life ("more wine, garcon!"), and a catastrophe came and swept it all away. It really doesn't matter if you think the story of Noah's Ark really happened or not. Don't get stuck there. Jesus' point with this advice is that we live in a world where things can change very quickly, overnight, neither predicted nor controlled.

I recall a pastoral visit several years ago with a couple in my parish, Al and Liz Barry. (They've given me permission to share this story.) Part of a pastor's job description is that he or she will bring gospel comfort and hope to the dying, but in this case it was the other way around. Liz and I gathered there at Al's bedside for Holy Communion on a Wednesday afternoon in December. Their faithful dog, Daisy, was there too. Liz told me that Daisy would often wake her up in the middle of the night when Al needed her.

We all gathered around Al's bed and I read this same "end of time" passage from Matthew 24. On the way to their home I thought about choosing another passage (something a bit lighter), but I'm glad I stuck with this old Advent theme. I read the story and we talked about it. Al said, "You know, my own life has been like that. We've been successful in our careers—very busy and successful, running around doing lots of things. Since I've been sick, this time has been a gift to us. I'm sad. We're sad. But it's been a gift to focus on God each day, focus on his love for us each day. I have grown so much in my own faith through this illness. I would never have chosen this path for my life, but in some ways it's been a gift."

"Keep awake," says Jesus, not so much a coercive warning, but rather as an invitation to notice the mysteries of this great gift of life. "For you do not know . . . you don't know on what day your Lord is coming." Al Barry died three days later. But he was also one of the most fully awake people I've ever known.

In a beautiful tribute to his son, Adam, Richard Lischer writes:

> There are only a few plots in the world, but every one of them hinges on death. Death is the ultimate sanction. It lends its edge to every tale, whether an action-adventure film or *Romeo and Juliet.* Everything in the story either anticipates death or

responds to it. *Pay attention*, the author or screenwriter warns, *somebody might die*. The only mystery is: by what contrivance of plot will it happen or be avoided?[2]

*

I suppose it might be tempting for a preacher to use this Bible story in a manipulative, fearful sort of way. Karl Malden plays a preacher in the old Hayley Mills movie, *Pollyanna*, who delivers a chandelier-rattling sermon one hot summer Sunday titled "Death Comes Unexpectedly!" with parishioners sweating and squirming in their pews.

With few exceptions, finger-pointing sermons (complete with threats) don't really help people change all that much. I was in downtown Chicago several years ago, came upon a street preacher with a microphone on Michigan Avenue, had a bit of time, and decided I'd give the guy a listen. I stayed about thirty minutes and was surprised that we actually agreed on many of his concerns. But I also noticed that most people ignored the poor guy—probably because he was yelling at them.

People really do want to change. I recently discovered an Internet website titled ivescrewedup.com, an online confessional where people need only list their age and city of residence. Here are a few confessions: "I confess that I've stolen about $15,000 while working for a family member." Said another, "I am struggling with self-harming, bulimia, and anorexia, but no one has noticed." And yet another: "I confess that I have had premarital sex repeatedly with multiple partners."

There's a lot of darkness in our lives—a huge need for confession, repentance, and forgiveness. It's easy to conclude that Jesus is yelling at us in this old passage from Matthew. "Shape up while you've got time, or else!" But I think that's missing the point. For Jesus is not an in-your-face sort of Lord here. In fact, he likens himself to *a thief* who comes in the night. In other words, Jesus refuses to be obvious about his return. He will not appear on Hollywood Squares as a game-show contestant: *I'm back*. His return will not be announced on the six o'clock news so that we can squeeze him into our busy calendars. Jesus' return is unscheduled, unexpected, unscripted. He will come like a thief. And why will Jesus come this way? Well, you know why. "You said Tuesday, Jesus? I don't know. How does Thursday look for you? Can we meet then?" Jesus

2. Lischer, *Stations of the Heart*, 169.

knows that our meetings with him tend to get postponed for a variety of "compelling" reasons.

As much as anything, this old story is concerned about the *dailyness* of the Christian life. Jesus wants us to live each day as if it's truly our last. Not out of fear. But to invite us to true and full "wakefulness" to what this life is for. Jesus does not return to "get" us. He's already *gotten* us, as I understand the promise. He got us real good in our baptisms.

*

I'll admit it. Sometimes I do wonder about how I will die and when. But the far more interesting question is how Jesus (alive inside us, his church) invites us now to live. Advent is hands down the season of the church year when the church is most out of step with the surrounding culture. Here's a little experiment you might try. In the next few days, try taking this Bible story from Matthew to any shopping mall in your town. Find a little bench. Read this story again to yourself. Not out loud, just to yourself. And then look around. Advent is a jarring alternative to the American holidays.

So keep awake. Not because Jesus is out to get you, but because in baptism he's already gotten you.

For further reflection:

1. Ponder the connection between the words *Advent* and *adventure*.
2. Look up the word *apocalyptic* in a Bible dictionary and discuss how this ancient biblical genre might be rescued from Christian fearmongers.

2. Ready and Waiting

"Now when these things begin to take place, stand up and raise your heads, because your redemption is drawing near"
(Luke 21:28).

RIGHT AFTER JESUS SHARES these dire warnings about the end of the world, Luke's gospel reports what seems to be a rather innocuous detail: "Every day he was teaching in the temple, and at night he would go out and spend the night on the Mount of Olives" (21:37).

I'm drawn to this little detail. Just before and after Jesus spoke about signs in the stars and the sashay of planets and the churning seas, he went camping. Just before they came to get him for the trial and just days before he died, Jesus slept out for several nights in a row. We're told earlier in Luke that "the Son of Man has no place to lay his head" (9:58), but this sleep-out (presumably alone) seems to be a conscious choice by Jesus.

Did he build a small fire and watch it get dark? Did he lean back and lace his fingers behind his head, staring at the evening sky? Was the moon waxing or waning that week? Or was it so ink-black dark and still that his entire body blended into the night? I suspect that Jesus thought about quite a bit on the mountain each night, camping out alone. If you've ever camped solo, you'll recall how much more there is to see and hear.

When our children were very small I used to love to walk outside late at night and look back at our house, entirely dark except for a small light that would help guide me back in. I'd stand in the darkness and think of the three kids and a great wife, all sleeping inside. And I would often lie down right in the middle of the driveway and look up and think about the contrast between the dim light in the house yonder and the celestial lights so far away—the nearness of Christ at Christmas and the amazing grandeur of God that fills the cosmos; just looking and looking at layer upon layer of time and space. Upon returning inside, it was an overpowering thing to stand over their beds and pray, and just watch them sleeping; welling up with gratitude. Watching a child sleep is a good time to pray and wonder about life and our place in the whole scheme of things.

The reason I like to think about Jesus camping out every night for a period of time is that it's important for me to have images of the man simply thinking, off alone somewhere—considering his life, this life, the life to come. Perhaps you've noticed an almost-breathlessness to the Gospels. *He heals, he teaches, he preaches, travels this way and that.* One story quickly blends into another. The image of Jesus camping under a night sky slows down all the gospel action. Even Jesus needed time to think and reflect quietly. The message here is pretty clear: so do we.

*

You may already know the origin of the Advent wreath in Christian tradition. About this time of year in Scandinavia, farmers would put away their tools in the waning light of the year, and clean and service their carts and farming implements for the coming spring. Families would take a wheel from the cart and bring it inside, decorating the wheel with greenery and candles. It was a way of marking time, but also an invitation to slow down and think—because you can't go anywhere on three wheels. If you doubt this, remove one of your Michelins and try driving to the mall.

The cartwheel in the middle of our worship spaces each December is an invitation to slow down and think about this life and the life to come, even while the culture we live in rockets through the month at a frantic pace. Someone has beautifully described Advent as "leisure to incubate."

Jesus camped out under the stars for several nights in a row just before his arrest and crucifixion. He no doubt thought about life—his own and the lives of his followers. And perhaps his reflections under the stars made it into his sermon the following morning: "There will be signs in the sun, moon, and the stars, and on earth distress among the nations confused by the roaring of seas and waves" (Luke 21:25).

We who take our Christmas with lots of sugar may be a bit puzzled by Jesus' words this time of year. Who has time to think about the coming kingdom when there's so much to do? "Be on guard," says Jesus, "so that your hearts are not weighed down with the worries of this life, and that day catches you unexpectedly, like a trap" (Luke 21:34). We may sing, "Oh come, oh come Emmanuel" every Advent, but what would it mean if he did?

"Now when these things take place, stand up and raise your heads because your redemption is drawing near." But if truth were told, we're a lot like one character in a Flannery O'Connor short story who says, "A man with a good car ain't got no need of redemption." And so we're invited to remove a wheel.

*

Here's an interesting story[3] told by a Presbyterian pastor. Her grandfather was attending his sixtieth class reunion. There was a break in the weekend agenda so the granddaddy and three of his old classmates grabbed their clubs and headed out to one of the local golf courses. They rode in carts, laughed a lot, and swapped old stories. One of the friends in the foursome teed off somewhere on the back nine. Still with club held high, after a great shot, the man looked at his three friends and said, "Gentlemen, you'll have to excuse me." And with those words, he fell down dead. Not a bad way to go if you love golf, but a rather jarring goodbye for those stranded on the back nine with a body.

Advent is a gift to the church, inviting us to stand on tiptoe, alert and watchful. Advent invites us to honestly consider our place in the world, our attachments, and where our true investments reside. Such important reflection need not be morbid. But it might strengthen our faith so that when our time comes, we can say without fear: "Ladies, gentlemen, you'll have to excuse me."

*

I've always loved the words of Charlotte near the end of E. B. White's classic barnyard story *Charlotte's Web*. Charlotte is about to die and Wilbur is overcome with grief, wondering aloud why a spider would ever help a pig: "You have been my friend," says Charlotte. "That in itself is a

---

3. Gillespie, "Emergency and Rescue."

tremendous thing. I wove my webs for you because I liked you. After all, what's a life, anyway? We're born, we live a little while, we die."[4]

As Jesus camped those nights, fingers laced behind his head, looking up at the stars, he probably knew that his own death was only days away. Maybe he walked to the brow of the hill those nights on the Mount of Olives, and looked back towards the lights of the city, imagining the occupants of the various homes.

Does he look back today at the lights of our cities and towns, the driveways of our homes, from a certain vantage point?

For further reflection:

1. Recall the last time you spent time alone, looking at the stars. How does this perspective shape the living of these days?
2. Describe how you might try to "remove a Michelin" this Advent.

---

4. White, *Charlotte's Web*, 164.

3. The Odd Gift of Endings

"So teach us to number our days, that we may apply our hearts to wisdom" (Ps 90:12, KJV).

Not long ago, after visiting a parishioner recovering from surgery in Mountain Rest, I hopped over to Highway 107, swung into the state park, changed out of my dress shoes, and started walking down the Foothills Trail. Hardly anyone was around. It was about 3:00 PM and warm with beautiful light angling amazingly through remaining leaves; one of those perfectly blue afternoons that make you think about the sweep of your life and time passing. I hiked for about twenty minutes, maybe a mile, and found a place to sit and think and pray.

I recently helped my parents move from Chattanooga to Clemson after we all agreed they could no longer safely live alone. My mom's been ready to move for awhile, but Dad (after sixty years in the city) wasn't so sure. It's hard to leave friends and church and a doctor who knows all about your strengths and flaws. Hard to leave your neighborhood barber who hugged my father (his first customer in 1957) and said through tears after the last haircut, "This one's on me." Hard to admit physical and mental limitations that will come to us all.

We wandered from room to room in silence after the house was completely empty, the small home in East Brainerd where I grew up and (with my friend Jimmy) smacked golf balls over I-75 with a three-wood teed up in the front yard. Four of us stood in a tight circle in the bare den and the son who is also a pastor prayed a parting prayer that included this petition: "And Lord, thanks also for protecting my little brother Lee on those late nights when he removed the screen and snuck out the back window to cavort with friends leading him who knows where."

There's a great scene in the movie *Smoke* (1995), starring Harvey Keitel and William Hurt. Keitel plays a guy named Augie who runs a tobacco shop in busy downtown Manhattan. Augie has this unusual habit of taking a single photo each morning at the same time out in front of his shop—each day, same exact time, 365 photos each year. He never misses. Different people inhabit these photos, but the buildings and the camera angle are essentially the same. Augie has dozens of photo albums filled with pictures of his little street corner, spanning several decades of time.

It's a very private hobby. Not many people know about it, but one night Augie decides to show the albums to his friend (played by William Hurt), who is amazed but flips through the pages hastily and says, "But they're all the same."

Augie starts to collect his photo albums, a bit offended. "You're missing it. You'll miss the point if you look at them that way. You'll miss the people. All these people who have come to my little corner in this little part of the world all these years. And you'll miss the light. How the earth turns at different times of the year. How the sun hits my corner at a different angle in the spring from the fall. You may as well not look at them if you're gonna go that fast."

Endings help us notice details of wonder like those noticed by Augie. It would be a rather strange existence if things just went on and on. I went online recently with a question and discovered that 152,000 people die each day around the world. That's almost 3,200 during the time it will take you to reflect upon this essay, about the population of my little town. A lot of people, yes, but consider the alternative in a world *without* endings. Endings, oddly, are often an unusual gift. Endings help us to number our days; to reflect upon what people mean to us; to take note of what's wonderfully around us—in grace and at no charge.

As I walked back to the car on the Foothills Trail, I took in the last light of the day and recalled words from my father, almost ninety, as we were leaving the house in Tennessee after that final prayer. "Promise me," he said. "Promise me that when I die you'll take my ashes back to Chattanooga to the church. Would you please do that?" My mom tried to hush him, but his words felt like those of some Old Testament patriarch talking to his sons towards the end of a life. We promised.

Perhaps we should regularly give thanks even for all the difficult endings in this life; endings that help us pay close attention to what's here, unbidden and unearned, offered up in a daily and repeating menu of wonder, calling forth praise.

For further reflection:

1. Describe an "ending" (perhaps painful) in your own life, without which you'd be a very different person.
2. With Augie, what place in your neighborhood would you like to photograph each day at the exact same time?

4. The Ax at the Root

"Even now the ax is lying at the root of the trees" (Matt 3:10).

I REMEMBER THIS GUY named Gus while hiking the Appalachian Trail through Pennsylvania over thirty years ago. My wife, Cindy, and I were on a rather remote section of the trail, hadn't seen anyone all day, rounded a bend, and out jumped this crazy-looking guy from the bushes, waving a machete. I was certain, at first, that we'd entered a dark scene from a Stephen King novel. Who in the world carries a heavy machete on the trail except someone with a screw or two fairly loose?

But Gus was a harmless, if rather eccentric, sort of guy. We'd startled him. He hadn't seen anyone for a couple of days. We hiked with Gus for most of a week and came to like him very much, admiring his knowledge of plants. The following winter we received a post card from Key West, but haven't heard from him since. I still think about Gus from time to time as I come upon a blind curve on trails I happen to hike.

*

John the Baptist jumps into our path each December on the way to the manger. We know he's out there in the wilderness, an annual character in any serious Advent journey. But the startling appearance in his skimpy wardrobe with accompanying meager diet still seems so jarring amidst the Christmas lights, joyous angels, and sugar plum fairies. There's a part of me that always asks: *What's this guy doing here anyway, ruining Christmas for us all?*

4. THE AX AT THE ROOT

Perhaps you have a manger scene at home, retrieved annually from the attic—Mary, Joseph, the baby; shepherds, a trio of wise men. We have manger and crèche scenes from all over the world in our house. My wife's maiden name is Christmas (no kidding). She loves the season even though she married a Scrooge. We have multiple boxes of Bethlehem delights, hailing the wondrous birth. The holy family hangs out in our den all the way until Ash Wednesday.

But I'm wondering if you have a miniature facsimile of John the Baptist placed on the mantle alongside the other starring characters? Somebody gave us John a few years ago and he has a place in our library on the shelves. But he's not been given permission to enter the holy of holies: the Christmas tree room. I may sneak him in this year and see if anyone notices.

There's something about John the Baptist that takes us by surprise every year. He jumps out at us from the shadows like a Rottweiler who hasn't eaten in awhile. He doesn't have a machete, but he does carry an ax and I've no doubt the man means business. I know he's coming, but he jumps out from behind centuries of bushes on our Advent trail and surprises me every year.

I find it interesting that *all four* Gospels begin (in the early chapters) with John the Baptist in the wilderness, calling God's people to repentance and change. But *only two* of the Gospels bother to mention the birth of Jesus and the details we've come to know and love. John stands in a long line of prophets (some thought he was Elijah, back again) who confronted safe and comfortable faith. "There's nothing safe about God," John seems to say. "You see this ax lying here? God means to chop away all this stuff in your life that gets in the way of producing good fruit. The Coming One will baptize you with the Holy Spirit and fire" (Matt 3:11). The Greek word here for "fire" is interesting. It's the word *pur*. We get our English word *purify* from this same root. Jesus means to come into our lives and burn away the chaff, purifying our lives with his love, grace, and yes, judgment.

This is not a popular image of Jesus, especially for Lutherans, and especially during Advent. The story seems too sweet to accommodate someone like John. We want to swaddle and coo over and protect little Jesus from mean old Herod. In doing so, it's easy to forget why he came.

One of my earlier books is a slim volume on the topic of sanctification.[5] It's an important word that Lutherans tend to forget because we've

---

5. Honeycutt, *Sanctified Living*.

been steeped in (and brought along by) the important phrase: "justification by grace through faith"—Luther's great Reformation insight fueled by his close readings in the book of Romans and many other places in the Bible. Lutherans have forgotten much of the Bible, but we do know that a core teaching of the faith is the forgiveness of sins won by Christ on a cross.

A challenge among Lutherans is that we often think that's the entire extent of Christianity. I've always loved the story of a Lebanese seminary student who came to the United States to study in a mainline Protestant seminary. In exasperation, he finally said in class one day: "All you Americans care about is justification! You love sinning and being forgiven, sinning and being forgiven, but no one seems to want off that hamster wheel. Have you ever heard of sanctification? Is anyone interested in learning to sin a little less?"[6] It's tough for Lutherans to talk about these things without feeling that we're compromising our core conviction of grace. Jesus certainly came to this world—was born joyously into it—to forgive our sins. But even a cursory examination of his teachings reveals that he also came to show us a new way to live together. There was a post-communion prayer in one of our old worship books that we've now largely retired: "Almighty God, you gave your Son both as a sacrifice for sin and a model of the godly life." It's not one or the other. Jesus is interested in both.

And so John shows up every Advent to remind us. He shows up with ax and fire. Not so much to threaten infidels like me, but as a reminder that following Jesus, paying attention to his teachings, means that I'll have to knock off and cease certain behaviors. That I'll be open to the change that the Spirit is trying to effect in me. That I won't be content with sweetness and sentiment when it comes to church life. "The ax is lying at the root of the trees." Jesus means to forgive us, but he also means to change and convert us more and more into his likeness. Machete time with our Lord.

I won't lie. This is hard and often uncomfortable work. And it may be that we've missed this about Jesus even though we've been a member of a church all our lives. "Do not presume to say to yourselves, 'We have Abraham as our ancestor'" (Matt 3:9). John is basically saying: "Don't think that four generations of your relatives connected to a congregation gets you any special consideration in your stature before Christ." Jesus is coming with fire and ax to burn and cut away all that separates us from

---

6. Taylor, *Speaking of Sin*, 86.

4. THE AX AT THE ROOT

God, regardless of one's personal congregational pedigree. John is telling us the truth. And I think we long to hear the truth—long for national leaders who will speak honestly and straightforwardly with us. Who will not lie to us or lead us on. John spoke the truth in the wilderness and people flocked out there to hear him.

*

It might be wise each Advent to recall a scene from *The Lion, the Witch and the Wardrobe*, the opening book in C. S. Lewis's stories about Narnia. The kids—Edmund, Lucy, Peter, and Susan—step through the wardrobe into a new land and begin to sense the evil of the White Witch and the hopeful returning power of Aslan the Lion to the woods. (Aslan is the Christ figure in these stories.)

The children are befriended by the Beaver family and the conversation turns to the fears of Mr. and Mrs. Beaver, but also their hope in Aslan, the great Lion:

> "Ooh!" said Susan, "I'd thought he was a man. Is he—quite safe? I shall feel rather nervous about meeting a lion."
>
> "That you will dearie, and make no mistake," said Mrs. Beaver, "if there's anyone who can appear before Aslan without their knees knocking, they're either braver than most or else just silly."
>
> "Then he isn't safe?" said Lucy.
>
> "Safe?" said Mr. Beaver. "Don't you hear what Mrs. Beaver tells you? Who said anything about safe? 'Course he isn't safe. But he's good. He's the King, I tell you."[7]

We prepare in Advent for the coming of Christ—a Lord who intends to change us with his teachings and his grace; his very life.

One who is always good, but never quite safe.

For further reflection:

1. Why is actual change and growth over time important for a follower of Jesus?
2. Honestly confess to a friend the things that need changing in your life this season with the help of Jesus.

---

7. Lewis, *The Lion, the Witch and the Wardrobe*, 75–76.

5. Fire and Soap

"For he is like a refiner's fire and like fuller's soap" (Mal 3:2).

There was a man in one of my former parishes (let's call him Stephen) who was not particularly well-liked. And it's possible I'm even being generous here. Stephen was a grumpy and ornery older man (harmless in most ways, but ornery) and most people just steered clear of him. He enjoyed calling into question my pastoral credentials and made a habit of staring at unruly children. I worried a bit about Stephen; asked others about his background (attempting to discover something from his past that made him behave so badly) and tried to reach out to him. No luck.

People in the church had a habit of saying, "Oh, that's just Stephen. Don't worry. He's always been that way." But I did worry a bit. And, after a point, that very common statement about Stephen left me wondering. What does it reveal about another human being when we say, "Oh, that's just the way she's always been," as if some people are simply incapable of change?

But more broadly, what does such thinking reveal about our true beliefs about God? Are even God's hands tied with some people when it comes to change?

I was thinking of Stephen when I learned of a popular headline that appeared in *The New York Daily News* just after the shooting in San Bernardino in December of 2015. The headline read: "GOD ISN'T FIXING THIS." The headline was a reaction to those in our country who say we should pray more if we want less national gun violence.

Please don't think I'm equating Stephen with the deranged couple in California. There are various degrees of orneriness in the world. I get

5. FIRE AND SOAP

that. But the catchy headline made me wonder: What *does* God fix? And what are we really saying when we say even God's hands are tied with some people who seem incapable of change? Whether they're an ornery parishioner, or a criminal on death row, or people with religious convictions gone haywire?

*

There was a time in my early pastoral life that I believed people failed to read the Bible with any consistent regularity because we were all such busy people—just not enough time in the day. Running hither and yon, we never got around to the Word of God because of the frantic pace of our culture. Some important things had to go and the Bible became one of them because, well, we are a busy bunch with vital things to do. I'm not being cynical here. I really believed that once upon a time.

However, I do not believe it anymore. To put it more precisely, I don't believe that's the *primary* reason we fail to read the book. Here's what I've come to believe deep in my pastoral heart. Many people, even active, churchgoing Christians, do not read the Bible with any regularity *because we're afraid of what we might find there.*

A huge chunk of the Bible means to change us. Transform us more and more into the likeness of Jesus. *Convert us,* to use a word that isn't found in many Lutheran circles. And frankly, Jesus is a loser. Or, to put it another way: *he wins by losing.* He will not play the dominance game because he knows of a much higher power than any wielded on earth. It's a very odd story with a cross at the center.

If we're honest there are a lot of stories out there that captivate our imaginations. The story of how to make a lot of money. The story of how to live forever with my amazing and beautiful bod. The story of how to "kick ass" and not take this anymore.

These competing stories (compelling stories to be sure) are why many do not read the Bible with any regularity. Because what we read there compared to how we choose to live our lives is often just too much to bear or think about. In short, the Bible invites us to see life from God's perspective rather than our own narrow lens. And frankly, this is a lot of hard work. It's exhausting work, if you want to know the truth.

*

The book of Malachi is the last in the Old Testament. Not much is known about the book's namesake. In Hebrew, Malachi means "My messenger." He preached about 450 years before the birth of Jesus and was mostly interested in faithful worship practices. Malachi was hard on priests (like me) and people who went through the motions of temple liturgical customs.

But Malachi was mostly interested in helping people get an accurate understanding of the Lord God. God, according to Malachi, was no cuddly teddy bear in the sky. God was loving and forgiving, yes, according to this prophet. But God was also jealous and incredulous and shocked by human behavior. God, in short, got ticked from time to time. Malachi's job (as divine messenger) was to let Israel know these things.

He says: "This God that you delight in, this God about whom you sing dazzling hymns of praise, he's coming all right. Oh yes. But who can endure that coming? You? Me? God is nobody's Santa Claus," Malachi seemed to say (3:1–2). "God has an agenda to change us. To purify us all with fire and cleanse this place with soap." It's not a message many wanted to hear back then. Fire and soap. I daresay not many want to hear it now, which leads back to my premise about our Bible reading habits.

But Malachi's message, though rather harsh and direct, is just about the best news any of us could ever hear. *For it reveals a God who loves us enough not to leave us as we are.* "Just as I Am" we come to God, claims the old hymn. But God will not leave us that way. Is that good news or bad? Depends. I like to think it can be very good news.

*

God's word came to John the Baptist in the wilderness (Luke 3:1–2). Interestingly, this word did not come to the other seven men (count them) who are named in Luke. All seven were privileged and powerful and very well-known; leaders of the known world at that time, guys who made the headlines. Luke takes time to list them, name their powerful positions. But the word of God bypassed them all. Curious.

What does this mean for us? What does it mean concerning how God changes people? I do know that I am fairly skilled at keeping God at arm's length. Heck, just keep the TV on all the time. That's a start at keeping God away.

*

I have a pastor friend[8] whose church once worked with a family that really needed help. The father in that family was an alcoholic and abusive. The family (including the father) came to worship for several Sundays, several months, after the church assisted them with food and clothing. And then they stopped coming and moved to another town and the congregation lost track of them.

One day my friend was out on the church lawn. It was spring and a man walked up and spoke. He'd changed so much that the pastor didn't even recognize him. "Good grief," said the pastor. "You've really changed. What in the world happened?"

The man paused a second. He said, "I really want to thank you for what your church did for my family, pastor. We really needed help at that time and you helped us. But it was when we started attending another church that I really started to change. They told me God was coming. And that God can change lives. They really shook me up and made me think hard about how I was hurting people. I guess your church gave me the equivalent of aspirin, and that was good. But what I really needed was a massive dose of spiritual chemotherapy."

*

In Advent, Christians make a renewed commitment to meet God in the wilderness of our choosing. Find a quiet place. Return there regularly. Allow this life-changing word, the holy gift of Holy Scripture, to penetrate your routine; your expectations of this season.

God is like fire. He comes to purify. God is like fuller's soap. He comes to cleanse us all. God is coming. He will not leave us alone.

It's one of the ways God fixes things, in God's good time.

---

8. The story comes from Will Willimon, retold here as I remember it.

For further reflection:

1. Do you know anyone like Stephen? How might a congregation caringly confront the behavior of people like him?
2. Why did God's word seem to bypass those seven powerful men mentioned in Luke and find a voice with John out in the middle of nowhere?

6. The One

"Are you the one who is to come, or are we to wait for another?"
(Matt 11:3)

DURING ADVENT, JOHN THE Baptist is found in two interesting places: the wilderness and jail. He asks a question from jail that I think is one of the all-time biblical classics. "Are *you* the one? Are you the one we've been waiting on all this time?" We cannot know exactly *how* John asked this question. The Bible is limiting in that it doesn't always reveal a speaker's mood or tone—whether it was timid, bold, or sassy, for example. We can't always know how a person's voice may have sounded; its inflection or pitch. And both are major players in how we interpret meaning from a biblical text.

When we read the Bible, or any book for that matter, we are making decisions about tone and tenor (rather unconsciously) by the clues the author gives the reader. One of the most overlooked and important tools in biblical interpretation is slowing down, slowing way down, and making some educated guesses about how characters in the Bible may have actually *sounded* in various situations. How did *Mary* sound when the angel brought the news? How about *Joseph*, even though the Bible tells us he never speaks? How did *Jesus* sound when he knelt and prayed that night in Gethsemane? How about *Jeremiah* in a cistern? *Paul* when he was struck blind on a Damascus road? *Hannah* when she learned she was pregnant? Or *John the Baptist* here in jail?

Practice this out loud, make some educated guesses about tenor and pitch, and I guarantee the Bible will come alive for you in ways silent reading cannot touch. In preparation for a sermon, I'll read aloud dozens of times the text I'm preaching on—at traffic lights, in nursing homes and hospitals, in my office, even in the bathroom—listening for nuance that comes alive; details long ignored that leap forth with new meaning.

Here's how I think John the Baptist probably sounded: "Are *you* the one? Are *you of all people* the Messiah we've been waiting for all this time? Or should we now wait on somebody else?" How do I know he sounded this way? Well, I don't know for sure. But it's a pretty good guess given the following: a) We already know John is fairly outspoken given his preaching track record in the Jordan River wilderness; b) We know that John is in prison and such a state makes anybody a little edgy; and c) We know (and John knows) that he is about to lose his head for exposing Herod's adulterous fling with his own brother's wife (Matt 14:1–12).

John's question from prison cannot be timid or posed just to pass the time of day. Given his situation there behind bars, John is a little miffed; beginning to doubt Jesus just a bit. "Are *you* the one? Are *you* the messiah? Are *you* the one who was supposed to come with spirit and fire and burn away injustice? Are *you* supposed to be the Savior of the world or something?" The obvious answer to all these implied questions is this: "Then act like a Savior, bucko."

I spend some time on voice inflection because until we take an educated guess at tone and tenor, the Bible will remain a dusty old book of dusty old stories printed on a page, and the words will have a hard time finding voice in our hearts. When we play around with how a biblical character may have actually sounded, however, we find the words forming in our own throats and gut and hearts. The stories are now portable.

Isn't this true of the story of John in jail? When we say *Are you the one?* and try to decipher how it was first said, it's not too long before John's question becomes our question. Whether we are new to church and just starting out on the journey of faith, or whether we are seasoned pew veterans, John's question posed to Jesus will always be a live, not-entirely-settled question for those with a vibrant faith—a faith that really matters in a world such as ours.

With myriad religious options set out for us like candy in the "spirituality" section of most any bookstore, we ask of Jesus: "Are you *the one* amid so many choices?" In a world of cancer, hunger, agony, and great suffering, we ask of the sufferer hanging on the cross, "Are *you* the one who will help me find meaning in the face of great paradox?" In a nation where it's far easier to center our lives around materialism and comfort,

6. THE ONE

we ask of the Lord who calls us to self-denial, "*Are* you the one who will help me discover my true self?"

Until a Christian asks questions like these and risks boring in like John the Baptist, faith may remain static or perhaps immaterial and have little real impact on our lives. "Jesus died and rose. Yeah, I believe that. What else is new?"

It's possible that people who ask questions like John's may be closer to the kingdom than those who seem smugly certain of Jesus. In a lecture titled, "Why I Am Not a Christian" (1927), Bertrand Russell, the twentieth century's most famous atheist, described why people believe in God and what they expect of God. "Most people believe in God because they have been taught from early infancy to do it, and that is the main reason . . . the next most powerful reason is the wish for safety, a sort of feeling that there is a big brother who will look after you."[9]

One can never know all of anyone's reasons for believing in God and they may not match Russell's at all. But in my experience, his answers are pretty typical for many, many believers as we face a new and different century for the church in this country. It's what we've been taught. And we need a Big Brother. Is it okay to have these reasons? Maybe. But I'll say it again. I can't help but believe such a faith will eventually become simply immaterial to our daily lives and have no real impact on how we live.

*

The big question is not whether God exists. Not really. The big question (and this is the Bible's central question) is: *What is God like?* That was John's real question from prison. He wasn't questioning God's existence or the fact of the coming Messiah. He was confused about *the nature* of this Messiah. Jesus, after close examination, didn't seem to square with John's expectations of how a Messiah should act and behave.

I'll never forget a letter I received from a good friend in Maine. He doesn't believe in God. But in all his letters he never asks me to try and prove God's existence. He wants to know what *sort* of God I believe *in*. "What do you mean by God?" he once wrote. "Who God? What God? Where God? Define God."

---

9. Russell delivered this lecture on March 6, 1927, to the National Secular Society at Battersea Town Hall in London.

We, of course, can never "define" God, but Christians should be prepared to say how Jesus *reveals* God's nature for them. "Are *you* the one" asks John. "Are *you* the one?" asks a lively person of faith. If our answer is "yes," we should be able to say how and why Jesus *is* one who reveals God. If we can't, then it is very doubtful that our "faith" will have any real impact on how we live. We simply believe in Jesus because we need a big brother.

*

"Are you the one who is to come, or are we to wait for another?" How did John say that from prison so long ago? What was his tone, the inflection of his voice? John's question, when we really hear it, gives us permission to ask the same thing. "Are you the one, Jesus? Are you the one?"

The choice to throw my hat in with Jesus cannot be based on proof or certainty. Jesus says, "Go and tell John . . . (Go and tell Frank) . . . Go and tell those who would follow me *what you hear and see*" (Matt 11:4).

What do you hear and see in these days of Advent? What is Jesus doing in and through your congregation? Recall Jesus' answer to the disciples of John. "The blind receive their sight, the lame walk, the lepers are cleansed, the deaf hear, the dead are raised, and the poor have good news brought to them" (Matt 11:5). I know people who are *seeing* with a brand new pair of eyes. I know folk who are *walking* in a whole new way. Others who are *cleansed* from a past that held them in bondage far worse than leprosy. Some, right in my home church, who have been *raised* from a dead end.

*

"Are you the one, Jesus? Or should we shop around for another?"

What a great question for Advent, for life. Let it roll around on your tongue, in your mind, in your heart this season.

"Are you the one above all others?"

A faith that truly matters may very well begin right here, with this question.

For further reflection:

1. Is God's existence or God's nature more important in your faith journey these days? Why?
2. In your Scripture study this week, try reading a Bible story aloud and making decisions as a reader concerning tenor and inflection. If you're in a group with others, how do the various oral readings shape the story's interpretation?

7. Mom of God

"But Mary was much perplexed by his words . . ." (Luke 1:29).

SOMEBODY ONCE ASKED ME a question around this time of year that I've never forgotten. A very good question: "Why didn't God just send an E.T.-type character from outer space to our world? Why did God have to choose somebody like Mary and pretty much ruin her life?"

The Bible says Mary was "perplexed" and ponderous after the angel's visit and the prediction of the miraculous birth. If Mary had written Luke's gospel, I wonder if she would have chosen different, stronger words. We rightly focus on the Savior's birth this time of year, but I've always had a lot of sympathy for the Savior's mom.

I cannot imagine that Mary was wildly happy about the news there at the beginning. Can you really see her turning cartwheels like in a Rodgers and Hammerstein musical or throwing back the sash of her apartment window yelling, "Yes, Nazareth! Yes, I'm the lucky girl! I get to carry God's baby! Won't Mom be proud of me?!" I just can't see any of this. Mary was perplexed. She was afraid. But I think the poor woman also felt *interrupted*. Her soul eventually "magnifies the Lord" (Luke 1:46) and all that, but at first, with an angel standing in her kitchen, she must have felt interrupted.

Among the many facts of time and place crammed into the first few words of this story (Luke 1:26–38) is this crucial tidbit: Mary was engaged to a guy. *She had plans.* Her wedding was on the foreseeable horizon. Don't you think she daydreamed about her future together with Joseph? In other words, Mary already had a life when Gabriel came knocking. It wasn't like her calendar was clear for this new, exciting venture, or she

7. MOM OF GOD

was out looking for something delightfully different to spice up her dull days. No, Mary had a life!

We also have a life. Rare is the person who can say, "Thank you so much for interrupting my vacation in your hour of need." Or, "Sure, please sign me up for an extra stint of jury duty next time." Interruptions come to all of us, but please be honest about that first gut reaction. Even among the most gracious, they're usually not welcome.

But Mary says "Yes." She says "Okay" to uncertainty. And thirty years later (or maybe thirty-three, depending on which Gospel you consult for Jesus' age at death) you have to wonder if Mary ever had any regret about giving the go-ahead. Because you have to admit it must have been very weird to be the mom of God.

*

They were all in the holy city once, a family vacation. Mary turns around at a vendor stand (maybe she's been distracted by the beautiful weavings and baskets) and suddenly Jesus, her twelve-year old, is missing. Jesus is separated from his parents for three days. *Three days.* They finally find him in the temple among the teachers. Mary says, "Son, we've been looking for you in great anxiety" (Luke 2:48). Now there's an understatement. Do you recall how the lad answers his mom? Basically this: "Chill out, would you Mom? Didn't you know I'd be right here?"

They were at a wedding together, Mary and Jesus. Many think Mary was probably in charge of the reception. Tradition says she was a relative of the bride. The wine runs out and she states the obvious to her talented and precocious son. "Woman," he says. "Woman, what is that to you and me?" (John 2:4). Now I don't know about your family, but this seeming impertinence would not have gone over in mine.

Jesus was teaching once. A large crowd. His family shows up. Mary was among them. But they arrive not for theological edification or due to family pride. They're worried about Jesus' sanity (Mark 3:21). They've worried about his sanity for quite awhile. They show up to "restrain" Jesus; haul him off to a safe and quiet place with attendants and perhaps a nice room with a view of the water.

Another time the family shows up. Mary is again with them. They just want a little time with Jesus—they see so little of the boy these days. Can't he spare a couple hours to go on a picnic in the forest, frolic at the sea for an afternoon for a family reunion? A message comes to Jesus: "Your mom's outside. She and your brothers are waiting to see you." Jesus' reply would have stung if Mary remembered it on Mother's Day: "*Who are my mother and brothers? They're not outside.*" He points to his disciples. "Here they are. This is my real family. Whoever does the will of God is my true kin" (Matt 12:46–50).

Oddly, there is *not a single scene* in the Gospels where Jesus gives his mom a gift, writes her a sweet card, or spends time in her kitchen eating chocolate chip cookies. The only time that Jesus gives his mom *anything* is when he's hanging there on the cross. Mary is standing at the foot of the cross and Jesus points to one of the disciples. He points to this guy and says, "Woman" (still calls his own mom that, please note). Points to a young man standing on the ground and says, "Woman, here is your son" (John 19:26). It's like Jesus is giving Mary the son she's never had.[10]

She had a very strange life. At the end of it, you have to wonder if Mary thought back to that evening in her kitchen with the angel Gabriel. You have to wonder if she would have changed anything. I think she would have said "yes" all over again, which says a lot about her in my book. With Mary, God also asks us to carry the child Jesus in our lives—to bring him to term and maturity[11] in our hearts. What will it mean if we also say "yes"?

*

In London, after the second World War, there was an orphanage some soldiers visited on Christmas morning—"Queen Anne's Orphanage" in the heart of the city. The soldiers had been walking by on the street and heard a celebration going on inside. The house mother gladly received them and explained that the children's parents had been killed in the bombing raids. The orphanage was a sparse place—no tree and no presents. The soldiers moved around the room and passed out small gifts from their pockets: Life Savers, chewing gum, coins, pencils.

One little boy, though, stood back from the men. He was quiet and very shy. One soldier approached him and asked, "And you, little guy, what do you want for Christmas?" The boy slowly answered, "Will . . .

---

10. I'm indebted to Frederick Buechner for this insight.
11. See Eph 4:11–13.

will you hold me?" The soldier picked up the little boy, nestled him close, and held him tight.

God asks Mary the same question: *Will you hold me?* And that is the question posed to all Christians at Advent. Will we hold Jesus and carry him with us no matter the interruption or inconvenience?

Give us courage, gracious God, to give our consent to your divine intrusion into our well-planned lives. That with Mary of old we might all confess: "Here am I, your servant; let it be with me according to your word."

For further reflection:

1. Try to find a recording of "Let It Be," the hit single recorded by the Beatles in 1970. In interviews, Paul McCartney is rather evasive about the song's origins. Do you think he may have had Mary's old story in mind as he wrote this song?

2. Reflect upon a recent interruption in your work/life. Describe your reaction to the interruption and any surprises you may have experienced as a result. Could God have been the source of this interruption?

8. Jesus, Son of Joseph

"Her husband, Joseph, being a righteous man and unwilling to expose her to public disgrace, planned to dismiss her quietly" (Matt 1:19).

OKAY, PRETEND WITH ME and I'll lay it out straight for you. You're a man, an engaged man. And your fiancée comes in with a bit of news. She's pregnant—a bun in the proverbial oven. You can weather this news. After all, you two won't be the first couple who've rushed up a wedding date. You are calm. You can handle this. Your in-laws are understanding people. Things will be okay. Settle down. Take a deep breath.

But then this. She hems and haws and blushes and stammers a bit and then blurts it all out. She says the baby isn't yours. *Silence.* It takes no time and a world of time for the news to reach your ears. You are reeling. You see the pain in her face and feel deeply for this woman you love; the anguish in her eyes as she tells you the truth. You both begin to tear up.

But you also can't help feeling betrayal and anger mounting from way down, deep down. Who has she been with? How did this happen? How could she have lied to you? A thousand things race through your mind. Wedding plans called off. Awkward explanations to friends. The taking back of rings. You love the woman standing in front of you, but this is not your baby. And there are limits to a person's care, a man's patience, are there not? You feel for her. But you are no saint. This is not your responsibility now. Things have changed now. Everything has changed.

Her eyes tell you there is even more to the story than she's revealing. She is silent. So you ask. Indeed you fly into a rage. You'll get to the bottom of this deception. And so she lies to you now. Tries to cover up her infidelity with a wild story that *The National Enquirer* wouldn't even believe. She's either lying or crazy, maybe both. You thought you knew her better than that. You thought she was one who could take responsibility for her mistakes. She is sobbing uncontrollably. But you cannot hold her. Not now. There is nothing else to do. It's *over* now. Thank God you learned this about her before it was too late.

*

The Bible today tells us that Joseph was "a righteous man." The word *righteousness* has fallen on hard times. We normally use it in a contemptuous way, as in the phrase "*self-righteous.*" Lutherans are extremely wary about the word and very fond of accusing folk of "works righteousness" when any discussion about grace and good works occurs. As if righteousness is a bad thing.

"Joseph was a righteous man," says the Bible. And that meant he followed the law revealed in Holy Scripture. He knew all of the rules and obeyed them. He was a good man, a righteous man. He wanted to do the "right thing." And doing the right thing in the first century meant calling off the wedding. An engagement, a betrothal, under Jewish law was a serious, legally binding period that was much like a marriage without the consummation of sex.

So under Jewish law these two lovebirds were essentially considered "hitched." It took a lot to break a betrothal. Adultery, for one, would do it. So when Joseph hears the news, he wants to do the right thing. Joseph loved God's law. He loved the Torah and he loved Mary. But he didn't go in for "fooling around." So Joseph plans to "dismiss" Mary "quietly." Before you jump on Joseph, know that it was common back then to dismiss such a woman *rather loudly*. According to the book of Deuteronomy, Mary could have been stoned to death (22:23–44) for what people would surely recognize as a fling with another man. Even before the dream, though, Joseph wants to protect her. He plans to send her away quietly. He was a righteous man. He was probably named for that other famous Joseph in Genesis; that other dreamer (Gen 37:5–11).

And so Joseph wakes up and chooses *the hard way*. He was a righteous man and no one would've blamed him for calling the whole thing off. But he quietly chooses the hard way. And you know it was hard. How does one explain such a thing to your family and friends? You don't. Joseph swallowed his pride and reputation and put up with the rumors and whispers without a word in order to protect Mary. In fact, Joseph never once speaks in this story or anywhere in the Bible. He does more than he says. Which is not a bad way to look at righteousness.

*

Jesus says a little later in this same Gospel, in the Sermon on the Mount: "Do not think that I have come to abolish the law . . . [but] unless your righteousness exceeds that of the scribes and Pharisees, you will never enter the kingdom of heaven" (Matt 5:17, 20). Joseph's behavior in this old Christmas story *exceeded* the law. Exceeded what was expected and required of him. He chose the hard thing—a difficult, crucifying choice.

Joseph's quiet choice seems to foreshadow another quiet choice of another man who stood by the whole human race and wouldn't turn his back. Jesus apparently learned a lot from his earthly father. For Jesus also chose the quiet, hard path. You normally hear him attached to his mom: Jesus, son of Mary. But I like the sound of this phrase also: *Jesus, son of Joseph*. He grew up to be his daddy's boy.

*

Christian growth (let's call it righteousness) is imparted to us by a loving God as a divine gift. But righteousness has a better chance to work its way in us precisely when *we* choose this hard path when two choices are available. The one "less traveled by," as Frost put it. Again from the Sermon on the Mount in this same Gospel: "Enter through the narrow gate; for the gate is wide and the road is easy that leads to destruction, and there are many who take it. [But] the gate is narrow *and the road is hard* that leads to life, and there are few who find it" (Matt 7:13–14).

Joseph the carpenter chose the hard path when an easier one was surely available. So did his son. Joseph exhibits the behavior his baby will grow up to preach about. Joseph's quiet, difficult choice is central in Matthew's version of the Christmas story. Not the Virgin Mary, curiously. Luke places her on center stage. But not here. It's the dad.

"For the gate is narrow and *the road is hard* that leads to life, and there are few who find it." Without words, Joseph shows us the sacrifice of the hard path at Christmas. His Son will soon follow. Ditto for the Son's children who call themselves disciples, marked in baptism with the cross of Christ forever.

For further reflection:

1. Discuss this line from the essay: "Joseph never once speaks in this story or anywhere in the Bible. He does more than he says."
2. Read slowly Matthew 7:13–14. In your own words, try to restate the gist of Jesus' wisdom in this passage.

9. God Con Carne

". . . you will find a child wrapped in bands of cloth and lying in a manger" (Luke 2:12).

A WONDERFUL SIXTEENTH-CENTURY PAINTING by Pieter Bruegel (*The Adoration of the Kings*, 1564) depicts the magi who finally arrive at the manger. The wise men are a little late and actually don't appear on Jesus' birthday with the shepherds and the rest of the Christmas cast (see Matt 2:1–12). In this old painting, the magus who seems the oldest kneels before the babe. Jesus displays his full humanity for the old man who leans in closely to get a better look, his gaze precisely at the level of the baby's groin. "Get a load of this, Mister Man of Science," the baby Jesus seems to say.

At Christmas, the church gathers to celebrate the utter humanity of God who broke into our world with skin and full plumbing. Theologians call this *the incarnation* and the literal renderings of this word are a little startling. For example, *chili con carne*, "spicy stew with meat," comes from the same root as *incarnation*, as do *carnivore, carnal,* and *carnage*.

I remember Ferdinand the Duck in the movie *Babe*, which is generally about a precocious pig who thinks he's a sheepdog. Ferdinand learns the ugly truth about Christmas dinner—who exactly serves as the main dish—and shouts his dark discovery from the rooftop to the rest of the barnyard. "Christmas means carnage! Christmas means carnage!" For those who recall the eventual dark fate of the baby Jesus, Ferdinand ironically isn't far from the truth.

Carnivore, carnal, carnage. All these words have something to do with "flesh." We claim at Christmas that God once came into the world in a small, out-of-the-way town, enfleshed in the baby Jesus. Someone has pointed out rather graphically (if not crassly) that it might be better to explain the incarnation by using the phrase *God con carne*. That is, "God with flesh on." And so baby Jesus offers an eyeful in Bruegel's painting to make sure these learned men of stars and sky know precisely what's at stake.

*

Whether you celebrate Christmas as a time to gather with family or because you love to sing the old carols; whether you're a true believer or you're really not sure what you believe; whether Jesus completely defines your life or simply gives us all an excuse to throw a little light on winter's darkness—regardless of your faith or perhaps lack of it, the incarnation is the very centerpiece on the Christian family table of fantastic theological claims. The marvelous array of Christian writing, art, and hymnody all rely on the verified plumbing of this little baby.

From Rembrandt to Raphael, from Handel to Haydn, from Dietrich Bonhoeffer to Dorothy Day, *God con carne* was not just an idea. "This will be a sign for you: you will find a scroll of philosophical precepts written in golden calligraphy, wrapped smartly in bands of cloth and lying in a library." No. For so many saints known and unknown to us, Jesus reveals God in a pinch-able way and gives the immortal and invisible creator both a body and a name.

Unlike any other religion in this regard, Christians do not strive to know God as much as God strives to know and communicate with us. And this is difficult for God. Writer Philip Yancey:

> God is infinite, intangible, and invisible. If I may use such language, we humans have little sympathy for the problems that must confront a Being who desires to relate to us. Baron von Hugel drew the analogy of a man's relations with a dog. The parallel was generous to us. An infinite God relating to human beings presents far more of a challenge than a man relating to his dog—perhaps a man communicating with a wood tick is a closer analogy.[12]

Suppose the church can indeed entice you to swallow the incarnation. Then it only follows (claim twenty centuries of theologians) that if

---

12. Yancey, *Reaching for the Invisible God*, 109.

God can show up on barn straw, *then God can show up anywhere*. If God can fill up a baby's flesh, then God can fill any flesh. Jesus says as much in the New Testament. "I am the light of the world," he says in John's gospel (8:12). No, wait a minute, "*You* are the light of the world," he says in the Sermon on the Mount (Matt 5:14). Well, which is it anyway? Won't you make up your mind, Jesus? It turns out that Jesus at Bethlehem is only the beginning of God's enfleshed appearances. God intends to get into our own skin. And from here on out there's no telling where God might show up. So if the church can lead you to buy the incarnation of Jesus, then we'll also help you believe other fantastic claims—such as divine presence in bread and wine, in water, in Christian community, indeed, in all of creation.

Fyodor Dostoyevsky, who came to Christianity only after wondering if God was in the world at all, once wrote these poignant words sometime before his death in 1881 in Russia, illustrating one possible response when a person is really grasped by the reality of God's incarnation. "Love all God's creation," he wrote, "the whole of it and every grain of sand. Love every leaf, every ray of God's light! Love the animals, love the plants, love everything. If you love everything, you will perceive the divine mystery in things. And once you have perceived it you will begin to comprehend it ceaselessly, more and more every day. And you will at last come to love the whole world with an abiding, universal love."

If God can show up as a baby, then God can show up anywhere. *God con carne*—filling Jesus, filling his church, filling the whole world.

For further reflection:

1. Orthodox theologian Alexander Schmemann (1921–1983) has described Christianity as "the end of all religion." Instead of religious adherents ceaselessly striving to gain access to God, Christ reverses the trend and comes to humanity unbidden in the incarnation. Do you agree with Schmemann's assessment? Why or why not?

2. Discuss Yancey's analogy of the wood tick. Can you think of other apt analogies?

10. Unacceptable

"He came to what was his own, and his own people did not accept him" (John 1:11).

For many years, at some point during the Twelve Days of Christmas, I've read the verses from John 1:1–18 into the wind, slowly, line by line, usually after a long hike on the Feast of Saint John the Evangelist (December 27) from the summit of Table Rock (3,124 feet), one of the most prominent peaks in upstate South Carolina. As I read, I'm reminded of the incredible claims the church makes about Jesus. "He was in the beginning with God. All things came into being through him, and without him not one thing came into being" (John 1:2–3). *Not a single thing.* And so I might stop right there and confess that in the last twelve months my ministry has often missed the grandeur (the size) of this messianic undertaking, wanting to pin Jesus down, selfishly capture him as the "local chaplain" for me and mine.

And each line of this famous passage from John is like that. I speak the verses into the weather and silently wait for images and memories from the past year to surface. And I pray. Or confess. Or give thanks. Or make a vow to start again.

Every year it's a different line that most grabs my attention. This past year it was verse 11: "He came to what was his own, and his own people did not accept him."

I cannot imagine what it would be like to be found unacceptable by your own people. But I know it happens. I've been told by people that they can never go home again—some because of their sexuality; some from a mistake they've made that seems unforgivable; some due to a long-ago argument where reconciliation seems impossible.

"Jesus came to what was his own, and his own people did not accept him." There are a variety of instances of Jesus' unacceptability among his own people in the Gospels. There's the time his own family thought he'd gone over the deep end psychologically and came to get him, interrupting his teaching. There's the time he came home and served as lector in worship one Sabbath day. All smiled at his speaking ability until Jesus started preaching on the lesson he'd just read. Then everybody in worship that day tried to toss him off a cliff—these were people he'd known all his life. "His own people." And there are many other instances of rejection (including the crucifixion) by people who weren't strangers. These stories come up regularly in the church's Sunday lectionary cycle. That Jesus was rejected by his own people should not surprise us.

What struck me this time on Table Rock as I spoke this line into the wind at year's end was that I (by virtue of my baptism) am certainly among "his own people." I am one of his own people and find so many of his teachings objectionable, unacceptable—maybe not the hearing of the teaching, but living it. It hit me outside in the wind that it was unfair to make the unacceptability of Jesus a reality just from 2,000 years ago alone. So much of what Jesus says is quietly unacceptable to me; unacceptable perhaps to much of his church, his own people.

If you doubt the truth of this, try the following exercise: compare what Jesus says about peace and reconciliation to the vast size of our national military complex, adding in all the other nations across the world and their respective forces. Compare the size of my home or yours and its contents to what Jesus says about possessions and ownership. Compare what Jesus says about forgiveness to our penchant for retaliation and revenge. Compare my set of friends with Jesus' friends. Compare what Jesus says about wealth and money to what I keep for myself.

None of this is meant to inflict guilt. It's mostly a confession—a confession that I am often so very far afield from the basic teachings of Jesus. And I'm one of "his own people." John 1:11 is not just about people from two millennia ago. It's about me. "He came to what was his own, and his own people did not accept him." There's much of my life where I fail to allow Jesus realistic and practical entrance. I confessed this into the wind from the top of Table Rock.

10. UNACCEPTABLE

*

"And the Word became flesh and lived among us . . . full of grace and truth" (John 1:14). Jesus is full of both, we're told here: grace *and* truth. Sometimes as a Lutheran I want his grace, but I don't much care to hear his truth. Keep it! His truth sounds nutty. His truth sounds so out of step. His truth may not please everyone in his church (his own people).

And so we may stop taking Jesus seriously; start reading him selectively. Adopt another story, another narrative, that really (honestly) directs our days and decisions a heck of a lot more than the story of Jesus. It's easy to worship a little baby on the straw—so cute, so sweet. It's a lot harder to follow the man when he grows up. "The true light, which enlightens everyone, was coming into the world. He was in the world, and the world came into being through him; yet the world did not know him. He came to what was his own, and his own people did not accept him."

His own people did not accept him.

So here's a challenge in the coming year. And you don't have to climb a mountain or even leave your home to accept the challenge. Here goes: in a land filled with so many desires, so many preferences, and so many opinions about so many things, strive to make decisions and plans based upon the teachings of Jesus, not based upon something easier or more popular. This will mean, of course, that we know the teachings of Jesus, in all their vast strangeness and oddness; his own people consciously choosing to accept him.

Deciding over and again to welcome both his grace *and* his truth.

For further reflection:

1. What's the difference between the words "grace" and "truth" in your own life? How do the two words function in the days given to us by God?
2. Has there been an event in your life where you took a courageous (but unpopular) stand that friends or family found unacceptable? If so, describe that event.

II. EPIPHANY

Introduction to the Season

NORMALLY ASSOCIATED WITH DIVINE revelation and manifestation, a quick dictionary check[1] of the word *epiphany* also suggests: "a moment when you suddenly become conscious of something that is very important to you." This season of the church year is filled with epiphanic stories involving learned men of science bearing gifts and following stars; a heavenly voice at a river; and encounters with long-dead heroes on a mountain peak. We'll get to those, but first the story of an old and gifted friend who also reveals the meaning and theology of the Epiphany season.

*

I picked up the phone one autumn long ago, wet from the shower, and the operator's voice sounded rightly suspicious, almost disbelieving. "I have a collect call for the Reverend Frank McIntosh from Alvin, Simon, or Theodore."

I think it was the little word *"or"* that made me laugh the hardest that afternoon; a choice of chipmunks. Or maybe his playful insistence upon referring to me with the name of his hometown dentist, the "tosh" such a fun-sounding syllable. After my go-ahead to the stunned operator, he chortled with a wonderful South Carolina accent, "Do you know who this *eees*?"

---

1. Cambridge Dictionary (online).

Who else could it be? Just prior to entering seminary, I met Bobby at Camp Hope near Clemson on Lake Hartwell. He was a member of a cabin group of mentally challenged campers that summer known as "The Fried Pies." Bobby's personality includes what textbooks used to call "idiot savant." He remembers all sorts of lists and numbers: radio call letters in every South Carolina town; names and situations of extended members of any family he's ever come to know; and detailed information concerning obscure hobbies like sanitation and the accompanying machines required to keep towns tidy. As a boy, Bobby stood silently for hours on the corner near his house and learned the detailed intricacies of his town's mechanized street sweeper.

Bobby still walks with a gait that appears agitated—hands open and parallel, chest-high and shaking in rapid movement; head bobbing up and down—but is mostly an aid in helping his intricate brain retrieve something witty or astonishingly obscure. I always recall portions of Psalm 139 when I'm around Bobby: "For it was you who formed my inward parts; you knit me together in my mother's womb. I praise you, for I am fearfully and wonderfully made." Bobby has felt his share of ridicule and stares. But in church every Sunday near his group home, he's also reminded of his gifts. He helps the men of his congregation prepare breakfast before worship each week; the marvelous leveling effect of food.

I recall a time when I picked Bobby up from his residential facility and we drove to a nearby Hardee's, placed our burger order, and settled into a booth. "Okay, Frank McIntosh, I have a question for you." He let the statement hang in the air for several seconds. "Do you think . . . do you think I'm *retarded*?" I'm pretty certain I've never been asked a question to which I was so eager to reply "no," but the contortions of his face suggested a recent history. I didn't answer right away; I asked what he thought about the word and why others felt a need to use it to describe him.

What followed was a remarkable conversation about our friendship and our differences and his sometimes painful attempts to get other people to understand him. He talked about how it felt when people looked at him strangely when he was at the mall with his friends and why God had chosen to make him this way. And it was like time stood still during our conversation. The nervous shaking of his hands was gone. He looked hard into my eyes and did not turn away. "No, Bobby," I said, using a word I'd come to despise. "I don't think you're retarded."

A letter arrived just before the wise men made their annual journey one recent Epiphany. "This is your old friend, Bobby. Do you remember that time when you were naked as the baby Jesus outside the shower and received a phone call from the singing chipmunks?"

Almost forty years have passed since that call. And yes, Bobby, I do remember. And give God thanks for such an old and gifted friend, so wonderfully made.

1. King Herod's Fear[2]

"When King Herod heard this, he was frightened, and all Jerusalem with him" (Matt 2:3).

IN THE OLD SILENT movies, the director would often employ a device known as an "iris-out." Beginning as a large circle on the screen revealing a fairly wide panorama of visual information, the diameter of the circle slowly closes upon a small detail that doesn't seem all that important at the time, but actually serves as a crucial transition into the next scene. A little tidbit I'd never really noticed in a story about stars, night journeys, and lavish Christmas gifts for a new baby is my new "iris-out" for the Epiphany season as the church year moves from manger to the risky ministry of Jesus.

When the magi visit King Herod that night so long ago, those wise guys ask a question about the whereabouts of a certain child. The text reports that Herod, upon hearing this question, "was frightened." This strikes me as very strange. I'd understand if his royal highness was alarmed, or maybe even confused, but that's not his first reaction. King Herod is afraid. Literally quaking in his boots concerning the birth of a small child who (please don't forget) is still wearing diapers. One of the most powerful men in the world becomes utterly undone by a simple question: *Where is the King of the Jews?*

"Now wait a minute," Herod must have pondered. "I thought that *I* was King of the Jews"—and this important man of means had indeed been given jurisdiction over this pesky tribe of people by the big boys in Rome. So help me here. What is it about this question posed by the magi

---

2. This essay first appeared (in slightly different form) in Honeycutt, "Herod's Fear."

(Persian strangers from the East) that would make Herod's knees knock? "And all Jerusalem with him"! (Matt 2:3). Why is such a powerful guy so utterly spooked by such a pitifully impotent threat who requires burping and a lullaby before a good night's sleep?

Danish theologian Soren Kierkegaard died in 1855. His writings were not well received in his hometown of Copenhagen, and it is said that Kierkegaard died alone and friendless, an outcast from the church. He is not the easiest guy to read; I've tried. But here's a short sampling of his writing that makes perfect sense to me. Kierkegaard is explaining the behavior of the scribes (Herod's head honchos in interpreting these biblical matters) on that night when foreigners followed a star: "The scribes, meanwhile, were much better informed, much better versed. They had sat and studied the scriptures for years, like so many dons. But it didn't make any difference. Who had the more truth? Those who followed a rumor, or those who remained sitting, satisfied with all their knowledge?"[3]

Kierkegaard may be a tough theological nut to crack at times, but here I understand the man perfectly, because he's essentially describing me. Do I really need to know any more about Jesus before I set out? Do I not have enough scriptural information about the man to send me on my way? Or is it simply easier to enjoy the perks and allowances of a resident scribe?

Here is the key to understanding Herod's fear (and perhaps our own). Jesus is not to be studied and admired from a distance, cozily tucked away in some manger twenty centuries removed, dying eventually on a sad cross. Our Lord's kingdom is a movement, an arduous and inviting journey; light in the dark of night where even the starry heavens collaborate in spreading the great good news. The entire cosmos delights in this birth.

Discipleship is always an exercise in exchanging kings, exchanging security, exchanging where we place our trust, our hope, and our gold. Christianity spells the erosion of an old order where we no longer look to earthly rulers for marching orders. Do you see why Herod was afraid? His entire system of governance by control and intimidation was crumbling.

In *The Lion, the Witch, and the Wardrobe*, the marvelous fable of C. S. Lewis now on the big screen, we see the utter panic in the face of the White Witch as her winter realm begins to melt away. She is threatened by what she hears as Aslan's reign emerges. The White Witch may not do

---

3. Kierkegaard, *Meditations*, 35.

away with all the babies in Narnia under age two,[4] but in the movie her fear is just as palpable as Herod's.

Please don't mistake this battle of kingdoms as only waged long ago and far away. There will always be a battle for our hearts with issues that involve ultimate trust and hope. And if this doesn't make us fearful at least occasionally, if it doesn't make our knees knock, then perhaps we haven't really heard the one called Lord.

The first word spoken out loud by a human being (Matt 2:2) in the book of Matthew is the word *Where*. It's a word that assumes a search is occurring. *Where is the king?* That single word must forever remain on the lips of Christians living in the world today, living in the United States. For false kings abound. And it is tempting to bow in all the wrong places in exchange for a host of passing securities.

Remember this "iris-out" for Epiphany. "When King Herod heard their question, he was frightened, and all Jerusalem with him." God bless the poor guy—if he only knew what we Christians know today.

A tongue-in-cheek confession from one (yours truly) whose evangelical knees regularly knock in scribal immobility.

For further reflection:

1. As a transitional exercise, what "iris-outs" from the previous season of Advent would you highlight?
2. Name a few improbable promises made by national political leaders in the twenty-first century, perhaps playing upon a perspective of fear.

---

4. See Matt 2:16–18.

2. Drenched in Divine Delight

"This is my Son, the Beloved, with whom I am well pleased"
(Matt 3:17).

AM I MISSING SOMETHING here? For heaven's sake, all the man did was stand there in a river and get some water poured over his head. Or maybe he was dunked; it's not clear. What really concerns me is that heavenly voice, booming affirmation over the river and across time and space.

Forgive me for being thickheaded, but "pleased' with what? What exactly has Jesus *done* to date to elicit such high praise from his heavenly Father? Search your Bible high and low and try to discover a single example of exemplary behavior recorded in any of the Gospels prior to his baptism. You'll find a good bit about his birth, a single story from his childhood (Luke 2:41–51), but little else prior to this watery event—no miracles, no teachings, no impressive deeds at all. Zilch. And if Jesus had been a rather precocious teenager, an up and coming young adult, I'd say somebody would have written it down. And none of the Gospels do.[5] Which means Jesus lived a fairly normal, nondescript life in those early years, nothing flashy or noteworthy.

So forgive me for asking what seems like an impertinent question, but what exactly is this heavenly voice so pleased about? What has elicited these divine cartwheels? It must not take a whole lot to make God happy, for the divine Father is absolutely beside himself with delight and pleasure for reasons that are altogether unclear to me. Jesus is standing there in the water, dripping wet, in need of a towel, and heaven goes nuts.

---

5. There are some rather bizarre examples of notorious childhood behavior (including an odd story of Jesus turning a bully into a bird!) in various apocryphal Gospels.

Please notice this watery story where Jesus is drenched in divine delight and showered with God's good pleasure. Notice it well because it just doesn't fit our modern notions of behavior modification and reward. "Now Johnny, first you learn to use the potty properly without messing your pants and then I'll give you an M&M." "That's right, Vivian, since you've been selected Student of the Week and are such a good little girl, you get to dust the erasers today." "Stewart, our profits are way ahead this year thanks to your hard work. Here's a little Christmas bonus to show our appreciation and there's more where that came from, if you know what I mean."

As far as I can tell, God must have failed "Behavior Mod 101" in college because his divine pleasure at the river with the man standing in the water has nothing at all to do with Jesus' performance record. For God is apparently delighting in (and pouring his spirit into) a son who has no miraculous vita, no impressive resume, and not a single recorded good deed to date. Not only does this tell us a lot about God, it also tells us loads about baptism.

Pastors, as you might guess, have to walk into a rather large measure of human misery on a fairly regular basis; it's part of the territory. But we also get to view some pretty remarkable things on a regular basis. Like watching two parents hold a new baby in the first days of life, just delighting in their child—just gazing in wonder and pleasure. I have a pastor friend who regularly visits the maternity ward on his hospital rounds (even if no one from his church is there) to remind himself that death and woe do not have the last word. Love has the last word.

Wasn't Jesus loved in just this way? With equal and surpassing delight? Jesus was doused with water that day, but he was also bathed and surrounded by God's good bliss and pleasure—which leads to a theory.

Have you ever noticed that it's only *after* his baptism that the miraculous works of Jesus begin? I've come to believe that Jesus' radical ministry of good works, his feeding of the poor, and his inclusion of people who were neither popular nor powerful are all a direct result of his clear identity as God's beloved. He was free to love others (even to the point of giving his life) because he knew of Another who loved him indescribably and infinitely. Ponder this: perhaps God's lavish, unconditional pleasure in Jesus empowered him to love so radically and freely; a love poured into him at baptism.

More pondering: what if the *same Spirit* poured into Jesus at the Jordan is also poured into Christ's church via baptism? Baptism is not

2. DRENCHED IN DIVINE DELIGHT

some magical ticket to heaven we get punched when the water is poured. As a result of baptism, our lives will begin to resemble the life of Jesus.[6]

*

A recurring problem in our relationships arrests the growth of so very many people. The unhappiest people I know (the most wounded people I know) fear deep down that no one delights in them; no one takes pleasure in them. They fear that they always have to earn approval, acceptance, and love. They've heard only criticism, never blessing.

It's impossible for such people to just *be*. They have to perpetually justify their existence to others. This is what it truly means to be *self-absorbed*—sadly spending much of our time trying to get others to love us. Never confident that love is there without condition, many fill their lives with trivia and trinkets and shallow friendships. Such people are often a hurt waiting to happen. Such a person is blocked from true love of others because they themselves do not feel loved.

The church's gospel invites us to love others, even those who are difficult to love. "You are my Child, the Beloved, with you I am well pleased." Yes, that was the voice that echoed across an old river centuries ago. But what if that same voice echoes across the waters of your congregation's font at every baptism? Here's one of our main callings as disciples of Jesus in his church: *to let the baptismal delight drenched upon us by a glad God flow through our lives to others.*

This specifically means that we'll spend a great deal of time blessing others: building the spiritual esteem of children; telling people how special they are and what gifts you see in them—in short, taking sheer delight in one another. There are so many opportunities to do this every day with a variety of people.

It took me a long time to learn this as a father. I guess I thought it was my role to always correct and guide with a strong hand; to morally instruct and always be the discipline guy. I missed a lot of opportunities to simply bless and commend and tell my children how delighted I was with them. This is such an important part of being a Christian, a baptized follower of Jesus—maybe more important than anything we do. Please, do not keep silent. When we bless and take pleasure in others, we are reflecting the very delight of God.

---

6. See Rom 6:1–11.

*

Remember: God went plumb bonkers over Jesus before he'd "done" a blessed thing. He was so proud of his Son. "This is my child, the beloved, with whom I am well pleased."

Do you believe those words were intended also for you? I hope and pray so. Because only then, from that clear and vocal identity of acceptance, can we slowly learn to love as Jesus loved. His ministry began in the water upon listening to the clear voice of his Father. Ours begins there, too. We are the walking wet; drenched in divine delight.

Who can we build up with a kind word? Who can we gift with the very delight of God? Anyone coming to mind?

Some advice: tell them.

For further reflection:

1. Why is it often so difficult for us to begin with affirmation rather than correction or criticism?
2. If you've been baptized, do some research on the date and circumstances of your baptism and begin celebrating the date with at least as much gusto as your earthly birthday.

3. Walk on By

". . . and as he watched Jesus walk by, he exclaimed, 'Look, here is the Lamb of God!'" (John 1:36)

WHICH OF THESE DESCRIPTIONS of the early disciples and their relationship to Jesus is more biblically accurate?

Description #1: Jesus is waking along and sees a pair of fishermen, brothers, casting a net. He calls Peter and Andrew; they drop everything and follow him. A little farther down the beach he calls another set of brothers, James and John, hard at work mending their nets. Jesus also calls these two. Right away they follow Jesus, leaving their daddy in the boat.[7]

Description #2: Jesus is walking along through an undetermined town. Perhaps Jesus sees a small gathering of interested observers, whispering and pointing. One of the observers is Andrew, mentioned earlier in Description #1, nowhere near a net. But here's the funny thing. Jesus walks right by these interested observers without a word. Ignores them is another way of saying it. Two inquirers (one is Andrew) scamper behind a rather aloof Jesus to ask questions.

So, which of these two descriptions is more biblically accurate? Oddly, they're equally accurate descriptions of discipleship—the Jesus who takes the initiative in finding us, *and* we who take the initiative in finding a rather elusive Jesus. The stories should not compete with one another. More and more I'm discovering that both are vitally important facets of the Christian life.

---

7. See Mark 1:16–20.

Lutherans get this right, I'm convinced: God acts, Jesus acts, to find us in our waywardness, our sin. We are called out of darkness into his marvelous light. The reason we baptize babies is not because they're so cute, but because the sacrament is God's action; God claiming a new child in a fallen world. Few things disturb me more than re-baptism. "Babies don't know what they're doing," is the rationale. "Now at an older age, they do." I once met a man who'd been baptized six times. The reason this is wrong-headed is that the sacrament (at whatever age) is about God acting, not about our relative worthiness or understanding. Baptism is grace in liquid form.

John Wesley, the great eighteenth-century frontier preacher of early Methodism, is known for a sermon titled "The New Birth" which he delivered almost 100 times in his career. "If any doctrines within the whole compass of Christianity may be properly termed fundamental," he preached, "they are doubtless these two—the doctrine of justification, and that of the new birth: The former relating to that great work which God does *for us*, in forgiving our sins; the latter to the great work which God does *in us*, in renewing our fallen nature."[8]

Lutherans are clear about the great work God does "for us." I'm worried sometimes that we (denominationally) are unclear about the great work God wants to do "in us." We need both portraits of Jesus that I sketched earlier. The Jesus who takes initiative, claims us, and realigns even family allegiance with his baptismal call. *And* the rather elusive Jesus who walks on by, beckoning us to take initiative in figuring out who he is; inviting active participation in our growth, our sanctification. This will conjure two words that may make some Lutherans squirm a bit: growth may *require* (the first word) our actual *effort* (that's the second). Squirmers may find comfort in Dallas Willard's words: "Grace is not opposed to effort, it is opposed to earning."[9]

"What are you looking for?" (John 1:38) asks Jesus who seems content to walk on by in John's gospel. These are the first words out of his mouth in this Gospel and I take them as a template for serious discipleship. A search is implied by the Lord; a quest. Without a sense for such a quest, the man ultimately cannot be known. It's not that he *wants* to walk on by. We may let him, in effect.

---

8. Wesley, *The Works of John Wesley*, 65 (italics in original).

9. Willard, *The Great Omission*, 61.

3. WALK ON BY

*

I saw a movie recently with my wife and son—an independent film, *Five Minutes of Heaven* (2009). The movie is set in Northern Ireland and stars Liam Neeson and James Nesbitt. One character in the movie is Protestant, the other Catholic. The two men are part of a Truth and Reconciliation project trying to heal old wounds from the decades of violence and mistrust in the region. As a nineteen-year-old, Neeson's character killed Nesbitt's brother, right in front of his eyes. The man who lost his brother was only a little boy at the time of the killing. All the characters in the movie are baptized Christians. Part of the artistry of the film, all through the attempted reconciliation, is the silent backdrop of various church buildings shown only from the outside. No words of Jesus are ever spoken in the film, but the silent church buildings speak volumes, as if to say: "Jesus has a place in this culture, but not in the streets."

In the town in Virginia where I used to live, there was an annual "Martin Luther King, Jr., Remembrance Day" hosted by the local peace education center. I went to the celebration for many years. We sang. We clapped. We heard testimonies of peace. We recalled King as a great man and heard some of his words. But after many years of attending, a strange silence kept bothering me concerning a key component of what fueled the civil rights movement in the first place. Something was missing. Jesus was missing. There was never a word about the man behind the man; the gospel teachings that led a good man to do great things. Never a word in all the times I attended. It's impossible to understand what King did without trying to understand Jesus. I invite you to give it a try, but you will fail.

Whether you live in Northern Ireland or Selma, Alabama, it's impossible to be the church without Jesus. Christians will first center upon this man, or it is something other than church that we are about. Can there be a Jesus-less church? No, but there can be a Jesus-less church that looks like a church from the outside.

*

Rather oddly, Jesus walks right on by would-be disciples in John's version of the story. They have to catch up with him, maybe breathlessly. Jesus will not push himself on us. We must want to get to know him, or he may walk on by.

"What are you looking for?" he wants to know. We must come to terms with this question. What *are* we looking for? Life as we know it with a little Jesus on the side? Or are we willing to allow Jesus into all facets of life, even the little nooks and crannies we hide away from anyone's view?

"They came and saw where he was staying, and they remained with him that day." *Remained.* May the church remain with Jesus through all our days, every day, until we confess, through diligent search and quest, that "We (too) have found the Messiah" (John 1:41).

For further reflection:

1. Why are Jesus' initiative and our quest both important facets of discipleship?

2. *What are you looking for* at this point in your life?

4. Sex and Saint Paul

"Do you not know that your body is a temple of the Holy Spirit within you?" (1 Cor 6:19).

IN MY LINE OF work, I hear a variety of comments at funeral homes from people trying to break the awkward silence of the moment. "Doesn't she look good?" I've honestly never really seen a dead person that looks all that great. They may look peaceful or at rest, but in short they truthfully look, well, *dead*.

Here's another comment, a close second place in popularity: "He's in a better place now." Traditional Christian theology does not embrace this immediate claim in the way we might think. We may sing the old spiritual "I'll Fly Away" on occasion, but the Apostles' Creed never states that souls somehow split away from bodies and glide up to heaven immediately after death. That's a very old Greek idea known as "the immortality of the soul," but it's not Christian theology.

Almost every week, many Christians say, "I believe in the resurrection of the body." I don't know exactly what happens at death. (Excepting Christ, no one knows, even those who claim to have come back from it.) But I do know that this old creedal line significantly parts ways with a very popular understanding of a division of body and soul.

Christian theology disagrees with the idea that the really good part of us, the spiritually pure part, goes on to the "Happy Hunting Grounds" while our bodies—often repulsive shells that smell bad, grow dandruff, and finally wear out—are expendable and transient. "I believe in the resurrection of *the body*," we say. Not the resurrection of a disembodied, ephemeral spirit.

Please don't get hung up on how this happens—what you'll look like in the hereafter; whether or not to cremate; whether or not to donate your organs to another needy body because you might need them later on. Our God is a creative God and will take care of such concerns. Instead, it's important to remember the *unity* of body and soul. Bodies matter. In short, *matter matters*. How we care for and honor bodies is not just some faddish frenzy to obtain washboard abs. Our care for the body has eternal implications, not just temporal.

Jesus took special pains after the resurrection to show the disciples that he was not a ghost. He invited the disciples to touch him and give him food.[10] He made a point that resurrection included flesh and bones. Again, I cannot say exactly what happens to a person at death and beyond. But I can say with certainty that the drafters of the creed assumed some sort of physicality in the resurrection; a body.

*

These reflections are a rather long introduction to some of Saint Paul's very strong concerns that serve as the centerpiece of this essay.[11] There is an inherent tension in Paul's writing between the ideas of freedom, liberty, and the health of the body. An ongoing wordplay exists in this passage between our individual bodies and "the body" that is the church. Paul is writing specifically about sex. (If that shocks you, it's important to recall that the Bible is absolutely full of sex.) Paul is centrally concerned here with fornication; the Greek word is *porneia*, from whence we get the word "pornography."

Prostitution was a commonly accepted practice in Greek culture. In Corinth, a port city, this was especially so. Few questioned the practice; spouses put up with it. Prostitution was as common as walking downtown for a loaf of bread. Brothels are rare in my small town (I at least assume they're rare and doubt anyone in the Lutheran church here in Walhalla will attempt to challenge that assumption), but common in Corinth.

In this teaching from First Corinthians, you'll notice that a couple of phrases are set off by quotation marks. For example, the very first words in verse 12: "All things are lawful for me." Paul is quoting a popular Greek slogan of his day. The idea was so popular that it could have been a

---

10. See John 20:26–29 and Luke 24:36–43.
11. See 1 Cor 6:9–20.

4. SEX AND SAINT PAUL

bumper sticker. All Things are Lawful for Me slapped on the back of your first-century Subaru wagon. Paul is careful here. He's written persuasively about the freedom of the Christian; how life in Christ liberates one from the law. So he quotes the bumper sticker, acknowledges its truth, but adds a caveat: *but not all things are beneficial.* He quotes the slogan a second time and adds a different caveat: *I will not be dominated by anything.* Paul resists legislative rules for sexuality, but does seem to suggest that sexuality is an area that can dominate our lives if we aren't careful.

And this fear is undeniably true in America today. We now have something reviewed and analyzed in various media sources known as "the sex life." I can think of no other facet of our beings that is given such attention and status. A guest on Oprah reports: "Oh, my sex life is rather stale these days." Magazines as mainstream as *Redbook* shout to me in the grocery checkout line: "Improve/Heighten/Enrapture Your Sex Life." Is *anything* assigned a "life" in our culture with such urgent consistency? It's almost like it's this other thing about us that needs isolating and constant examination. And when we admit this, I think we're getting close to Paul's entire argument.

Saint Paul is no sexual prude, as many believe. Instead, he wants to bring sexuality under the wider umbrella of what it means to have a body. If soul and body are eternally united in a person, what we do with those bodies, how we care for other bodies, does indeed matter. "All things may be lawful," says Paul, "but not all things are beneficial."

When I was a little boy in Chattanooga, before the interstate came through, there were some wonderful woods near our house. My friend Jimmy once swiped several magazines with certain well-known titles from his grandfather and buried those magazines in the woods in waterproof plastic bags. I cannot remember how many times Jimmy and I crept off to the woods, dug up those magazines, and got an eye-full from the pages. Each time I did this I felt bad, vowing that this final peek would be the last, even praying to God for strength to resist.

Such furtive peeks are a normal part of growing up, of course. As we age, however, there is a line that's easy to cross for any male or female. Often we justify crossing that line with the slogan offered in Corinth: "Who's this hurting, really? Isn't this just my own personal business? Aren't all things lawful for me?"

In response, Paul sounds like a fire-breathing fundamentalist when he shouts in the middle of this passage: "Shun fornication!" Flee from *porneia*! I really doubt that anyone's ever refrained from crossing a harmful sexual line simply because someone's told them not to.

But you will miss entirely Saint Paul's point if you think this is just an exercise in imperative scolding. Paul's main arguments are first couched squarely in the indicative: "Your bodies are members of Christ. . . . Anyone united to the Lord becomes one spirit with him. . . . Your body is a temple of the Holy Spirit within you" (1 Cor 6:15, 17, 19). Scolding and stern prohibition will never create a healthy child, a healthy man or woman (sexually or otherwise). But Paul is not really doing that here. Paul is reminding the church of the deep presence of God in our bodies—a temple, a physical abode, where the Spirit takes up holy and permanent residence. "My body was not hidden from you, while I was being made in secret and woven into the depths of the earth" (Ps 139:15).

What kind of home are we offering God in our bodies? This is such an important question as we teach physical and sex education to our children and grandchildren and as we think about sexuality and take care of our bodies as adults. "You are not your own," says St. Paul. "You were bought with a price" (6:19–20). God has taken up residence in every physical fiber of your being.

How can we help recall this deep indwelling of the presence of God *in our bodies*? The answer to this question may reside in a recovery of that old line from the Apostles' Creed: *I believe in the resurrection of the body*. Please confront wherever possible the old falsehood that physical concerns have nothing to do with the spiritual. Be suspicious of the conventional wisdom that makes this claim: "Gosh, we can't talk about that in church! That's not a spiritual topic!" In this old creedal claim, physical and spiritual are forever united.

What God has joined together, let no one put asunder.

For further reflection:

1. Are the ideas concerning "the resurrection of the body" new for you? Discuss how this old creedal claim might reshape convictions concerning how we care for human bodies.
2. Why is it sometimes difficult to talk about sex with our children?

5. Tonic for Demonic

"What have you to do with us, Jesus of Nazareth?" (Mark 1:24)

THERE WERE LOTS OF little places of fear and trepidation in my childhood. Under the bed at night. A dark closet that seemed especially foreboding. Old Mrs. Connor's house in the woods. (She was surely cooking gingerbread in there to lure children towards her hot ovens.) The attic of my grandmother's house in North Carolina gave me the willies every time I went up into it. The pictures of my dead relatives and the old letters they wrote seemed to come alive and float around that stuffy space. I soon needed air.

Lots of strange stuff lurks in the recesses of a child's mind. Darkness and evil are real; nearby. But there was one place that I knew was off-limits for anything sinister. And that was church—church was safe; holy. I figured my early boredom with it was a reasonable trade-off for the divine protection God was granting me during that sacred hour. And perhaps there were other extended perks of holy safety and protection that followed me around the other days of the week just for setting foot in a church on Sundays. Even our adult sensibilities of the sacred and profane suggest a church building as a holy, set-apart place, exempt from the cares of the world; a true sanctuary.

Jesus seems to encounter the demonic with some regularity during the Epiphany season. He deals with demons in Mark's gospel more than any other. He speaks with them, puts them in their place, and defeats them. A curious sidebar in Mark's gospel is that the disciples never really understand who Jesus is, even after he dies. In contrast, the demons know exactly who Jesus is. They recognize the power he is bringing into the world to send them packing. "I know who you are, the Holy One of God," says this particular unclean spirit (Mark 1:24). The disciples never come close to such a confession.

Have you thought much about the existence of the demonic? In one of my former congregations, somebody called the church office one morning and asked if we did exorcisms. Our church secretary, Amy (quick on her feet) said, "No, I can't recall the last one." The caller said, "Thank you. I'll try another church."

In the early church, some baptismal liturgies included an actual spitting at the devil (towards the western darkness) by baptismal candidates, before they were plunged into the water at the eastern rising of the sun. Cyril of Jerusalem (350–387) writes:

> When you renounce Satan, you trample underfoot your entire covenant with him, and abrogate your former treaty with hell. The Gates of God's Paradise are open to you, the garden which God planted in the east, and from which our first parent was expelled for his transgression. When you turned from west to east, the region of light, you symbolized the change of allegiance.[12]

Even though remnants of the ancient rites still exist in modern baptismal liturgies in the "renunciation" part of the service, I suspect many Christians attribute bizarre behavior—Hitler, school shootings, various hate crimes—to something explainable and rational: a psychological abnormality, an abusive parent, or some early deprivation. But here in Mark's gospel (just after his baptism) we have Jesus going head-to-head with a dark underworld. What do you make of this?

What surprises me most in this old story is the context for this confrontation. Look closely. Where does all this happen? You'd think we'd find Jesus in an obviously shady place—a local hangout for organized crime, perhaps a downtown brothel, maybe the equivalent of a first-century crack house. Instead, Jesus encounters demons (for the very first time in his ministry) in a worship space—a synagogue; *a sanctuary*. The one place I thought we were safe. Nothing in *The Exorcist* could rival what was going on right in the middle of church, let's say.

*

"One little word subdues him," writes Martin Luther in his famous hymn, "A Mighty Fortress." It's true. "Silence," says Jesus, and there is. But

---

12. Johnson, *The Rites of Christian Initiation*, 95.

not before convulsions and screams fill the air and saliva stains are left on the carpet. We have a bit of silence during the confession and following the sermon in my own worship tradition, but nothing like this. To the credit of this Capernaum congregation, nobody ran.

As he tells this old story, Mark wants us to notice that there's a lot at stake when we gather for worship; when we gather as church. The battle isn't always "out there" in somebody's obviously evil backyard. The battle for our ultimate allegiance is always occurring as the teachings of Jesus clash with the ways of this world. That's one reason many churches offer Holy Communion each week. That's why we have confession. That's why we cross ourselves and remember our baptisms, over and again. In short, we are at war spiritually.[13]

Please notice the rather odd response of this seaside congregation in Capernaum just after they witnessed an exorcism with one or more demons on the floor of their sanctuary. "A new teaching!" they report. *Say what?*

The spit is fresh on the sanctuary carpet and they call it a Sabbath school lesson. Now if a man came through the street doors in the middle of the sermon at your home church, behaving like a demoniac, and your pastor had even minor success in silencing this loud person or casting out an evil spirit or two, you might react in a variety of ways, but I seriously doubt you'd elbow your neighbor and say, "My goodness, a new teaching. Our crafty pastor is trying a new innovation in Christian education this morning."

*

What does this story mean for congregations like ours? The demons ask a question and it's also our question on some level. "What have you to do with us, Jesus of Nazareth?" Well, plenty.

This old story might help us see that Sunday mornings are not the safe, sweet haven of rest and sanctuary we sometimes seek. The story might also remind us that it's important to *prepare* for worship as we step into the space, rather than chatting up a neighbor right away. Why? Because this old story suggests that church is the community where demons (real or symbolic) are driven out. And how does this happen? *Through the teachings of Jesus.*

13. See Eph 6:10–17.

The unclean spirit appears in this story not before Jesus starts teaching, *but as a result of the teaching*. The text says, "Just then . . ." (Mark 1:23). Just after he started to teach. The evil spirit seems to sense the amazing potential of this teaching to transform and heal, so the demons arrive to interrupt and derail the instruction. Mark wants his readers to clearly notice: the words of Jesus will unbind and free this world from sin and evil, but those same words may quicken (post-baptism, please notice) our encounter with such.

*

Do you ever wonder what happened to the unclean spirit in this story? Jesus clearly casts the demon out, but where does it go? There is no mention that the spirit is annihilated, just defeated for the moment. It seems to be at large.

Jesus has power and authority over evil in the world. But evil still roams the earth in ways we cannot fully understand. "All threatening to devour us," says Luther in that same hymn. We cling to Jesus' teachings. His voice, still echoing down to us, silences the very real voices of darkness potentially inside us all.

Be silent. Come out of them.

For further reflection:

1. Examine your honest thoughts and feelings about the existence of evil in the world today. What do you really think about "demons"?

2. Baptism in this old story does not magically "protect" Jesus from evil, but instead seems to hasten the encounter, especially as he teaches. How does this story change a rather common notion that baptism somehow inoculates a person from future evil or calamity?

6. Furious with Jesus

"They led him to the brow of the hill . . . so that they might hurl him off the cliff" (Luke 4:29).

IN 1985, WHEN I graduated from seminary, nobody told me that preaching a sermon could get you killed. Nobody told me that people sometimes get mad at you for trying to speak the word of God. Nobody told me that usually loving people could get red in the face over a twelve-minute homily.

Just after the horrible news of 9/11, I preached a sermon about praying for our enemies; it was right out of the teachings of Jesus. This was at the height of Osama bin Laden's reign of terror and I suggested that we actually pray for the man; that if anyone could change his warped thinking, God could.

After the service, I saw her coming. She was not happy; livid, red in the face, even breaking through the pastoral receiving line. I thought for a moment she was going to hit me. "How *dare you* preach such a thing?" she hissed. "Especially with what's going on in our country right now. Who do you think you are?" I reminded her that I was indeed her pastor, "at least for the moment," I said rather flippantly (now regretfully), sometimes called by God to say difficult things out loud. It didn't help for me to say, "Hey, I didn't make this stuff up. Do you read the Bible with any frequency?" More invective and spitting of nails. It wouldn't be the last time a churchgoer had their pastor for lunch, so to speak, after a sermon.

II. EPIPHANY

*

Once upon a time, some irate parishioners led Jesus to the edge of town and tried to throw him off a cliff after he unwisely made a few pointed comments on the lesson for the day. In other words, he gave a sermon nobody liked.[14] I carefully research the topography around the church building before accepting a call. The beautiful campus where my last congregation gathered also included a rather lofty clock tower that would undoubtedly get the job done, but at least the church wasn't built on a precipitous pinnacle like nearby Tamassee Knob (elevation 1,620 feet) where the merest of pastoral shoves (oops) would do the trick.

Jesus went home one weekend and went to worship that Saturday, probably with his family and surely with people he'd grown up with. He read the lesson in his hometown synagogue. Maybe somebody in the congregation slept late and Jesus had to fill-in as substitute lector. He must have read very well. The story says that "all spoke well of him." Not some, all, at least for awhile. The sermon he preached that day created a lynch mob, oddly filled with people who'd known him all his life.

Growing up in Chattanooga, I once made our next-door neighbor, Mr. Henry, very mad because we kept hitting baseballs into his immaculate backyard. Mrs. Zott farther down the road didn't like it upon learning that certain teenage boys were sneaking over her fence and into her swimming pool to skinny dip after midnight. But Mr. Henry and Mrs. Zott were always warm and cordial whenever I came home from college. I cannot imagine how hard it must have been on Jesus to feel aunts and uncles (and once-friendly neighbors) roughly grab his shoulders and lead him out to the edge of town. Why didn't Jesus just read the lesson that morning, soak in all the adulation, and go home after worship to his momma's fried chicken? It must have been some sermon for the whole congregation to turn on their hometown boy like that.

Martin Luther once said that effective preaching is sometimes like surgery. He said most know that surgery is something we probably need, but nobody really wants to sign up for such news if they can avoid it. The townspeople in Nazareth were undoubtedly a bit like that. The stories Jesus alluded to that morning about a widow (1 Kgs 17:8–24) and a leper (2 Kgs 5:1–14) were stories from a Bible that the Nazarenes knew very well. Jesus wasn't springing a new teaching on them. He was reminding them of something they already knew. "But the truth," says Jesus, is that

---

14. See Luke 4:16–30.

6. Furious with Jesus

God loves outsiders as much as insiders. "The truth is that God loves foreigners, people who aren't anything like folk living around here, just as much as he loves us." This was a truth he (at the very least) implied; a hard truth to swallow for those at worship that day. A truth that almost got Jesus killed.

Reminding people of what they already know can birth quite a bit of canned rage. Have you ever told the truth to someone and it made them furious? I'd say you have. Has anyone ever told *you* the truth and it infuriated you? In Nazareth long ago, the story says "They got up." Please don't forget where these people were. They got up from old pews, the place where they'd heard the Bible all their lives; and they grabbed the preacher, the messenger, absolutely irate over his audacity. Jesus escapes this time. But there will be another crowd, another hill, another place where angry people will try to silence the voice of truth.

In Saint Paul's famous verses about love[15] (which were first written with *congregations* in mind rather than for moony couples standing at an altar), the old salty preacher says that we "have been fully known." I suppose it's comforting to be fully known by God, but such a state can also be terrifying because nothing remains hidden. Our prejudices, our hatreds, our old, festering wounds and grudges—*all exposed*. Jesus does this about as well as anyone I know. He will lead us to spiritual growth if we want such, but if we're really listening, *he will first make us angry*. If he doesn't raise your ire on a regular basis, then it's possible you may have settled for a sweet and domesticated Jesus who only coddles, affirms, and supports without condition.

Once again and for the record: it was very nice that morning when Jesus read from Scripture, but it was another thing altogether when he went to preaching—went to meddlin', as southern folk sometimes say. It's one thing to revere the Bible, a holy tome still (hands-down) the most popular book in America in terms of sales. But it's a different enterprise entirely to open its pages and be completely shaped by what we encounter there. They loved Jesus as a lector, but his application of a familiar word to their daily lives really ticked these townspeople off.

---

15. See 1 Cor 13:1–13.

II. EPIPHANY

*

I do a fair amount of thinking about folk who slowly become inactive in congregational life—people who join a church and then vanish. This should cause us great alarm because I've never met a person who is growing in Jesus Christ apart from the church. Without the regular reception of the Eucharist in your life, something is substantially missing.

In over three decades as a pastor, I've noticed that people depart from church life for a variety of reasons. Here are four of the most common: No one reached out in a time of crisis. The pastor did or said something that was offensive. Feelings were hurt by another church member. A general lack of feeling wanted or included caused the exit. When I talk with other pastors, these four reasons are usually near the top.

But here's a fifth (and largely overlooked) reason. People often leave church life over the teachings of Jesus, and much more often than you might think. Instead of taking his instruction to heart and allowing his Spirit to shape and form all facets of my life, it's sometimes far easier to flee. Jesus says many strange, offputting, odd things in the Gospels. Running the other way becomes an appealing option for any of us. If you've never considered fleeing from Jesus, then it may be that you're reading the man selectively. He can be offensive just about as often as he's comforting.

Please remember. "All spoke well of him." Everybody in that congregation loved him as a lector. He read so beautifully with his long flowing hair, but there were limits to the adulation. Jesus can make us pretty mad if we listen to him closely; angry enough to spit nails.

There's a lot of anger in the United States these days, but I truly doubt that we'd actually push Jesus over the side of a cliff to get rid of him. I suspect we're far too civilized for that. However, I do think it's possible to push him so far and so insidiously out of one's life that this second sort of pushing amounts to just about the same thing as what happened on that hill.

For further reflection:

1. Describe a time when someone so told you the truth about yourself that your response was anger more than acceptance.
2. Why do we need such people in our lives?

7. Jesus Gets Ticked

"Moved with [anger], Jesus stretched out his hand and touched him . . ." (Mark 1:41).

THE LAST ESSAY DESCRIBED one's honest anger with Jesus in reaction to his message, but this next story deals with the Lord's own anger and a tiny literary device that may or may not appear in the Bible you're using: *a footnote*. Consult a Bible with notes and annotations. Turn to Mark 1:41, and let your eye rest upon the word "pity." Jesus stretched out his hand and touched a leper because he was "moved with pity." But notice the footnote beside that word. It will direct you to the bottom of the page, where small italicized print reports: "Other ancient authorities read *anger*." Fairly strong and reliable ancient Greek manuscripts depicting the healing of a leprous man choose the word *anger* over *pity*. I realize this line of thinking may make a scriptural fundamentalist fairly nervous. Anger and pity are very different words. As my children used to ask on occasion, *What's up with that?*

The church makes bold doctrinal claims that Jesus was both divine and human, so it's important to remember that Jesus felt every human reaction under the emotional rainbow—anger, pity, grief, joy, exhaustion, elation, dismay. Name an emotion and Jesus had it because he was human, not a celestial robot.

What may be troubling is the Bible's inability to report clearly in this story exactly which emotion Jesus was feeling that day. Was it anger or was it pity? Why do we have this choice in the Bible? Did a similar scene occur more than once in the ministry of Jesus? Was an early scribe uncomfortable, maybe nervous, with one of the emotions and simply chose the other?

I consulted a variety of English translations in my possession to see what each did with this choice. The New English Bible was far and away my favorite because the editors chose to include the sense of *both* words. That translation reports that Jesus reached out to the leper "in warm indignation." Now that's quite an emotional balancing act, warm indignation, but perhaps Jesus could pull it off. I'd say it's fairly challenging to be warmly indignant, an obvious revelation that the editors of the New English Bible had a tough time choosing between "anger" and "pity" and therefore included the sense of both. For the record, I choose "anger."

Why choose "anger" for Jesus' reaction to this leper? The poor leprous guy comes to Jesus, begging, pleading, throwing himself in a puddle on the floor at our Lord's feet. Lepers, as you probably know, were cruelly segregated in the time of Jesus. They were untouchables. It makes biblical sense to think that Jesus felt "pity" for this man. I could certainly make an argument for that word, too. So why "anger"?

My choice centers upon the leper's statement: "If you choose, you can make me clean." It was a remarkable thing for the leper to say: "*you* can make me clean." Such a declaration stood in marked contrast to how leprosy was dealt with in the first century. Back then, ailments of the skin were thought to *theological* rather than dermatological in both origin and cure. So if you had leprosy—eczema, seborrhea, signs of psoriasis, boils, burns, a nagging itch, even baldness (all these afflictions were grouped under the heading "leprosy")—you came to see me, a priest, rather than a doctor. And I would make you jump through a host of little liturgical hoops before you were pronounced "clean" and admitted back into the community.

According to the Bible[16] (and Jesus knew his Bible), here's what would normally happen. The priest apprehends two birds. One bird was sliced open and its blood was sprinkled on the patient exactly seven times. The other bird was released as a sign that the disease had departed the afflicted. The ex-leper was then required to live outside the community for a full week as a sort of interim test to prove that the disease was now completely vamoose. On the seventh day the person shaved their head, beard (if applicable), and eyebrows. Oil was then placed on his or

---

16. In addition to looking up that scandalous footnote in Mark 1:41, you might also take a gander at the purity laws in Leviticus (chapters 13–14) for the odd but interesting biblical protocol for dealing with various skin ailments.

her right earlobe, right thumb, and right big toe. *Never the left, always the right*. Thus the leper was pronounced "clean." It's right there in the Bible.

Houses could also become leprous. Detailed biblical instructions exist for dismantling your house if the leprosy got out of hand. The stones were placed well outside the city in an "unclean" heap. (Better attack that bathroom mildew now before it's too late.) All of this was inspected and examined by an ordained priest who made holy determinations about leprous buildings, clothing, and people. I love this quote from an old priestly rule book: "Even if the priest be an imbecile, he alone shall quarantine [the leper]; for theirs is the judgment." What power the clergy had back then! Even *imbecilic* behavior was overlooked by congregations. I occasionally quoted from this old rule book when I was in the parish so that folk might overlook mine.

Our leper says to Jesus: "If you choose, *you* can make me clean." That statement is radical because it subverted the entire priestly protocol of released pigeons and oil on the right earlobe. This leper was completely bypassing the prescribed system.

Now I suppose Jesus could have reacted to that poor man in "pity." It's a rather pathetic state of affairs for a sick person to go through all that. But can't you also understand the emotional footnote? Isn't "anger" also an appropriate reaction from Jesus? Maybe Jesus was indeed "warmly indignant," but for my money, I think our Lord was just plain ticked at this foolishness. When Jesus said "I do choose," he was also choosing to buck a centuries-old system and largely tell the priests to take a hike (even though a priest still seems to have a role per tradition in public pronouncement, post-healing).[17]

*

I've taken some time with the historical details here because there's a tendency to read these old stories and say, "Thank God. Thank God we don't segregate people anymore like that poor leper, the poor man. Thank God we don't make people go through all *that* anymore." And once I talk this way, the story has me squarely in its sights.

Religion has a long embarrassing history of faithful people trying to prescribe who's in or out. It's one thing to claim "everybody's welcome

---

17. See Mark 1:44. Jesus gives a nod here to tradition, but the healed man seems to ignore the instruction.

here" on a church sign, but it's another thing entirely to live out that welcome, to be a gospel agent of hospitality for various kinds of people and cross the tracks as Jesus did. *Who does your congregation take time to invite and welcome into church life?* Your honest answer to that question might be revealing. Many congregations have a set of unwritten "purity laws" that sometimes govern local life together. In this old story, Jesus got angry about that. Or did he feel pity about that? In truth, both emotions are appropriate.

The next time you receive Holy Communion, think about the posture of kneeling at an altar. This was also the posture of this leper. He *knelt* before Jesus.[18] Kneeling and naming our need before Jesus is a great "leveler" and unites us much more than we might think.

"If you choose, *you* can make me clean," said that leper so long ago. As we seek to welcome others, remember these three words from our Lord in your own life: "I do choose."

He chooses us.

He chooses us all.

For further reflection:

1. Discuss how "ancient authorities" are not in unanimous agreement when it comes to making certain biblical word choices. Does this trouble you?

2. Given the range of human emotion, is there a particular emotional response that you have a hard time attributing to Jesus? If so, which emotion would that be and why?

---

18. See Mark 1:40. Uh-oh, a footnote in your Bible may say: "Other ancient authorities lack *kneeling*." I'm going with the word for reasons described earlier in the essay!

8. Spring Training

"You, therefore, must be perfect as your heavenly Father is perfect"
(Matt 5:48).

HERE'S AN AMUSING QUOTE from Michael Malone's excellent novel, *Handling Sin*, describing the lovable Raleigh Whittier Hayes, the book's main character who hails from Thermopylae, North Carolina:

> Hayes was a Christian, but if the truth be known, Christ irritated him to death. With the army in Freiburg, Germany, in 1959, he'd read the Gospels while cooped up in the infirmary, and he'd argued by pencil in the margins against the Savior. In his personal opinion, Christ's advice sounded like civic sabotage, moral lunacy, social anarchy, and business disaster.[19]

Although I suspect such an exercise is fairly rare, it's important for Christians to honestly admit that there are a fair number of things that Jesus clearly tells us to do that we don't do, and maybe have no intentions of ever doing. Please don't ask me the percentage of his teachings I tend to overlook, but to be honest I sometimes read a clear instruction from Jesus and often have no specific plans to try harder.

Want a for instance? I worked at the Hungry Bull Steak House in Clemson, South Carolina for several months in the winter of 1981. I was backpacking the Appalachian Trail south from Maine about halfway-through, needed money, and took some time off to wait for spring. I was the dishwasher (the very low man in the restaurant hierarchy) and took out the garbage and mopped everything in addition to running an old

---

19. Malone, *Handling Sin*, 20.

Hobart dish machine that was hotter than Hades. I'm convinced there's a lot of scalding steam in hell.

A rather bossy guy worked with me that winter at the Hungry Bull. He was the meatcutter and had no real authority over anyone who worked behind the scenes, but acted like he did—constantly badgering and belittling the people who had the grunt jobs at the restaurant. He mocked people at the breaks; made fun of them.

One day I'd had enough. Mister Meatcutter had crossed a line and taunted us with some bizarre expectation I cannot recall. I took off my apron for dramatic effect, left my steamy prison of dishes and cups, and got in this guy's face with a very slow and measured verbal fuselage that I think scared him a little. I never touched him, but intended to make sure he knew to back off.

The manager of the Hungry Bull appeared in my steamy station a couple hours later. He was not happy and called me into his office. He wanted to know why I had pushed his top employee into the bloody blade of a spinning meat saw. A lie, of course, but I'm sure a little asterisk now appeared in my otherwise sterling personnel file.

*

"Do not resist one who is evil. But if anyone strikes you on the right cheek, offer the other also; and if anyone forces you to go one mile, you should really go two. Love your enemies and pray for those who persecute you" (Matt 5:38–44).

Okay, Jesus, so I really failed at these instructions at the Hungry Bull that steamy afternoon back in 1981. But would I do that again today at age sixty? I'm not going to answer that, Jesus, because there are different anatomical understandings of that word *cheek* and I guess I could have offered that bully my left one. But you don't like my little joke, do you? I didn't think so.

*

I have a friend who was once a ranger for the National Park Service in Virginia, a job where he had to be nice all the time, even to nasty park visitors. He was in charge of a concession that was closing one afternoon at 4:30, exactly when it was supposed to close, but an angry woman with her three children insisted that the place really closed at five. She'd read it in a park brochure. My friend tried to be nice. He wore his park uniform proudly and told her politely that the park had to close. The woman would not listen to reason and finally said, "Well, if you won't let me in, you can just kiss my (you know what)." My friend somehow had the professional decorum to say, "Well, lady, from the looks of it that might just take me all day."

*

"For God makes his sun rise on the evil and on the good, and sends rain on both just and unjust. For if you love those who love you, what's the reward in that? Don't even tax collectors do the same?" (Matt 5:45–46).

I know, Jesus. I measure and guard my love. I don't mean to say the words I sometimes say. Okay, yes I do. I say them in my heart even before they're out of my mouth. And they feel pretty darn good if you must know.

*

And so you see how this works? We have trouble applying the teachings of Jesus to interpersonal relationships, not to mention interactions with countries that raise our national ire. Can you seriously imagine the Sermon on the Mount taken seriously in meetings of national security at the Pentagon?

I'll say it again. It's important for Christians to admit that there are quite a few things Jesus clearly tells us to do that we just don't do very consistently (or maybe ever) because the teachings sometimes don't make sense living in the kind of world we inhabit. Perhaps the ignored teachings vary from person to person, but it might be interesting to name a few with a trusted friend.

I think Jesus—the walking-around Jesus who was alive then and up and about in the world today—really means what he says. Now, right now. That's why confession and Eucharist are vitally important on a weekly basis as we fall short.

But also consider: what if these teachings are also *practice* for life in the next world? It almost goes without saying that anyone is around on the planet for just a short period of time. What I get so wrought up about (and emotionally chagrined over) is all pretty temporary. Conversely, the life to come with Jesus is not temporary at all; "eternal" describes it. "You, therefore, must be perfect." Now please note the rest of this verse: "As your heavenly Father is perfect." The word "as" is an important two-letter breath of a word here. Christians strive to do the things described in the Sermon on the Mount to mirror what is already happening perfectly in heaven. We attempt to obey the challenging and rather odd instructions offered by Jesus as practice, in the spring of our lives, for a reality that will always be. We are "children of [our] Father who is in heaven."

I've always loved what theologian Dallas Willard said about the next life: "I am thoroughly convinced that God will let everyone into heaven who, in his considered opinion, can stand it. But 'standing it' may prove to be a more difficult matter than those who take their view of heaven from popular movies or popular preaching may think."[20] Jesus describes in the Sermon on the Mount his will upon this earth, as it is now observed already in heaven. Heard that anywhere?

*

I'm told there is a Lutheran congregation in the Midwest with an unusual baptismal practice. Most of the members are born and also die in this small rural community. When a child is baptized, someone scoops the baptismal water out of the font and everyone in worship that day processes behind the water, singing, to the cemetery adjacent to the church building. The family of the newly baptized leads the way, holding the child. With words of hope and promise, the water from the font is poured directly onto the burial plot where the child will one day reside until Jesus calls his or her name again.

Baptism is not only our entrance into the next life, but also the blueprint for all the days between then and now. Between birth and death a Christian encounters a variety of testy situations that may involve bossy meatcutters, rude strangers, or any number of people who push our patience to the inevitable limit.

We are on the way, moving to another land where Jesus reigns eternal. Might as well start practicing for it.

---

20. Willard, *The Divine Conspiracy*, 302.

For further reflection:

1. Name a few teachings of Jesus that you find impossible (or impractical) to follow most days.
2. How do you feel about the Dallas Willard quote about heaven cited in this essay?

9. Analysis Paralysis

"Which is easier, to say to the paralytic, 'Your sins are forgiven,' or to say, 'Stand up and take your mat and walk'?" (Mark 2:9)

CONSIDER THIS HYPOTHETICAL SITUATION. The phone rings in the middle of the night. A church member, only in their twenties, has been injured badly in an automobile accident—drunk driver, stop sign, you get the picture. The drunk driver was able to walk away with hardly a scratch but the church member whom I know and love, completely blameless in the accident, is facing a series of surgeries that may result in a lifetime in a wheelchair.

Just before surgery in the middle of that long night, I'm called in to be with the family and a few close friends. Fear and anger alternately swirl around the room. We pray, of course. But before that prayer, in the midst of all that worry and emotion, I lean down and announce these words to that stricken young person: "Son, your sins are forgiven."

*

Am I getting the details of this old story (in Mark 2:1–12) right? Four friends carry a palsied man to Jesus. I love their pluck and nerve, navigating their buddy around the large crowd blocking the front door. Watch them sneak around to the backyard and carry their friend awkwardly up a ladder onto the roof. Watch them, utterly determined, peel back the thatch, dig through the dried clay, and create a rectangular hole large enough to accommodate a stretcher. (Jesus suddenly has a new skylight in his den, not to mention an urgent need for a vacuum cleaner.)

9. ANALYSIS PARALYSIS

Watch these four friends lower their pal down to Jesus, ever so slowly; carefully, lovingly. In some ways, this story is about bringing a friend to Jesus; digging for Jesus. The story exposes my half-hearted attempts at sharing Jesus with people who don't know him. So far, I love the story on quite a few levels. It grabs my attention; draws me in.

But after all the climbing, digging, and fumbling around on the roof; after the awkward nail-biting descent into Jesus' living room; after the teacher turns around and sees the faith of these five, their aggressive trust that he indeed can do something; after taking in the situation and the predicament of this paralyzed man who has probably suffered even more in that century than this one from pain and random taunts; after all this, our Lord looks at that injured man—quadriplegic, paraplegic, take your pick—and says something that possibly ranks in the top ten confusing statements Jesus ever made. Our Lord looks at the man and says, *"Son, your sins are forgiven."* First thing out of his mouth. No hello, no grimace, no emotional reaction at all from this man of compassion. If Jesus felt sorry for the guy, we just aren't told. "Your sins are forgiven." Such a statement would be met with much confusion should I (or you) utter similar words in that hypothetical hospital room described earlier. What in the wide world is going on here?

Surely Jesus is not equating this man's paralyzed predicament with some sin in his past. Such a repulsive idea leaps into my head upon first reading this old story. But I quickly remember the man "born blind" in John's gospel where Jesus silences any crass connection between physical blindness and something the man (or his parents) may have done to cause it (John 9:1–17). I recall two specific tragedies in Luke—gruesome murder and the collapse of a tower, together killing quite a few people—where Jesus clearly refuses to connect these mishaps with any sinful slip-up in the victims' past (Luke 13:1–5). Even today, it's a quick and convenient way to make sense of suffering: personal woe explained by pointing to implied personal misbehavior. And I'm not denying the regular truth that the two are often related.

But surely Jesus isn't making that connection in the story of this paralyzed man. Jesus said some rather direct things in his ministry that are hard for any of us to hear. But *surely* Jesus isn't trying to drag a confession (some dark admission of guilt and wrongdoing) out of this poor paralyzed man before any healing can take place. Jesus can be difficult to understand, hopelessly out of step concerning accepted etiquette. But he's not cruel. He never wears a Don Rickles mask and ridicules people. So I ask again: *what in the world is going on here?*

Here's my take on this story: unless we see ourselves, figuratively, as that paralyzed man—brought to Jesus by friends, lowered into his living room—this story will not make much sense. But once we make that figurative leap, all sorts of theological truths open up.

This old story hinges on a question posed by Jesus that no one ever really answers. Some observers that day wonder in their hearts why Jesus is speaking to this paralyzed man in such a way. (Their wondering is a little different from ours, but their perplexity is just as great.) So here comes the question: "Which is easier," Jesus wants to know, "to say, 'Your sins are forgiven,' *or* to say, 'Stand up and walk'?" *Which is easier?*

This is a wonderfully vexing question. Jesus could also have asked, *Which is harder?* I don't know how you might answer Jesus' question, but I'm certain he wants us to mull it over awhile.

Very often in this life, horrific incidents seem to chip away at our faith, our trust in Jesus—accidents, illness, paralyzed friends. For months after the death of a close friend due to brain cancer, I found myself breaking into tears at traffic lights, wondering who I was kidding with all this Jesus stuff. This story raises profound theological questions about the nature of illness and healing.

But if we read the story only on the level of a man in need of a health fix, I'm afraid we're missing how the story intends to bore into our lives in a much deeper way. *Which is easier?* asks Jesus. Which is harder? Forgiveness or healing? Or can the two be very much related?

In truth, I am that paralyzed man. And so are you. I've never spent time in a wheelchair and no one has ever carried me on a stretcher, but there is a paralysis within my soul that is even harder to analyze, more difficult to diagnose and get at—so cloaked and hidden that even the sharpest scalpel fails to uncover the problem. So Jesus asks: which is easier? The longer I've been engaged in pastoral work, the clearer the answer becomes.

Theologian Ted Peters writes: "Inherent in sin is the denial of truth. We cover our unwholesome motives and violent acts against others with a veneer of goodness. We sugarcoat our garbage. Everyone has a stake in hiding the truth of sin. This makes uncovering the mystery of how sin works difficult, because wherever we dig, lies rush in to fill the hole. Perhaps an objective or a scholarly approach to the truth of sin is foredoomed from the start. Perhaps the only way to get at the truth of sin is through confession."[21]

Which is easier? asks Jesus. Harder?

*

This old story begins to make sense upon awakening to the truth that *I am that man* paralyzed by sin: full of darkness, excuses, prejudice, missed opportunities. I need others, friends, to carry me to Jesus; lower me directly into his house with all the others around his door. The spatial movement in this story—descent and ascent—is important. This is the language of baptism: dying and rising. "Stand up," says Jesus, "and go home."

Our problems in American history and culture can be analyzed to death. Amidst the myriad problems incumbent in a still-new century, we tend to hand people many things: a counselor, a new book, the latest fad or therapy, a psycho/socio/linguistic answer to what's ailing us. And perhaps all of these are indeed helpful, although I often fear that our real paralysis is all the endless, sugarcoated analysis. All the ways we keep Jesus at arm's length.

Here's my take on this old story: until we *carry each other* to Jesus, until we assist one another in the lifelong descent of arriving prone and vulnerable at the feet of Jesus, not much will change. We need each other. We need friends like these four who dug through a lot, peeled away a lot, descending ever more deeply into Jesus' love which overcomes all darkness. Following Jesus into the depths will not be easy. Inviting others to accompany you is perhaps harder still. Oddly, it's always the narrow door (Luke 13:24) that leads to life.

His question haunts me. *Which is easier?* Forgiving sins or working an obvious, headline-grabbing miracle? Our answer to that question reveals the work Jesus will do in the lives of all the paralyzed.

For further reflection:

1. If your congregation's Sunday liturgy includes a corporate confession of sin, describe the nature of this confession and why it might

---

21. Peters, *Sin*, 9.

be important for you. Also: ponder the diversity and size of the collective sin confessed each week, simultaneously in the silence.

2. Discuss this quote by Thomas Merton (1915–1968): "The Bible may be difficult and confusing, but it is meant to challenge our intelligence, not insult it."[22]

---

22. Merton, *Opening the Bible*, 14.

10. Passing on the Mantle

"Then Elijah took his mantle and rolled it up, and struck the water; the water was parted to the one side and to the other, until the two of them crossed on dry ground" (2 Kgs 2:8).

ONE OF MY FAVORITE scenes in *Tuesdays with Morrie*, the best-selling book about two friends with decades of age difference, is when Morrie starts to talk about the subject of death. He is dying of Lou Gehrig's Disease. One Tuesday he looks at his young friend Mitch and says, "Everybody knows they're going to die, but nobody believes it. If we did, we would do things differently." Morrie then shares an old Buddhist tradition with his young friend, where every day you envision a little bird on your shoulder that asks, "Is today the day? Am I ready? Am I doing all I need to do? Am I being the person I want to be?"[23]

In the novel *The Passion of Reverend Nash*, a character named Mary Jane is dying of cancer. Her pastor comes to visit one afternoon and Mary Jane says, "There's so much resting and so little sleeping when you're going. No one tells you that, but it's true. What do you need to rest for, I don't know. But when I'm lying down, I close my eyes and swim all the rivers and ponds and oceans and pools I've ever been in. I'm working my way through them all. I started with the bodies of water furthest away ... all the swimming holes I was in as a girl, the swimming pools and the little streams and brooks we used to picnic by. I'm trying hard to remember them all. There are ponds that have come to me for the first time in fifty years. It's an amazing thing."[24]

---

23. Albom, *Tuesdays with Morrie*, 81.
24. Basch, *The Passion of Reverend Nash*, 51–52.

II. EPIPHANY

*

Early in the book of Second Kings,[25] an older friend is trying to say goodbye to his younger friend. Elijah doesn't really die in this story; he's one of two people[26] in the Bible who are taken into heaven without breathing their last. Many Jewish people leave an empty place for Elijah at their celebration of the Passover meal, believing that he will return just as quickly and mysteriously as he departed. Elijah never dies, but all the elements of death and departure are present here—denial, hanging on, grief, last will and testament.

Elijah has been a faithful mentor to his young prophetic apprentice, Elisha. They both know what's coming, but there's a little dance they go through that I've seen repeated in many families facing death and separation, including my own. *Three times* Elijah tells his young friend, "Stay here. There's something I've got to attend to." And we all know what that "something" is. *Three times* Elisha responds to his old friend by saying, "I will not leave you. As the Lord lives, I'll never leave your side." When a loved one is dying, going away forever, it's often hard to leave even for a moment, even to go downstairs and grab a bite in the hospital cafeteria. Something of this is occurring with Elisha and his old friend.

Various companies of prophets approach the young man who will soon inherit the mantle of leadership. "Were you aware, did you know that your master will soon be taken away from you?" Elisha replies like any of us might: "Yeah, I know, but would you please shut up about that?" He's just not ready to think of life without his old friend.

And so this old prophet and this young "prophet-to-be" take a little road trip together. You might take note of their three stops. Bethel is where Jacob had his fitful dream on a stone pillow that night so long ago (Gen 28:10–22) after he'd fled into the wilderness upon cheating his brother out of blessing and birthright. There in Bethel, angels climbed up and down a ladder reaching to heaven. God spoke to Jacob in that dream, reminding the poor boy that even cheaters and pretenders are still loved by God. Did our prophetic pair recall that dream as they stopped in Bethel for lunch?

The next stop on the road trip is Jericho, place of famous triumph where walls came tumbling down (Josh 6:1–27). I wonder if Elijah and his young friend paused awhile among the ruins, recalling the surprising

---

25. See 2 Kgs 2:1–14.
26. Enoch is the other; see Gen 5:21–24.

trumpets and how God is more powerful than the mightiest political superpower.

They finally come to the Jordan River, last stop on the road trip, holy waters of God's people where Jesus would eventually be baptized. Elijah does an amazing thing when they reach the riverbanks. Watch what he does with his mantle, the very item of clothing that his young protégé will soon inherit. Rolling up the mantle like a towel, the old prophet rat-tails the river and the pair of friends walk across on dry ground. Nothing needs to be spoken in reference to the history they share—how their great-grandparents once walked through the dry ground of an old sea on their way to freedom and liberation (Exod 14:1–31).

Do you see what's happening here? The old man is walking the young man through a long and shared history. They both know what's coming next. They both know the changes in the road up ahead. When Elijah finally gets around to broaching a conversation about a last will and testament, the young apprentice asks for something the old man inherited from so many others long dead. "A double share of your spirit," says Elisha—a spirit that finds its roots in an old dream, an improbable triumph, and freedom in the face of overwhelming odds.

*

I often wonder about people who may be visiting our congregations for the first time, particularly those who may have been away from church for awhile or those who have no church experience at all. This story from Second Kings recounts a feast of paranormality, one of the main characters whisked away in a whirlwind much like Pecos Bill, only to land on a mountain several centuries later, calmly chatting with Jesus and Moses, another Old Testament Hall of Famer.[27] It all seems so Oz-like. Dorothy! Toto! Come back!

"What kind of church *is* this?" newcomers might understandably ask. "I can halfway believe Stonehenge or the Great Pyramids, an errant UFO maybe, even a live Elvis. But come on. I've got my limits here. These people are crazy."

"The gospel," says Saint Paul, "is veiled" (2 Cor 4:1–6). Here in a still-new century, the church dares to tell and ponder veiled, unusual stories that seem like so many tall tales to outsiders; all of these stories

---

27. See Mark 9:2–8.

pointing to the craziest story of all where a man actually dies and lives to tell about it. "Listen to him," says a voice on that same mountain (Mark 9:7). Listen to the one who will take you on a road trip you'll never forget, stretching backward and forward across millennia.

*

Here on the 500th anniversary of the Reformation, we're at something of a crossroads as we give thanks for our common history and consider what's up ahead. This process of looking backward and forward has much in common with that road trip taken by Elijah and Elisha so long ago; one generation passing the baton to another. We often want to hold on to what's always been, sometimes pretending that nothing is supposed to change in church. It's always an important yet difficult task to hand over leadership to a new generation of Christians. Can we trust each other? Will the transition be faithful to our heritage?

The mantle that Elijah passes to his young friend will divide a river and clear a new path. Our faith inheritance that we pass on from generation to generation also parts rivers, rough waters, and leads to safe ground. One of our main tasks as church together is to keep telling the story, faithfully and creatively, so that we see our lives in the stories of Bethel, Jericho, and the Jordan—forgiveness, trust, freedom. When we tell it this way, the mantle is passed on, the future becomes less frightening, and the whirlwind of God lifts us across the centuries.

In the story of an old prophet and a young one, God is the author of change. Standing on a mountain many centuries later, chatting with the heritage that brought him there, a young prophet born to die was transfigured. It's how any of us changes: telling the story again and again, passing the mantle of faith, until the wind of God lifts us and takes us to places we can only dream about, where death does not have the last say.

For further reflection:

1. Give thanks for a wise and older Christian in your life without whom you'd be a very different person. In what ways did this person pass on the faith to you?

2. How does this odd story of two prophets serve as a transition to the season of Lent?

III. LENT

Introduction to the Season[1]

MANY FRIDAY EVENINGS AGO, when I was a much younger pastor, the phone rang in our home near the beginning of Lent. It was a man named Brian. I'd never met him; had no idea how he got our number. We had some company over as I recall and were enjoying laughter and a rather carefree beginning to the weekend. I could tell right away it was one of *those* phone calls. Brian was a stranger in town—no money, no place to stay, a broken-down car that needed a ball joint. Could I help him?

I must admit as I drove to meet him that my thoughts were not benevolent and filled with light. In fact, I wondered the worst about this person. How'd he get *my* number? What was he doing here when he lived in Ohio? I was inwardly annoyed and you are my confessors.

There he was, standing in front of a Texaco station, expectantly watching for my car. He was dressed in a jacket that actually had a plastic crucifix of Jesus sewn onto the back. He was beaming. I wanted to pretend I was someone else and drive the other way. We chatted and inspected his car. It too had a plastic crucifix, a rather large one, lashed to the trunk with rope. This had all the makings of a long evening.

As we drove to the homeless shelter, Brian chatted excitedly about his faith. He was on fire with it and knew the Bible well. I laid low. He said, "You know, I've got this great video about Jesus back at the car, and if you let me sleep on your floor tonight, we could watch it together."

---

1. This introduction first appeared (in slightly different form) in Honeycutt, "Upstairs and Down."

Time froze for a second and all of these biblical images flashed in front of the headlights. I thought of old Isaiah who urges God's people to "bring the homeless poor *into your house* . . . and not to hide yourself from *your own kin*" (Isa 58:3–9). I thought of Brian on our living room floor in a sleeping bag and I though of psychopaths and ax murderers and even though Isaiah mentions nothing about taking the homeless to a shelter instead, I decided to biblically paraphrase on the spot and lie a little. I said: "I'm not sure what my wife would think of that." Yes, blame the woman. *She* wouldn't understand. Her misgivings, not mine. He accepted my little lie. We arrived at the shelter. I said good night and went back to our home, our friends, dessert.

*

You see how this works? Jesus says, "You are the salt of the earth. You are the light of the world" (Matt 5:13–14). And so we are. On one level we acknowledge this. We gather in church to pray and sing and stand up for Jesus. We belt out "This Little Light of Mine" with fervent gusto. But the truth is that it's easier to hide from the daily nature of such a faith. Admit it. Jesus is just plain tiring at times. We are sometimes annoyed and a bit put out with the people he sends us. We just want to be left alone. We drop our dollars in the offering plate and say all the right words. Isn't that enough?

Isaiah 58 describes Israel just after they've returned from the Babylonian Exile. They are rebuilding a ransacked Jerusalem and they are careful to jump through all the proper religious hoops this time around. They want God on their side in case of future aggression. So they worship and pray regularly; they even fast, commendably. But it doesn't seem to "work." Problems and violence are all around them. The people get kind of uppity with God: "Why do we fast, but you do not see? Humble ourselves, but you don't seem to notice?" They say this to God! It's the old question: "Why are bad things happening to us very good and holy people?"

Speaking for God, Isaiah answers. "You call *this* a fast?" Uh-oh. "Is not this the fast I choose: to loose the bonds of injustice, to undo the thongs of the yoke, to let the oppressed go free?" Worship without justice and mercy is not faith, says Isaiah, it's an escape. You cannot hide in the sanctuary and close your eyes to the world.

The irony of Isaiah's words is that Israel's history is told from the angle of an oppressed people who were liberated at the Red Sea. Israel should know what to be about because they had been in the place of the people they were ignoring. But God popped them loose from Pharaoh's brickyard, brought them safely through the sea, and set them free. "How can you turn your back on your own kin?" asks the prophet. "These naked and hungry and homeless ones are a lot like you were." Rescued by God's light, Israel was expected to *be light* for others.

Christians have their own paradigm for this Red Sea event. It's called baptism. We are led through the waters from death to life; from darkness to light. We are set free for good works. It's not just a sweet gesture when we place a candle in the hands of the newly baptized and say: "Let your light so shine before others, that they may see your good works and glorify your Father in heaven" (Matt 5:16). Jesus once said, "I am the light of the world" (John 8:12). In baptism, he now says we are.

You are light. You are salt. I think it's instructive that Jesus never says, "You are sugar." You are the *sugar* of the world. No. The word never even appears in the Bible. But sometimes we equate being a Christian with being nice and sweet and well-mannered. He didn't choose that word: sugar.

You are light. You bring illumination to dark places. You are salt. You bring seasoning and a bit of feistiness to complacency.

And Jesus never says, "You *oughta* be light and salt," reprimanding us. That's a common mistake of preachers like me, by the way. Jesus says, "You are."

*

I met Brian the next morning outside the auto parts store. We had agreed to meet there. "Ten sharp," I'd reminded him as we said goodnight at the shelter. I halfway expected him not to show up the next morning. But there he was, smiling and wearing the plastic crucifix jacket. We bought a ball joint with money from the church discretionary fund. I dropped him off at his car. Jesus was still lashed to the trunk.

We talked a bit. He thanked me. We shook hands and said goodbye. He said something as I walked away that's haunted me ever since. "See you upstairs someday, Pastor." What? I hadn't heard him. "See you upstairs," he said again.

That's true, you know. The Bible tells us that God is preparing a great feast for us where the last are first and the greatest are the least. I suspect I will see Brian again upstairs someday, maybe still wearing the jacket.

But there's another side of the Bible we miss sometimes. It's about *downstairs*: "Thy kingdom come, thy will be done *on earth* as it is in heaven." The kingdom of heaven is not just something we go to. Jesus says it is coming in this direction, to us: we who have been led through the Red Sea waters, now God's light for a darkened world.

Fear not. Let it shine. Upstairs and down.

1. Dust and Return

". . . you are dust, and to dust you shall return" (Gen 3:19).

THERE ARE THINGS CHRISTIANS do in church on an annual basis that must seem downright odd to outsiders. We wash feet on Maundy Thursday as a sign of radical service. We gather around a fire on the feast of Epiphany and recall a certain star. We wear red on Pentecost because flames once rested upon timid disciples and got them going again. We decorate a tree in December not with sugarplums and fairies, but with old symbols that include a mother pelican who has pecked her breast hard enough to bring blood so she can feed her hungry children. These are all celebrations in the church year with multiple layers of relative weirdness. We have lots of strange little habits that take awhile for newcomers to embrace and understand. Conversion to Christianity, in many ways, is like learning a new language.

But I really think Ash Wednesday may win the grand prize for distinctive strangeness. A pastor comes at you with a glob of ash. On the prior Tuesday afternoon, I used to head out into my backyard, take sharp scissors to chop up the old palms used the previous year on the Sunday before Easter, kindle a small fire with a little rubbing alcohol, toss in a couple drops of oil for adherence purposes, and *voila!* The modus operandi that annually gives birth to these very ancient words: "Remember that you are dust, and to dust you shall return."

Imagine someone with no knowledge of Christianity peering through a window at your church and watching the Wednesday proceedings. And imagine a young pastor (like me) tracing a black cross on the foreheads of his children when they were tiny babies. It was enough to take my breath away. I halfway expected somebody to call the Department of Social Services.

*

Carlyle Marney was one of the most impressive pastoral theologians of the mid-twentieth century. He labored for many years at Myers Park Baptist Church in Charlotte, North Carolina. After a lecture once at Wake Forest Divinity School, a student rose from the audience and asked, "Dr. Marney, do you believe in the garden of Eden?" Without hesitation, Carlyle replied, "Well, yes I do. It's at 250 Elm Street in Knoxville, Tennessee." The student looked rather confused. "I thought Eden was discovered somewhere in southeast Asia." Dr. Marney replied, "No, I've got it on good authority that it's in Knoxville on Elm Street. That's where I stole some money from my mother's dresser, went down to the corner drug store and bought some candy, then came back and hid in my closet, eating it all. I thought I'd gotten away with something until I heard her walking through the house that evening. She sounded like God. 'Carlyle, where are you? What have you done?'"[2]

As a result of the disobedience, God says to Adam, "Eden's over. Remember that you are dust. Now get out of here and get on with your life." It's seems like a fairly jarring punishment for simply eating the wrong piece of fruit.

But try to look at the dusty remembrance another way. *Adam came from the dust.* That's how God created the old boy. "Then the Lord God formed man from the dust of the ground, and breathed into his nostrils the breath of life; and the man became a living being" (Gen 2:7). The wordplay in the Hebrew is even more revealing. The word for *man* here is *adam* (that's where we get our hero's name). And the word for *dust* is *adamah*. There's a rich and suggestive oral association between these two words. It's almost like saying humans come from humus.

So when a pastor traces an ashen cross on your brow and says, "Remember that you are dust," it should indeed recall the old Genesis story of disobedience and the modern story of local disobedience with which we all struggle. But the dusty proclamation you hear is also an ecological statement, a common kinship with this broken but gorgeous world. We are not *apart* (one word) from creation. We're *a part* (two words) of

2. See Gen 3:1–13.

creation. To recall that we are dust is something of a call to remember our ecological roots with the soil. "Yes, you messed up," God seems to say. "But I'm not kicking you out of Eden with no resources. Remember your kinship."

*

There's also a second half of the old statement we hear each Ash Wednesday: "And to dust you shall return."

We all have a term limit, right? We'll all succumb to something. And even this is a blessing. Read sometime the 1922 short story by F. Scott Fitzgerald titled "The Curious Case of Benjamin Button." It's an odd story (which became a movie) about a person who ages in reverse. But it's also packed with lines about life's meaning. Here's a quote from the movie: "I hope you make the best of it. And I hope you see things that startle you. I hope you feel things you never felt before. I hope you meet people with a different point of view. I hope you live a life you're proud of. If you find that you're not, I hope you have the courage to start all over again . . . . We're meant to lose the people we love. How else are we supposed to know how important they are?"

"And to dust you shall return." Perhaps we should not look at this truth with somber sadness, but rather gospel opportunity. How shall we live this wild and wonderful life knowing that our days are finite and numbered? In some ways, Lent is an invitation to wake up.

*

The other day I was walking alone on the Foothills Trail above the nearby state park. Nobody on the trail; a great day to think and pray. I was thinking about some problem that was bothering me. Pastors, of course, are not immune from problems. I was thinking about a certain problem and realized the sound I was hearing was coming from a small stream below the trail that was mostly out of sight and making the most beautiful sounds. I followed the music of the water for a little while and then ran out of time and needed to head home. On the way back to the car I noticed the exact place where the water came out of the bank and dropped several feet in elevation, gathering speed, tumbling over rocks, and making these great sounds. I saw the very beginnings of this creek where there was ample water, and then farther up the trail with no water at all; at least no water that I could see or hear. It just emerged mysteriously from a bank, hidden from view.

*

"Remember that you are dust, and to dust you shall return." Yes, maybe you should count Ash Wednesday near the top in liturgical weirdness, especially when viewed from a distance by an outsider.

But try to look at this old day another way. Like that creek emerging from an invisible source, perhaps Ash Wednesday came into being so long ago to give us an opportunity to reflect hard on our lives—where your life came from, where it's now going, and what you'll do with the time you have left.

The words sound ominous. And indeed they are. But perhaps they're meant to be liberating more than foreboding.

Remember that you are dust. You'll be returning there.

For further reflection:

1. Does it matter to you whether the garden of Eden was a real or perhaps figurative place? Discuss how the Marney story applies to us all.

2. How does our primordial connection to the dust of the earth (*adamah*) shape how we might care for this world in the days we're given?

2. Water and Struggle

"Jesus was led up by the Spirit into the wilderness to be tempted by the devil" (Matt 4:1).

SOMETIMES I GET CALLS from non-church members wanting sacraments for their children. I never refuse to talk or meet with them. But I do feel the need to clarify. "And why is it you want your child baptized?" I ask. "Well, I've always been taught that baptism wards off evil. I know the world's a scary place and I want to be sure my baby is safe." "Safe?" I ask. "Yes, that's what baptism is for, right? A way to be protected from the devil and hell? Don't you put some special water on them and say some special words and then they're safe? Sort of like an insurance policy, right?"

Modern baptism, even among those who should know better, is often perceived as a way to ward off and protect the newly dunked from evil, mishap, and calamity. Baptism as talisman. Baptism as rabbit's foot. Or, crassly put: baptism as fire insurance.

But if you look closely at Jesus' own baptism in the Gospels, he comes up out of the water and immediately enters the wilderness to struggle with the devil. And I do mean "immediately." In Matthew and Mark not even a single verse separates the two stories. In Luke, only a short genealogy. The Gospel writers want us to connect these two events. For Jesus, baptism does not *protect* him from evil. Instead, it seems to *hasten* his encounter with evil. In Matthew, Jesus is *"led up by the Spirit"* into the wilderness for the very purpose of being tempted by the powers of darkness. Strange thing for the Spirit to do, don't you think? "Lead us *not* into temptation," we pray. But by golly the Spirit does this very thing with Jesus. Baptism immediately leads to a struggle.

We're sometimes led to believe that baptism is a quaint rite of perpetual protection, but not according to the Gospels. Jesus doesn't just accidentally bump into evil out there in the wilderness. He is there to confront evil, stand up to it. Baptism doesn't protect us from this encounter either. In fact, baptism heightens and hastens the struggle. Sometimes when I explain this over the phone to young mothers wanting the best for their child, they conclude that perhaps baptism isn't what they want for their little one after all.

Ironically, it is children (not adults) who often better understand what's at stake in the world. They know that the world is a dark place and a war between good and evil rages all around us. When my son Lukas was very young, he used to play this game where he'd say, "Dad, I want you to name a movie and then I'll tell you who the bad guy in the movie is. Go ahead." And so I'd name about ten movies. And he had them all down pat. "*Star Wars*," I said. "That's easy. Darth Vader." *Beauty and the Beast*. "Gaston," he said. *Aladdin*. "Jafar." *The Little Mermaid*. "Ursala." *Hunchback of Notre Dame*. "Frollo." *A Bug's Life*. "Hopper." And on it went. A litany of villains. I'm sure the children in your own life are well-acquainted with their own list. They know who the good and bad guys are. Kids are ready to fight for what is right and good.

When we reach adulthood, however, we may face our own set of demons, but very likely we perceive them on an internal playing field, explained and managed by modern psychology. We may even dress evil up in a red suit and pitchfork and lampoon it. "The devil made me do it," we jokingly say. In short, we sometimes pretend evil doesn't really exist; that all human sin can be explained by theory and fixed (managed) with the right therapeutic world view.

Jon Levenson, a Jewish scholar, quickly points out the empty-headedness of such a position by recalling that Dietrich Bonhoeffer resisted the Nazis and was executed for his courageous resistance in April of 1945. Bonhoeffer referred to Hitler as the "anti-Christ." Levenson writes: "Had he not believed in the Christian theology out of which the Anti-Christ grew, would he have chosen his heroic path of resistance to evil? Or would he, like the pro-Nazi Christians, have chosen instead the path of compromise and accommodation? Or perhaps the neo-gnostic course: exhorting the Fuehrer to engage in self-discovery, with a view toward transforming his consciousness and discovering the divine spark deep within?"³

Baptism is not a cozy security blanket. Baptism will lead us into struggle with the powers of darkness. *With Jesus*, we will struggle with and not tolerate a system where bread is offered for some and not for all. Jesus could have turned the stones into bread. A little later, he will multiply a few loaves and feed thousands. Why one miracle later on and not a similar miracle now? Because, says Jesus, "One does not live by bread alone." Another way of saying this might be, "I cannot be fed alone apart from my brothers and sisters who are not fed at all."

With Jesus, we will struggle with a culture that is overly impressed with entertainment and performance. A culture that is drawn to a "Six Flags Over Jesus" style of encountering God. A culture that wants miracles (like jumping off the pinnacle of the temple) and not sacrifice.

With Jesus, we will struggle with our endless obsession with power, money, ease, and splendor. "All these I will give you," says the tempter, "if you fall down and worship me." He isn't only talking to Jesus here. We sometimes sell our souls for far less.

Baptism will lead us into *struggle*, not safety. Baptism opens our eyes to the very real temptations all around us. I don't care what you call the devil or how you choose to dress him up. But it's accurate to say that if we are not struggling with the dark powers of this world that divert us from God, then we are talking about something other than Christianity.

God will give us what we need for this struggle. Jesus refused to turn stones into bread. *But we are given the bread of heaven* in Holy Communion that is far more precious than any bought in a store. Over time this bread can transform even the stoniest of hearts.

We are given God's word. With each temptation, Jesus sends evil packing not with his own charisma, but through his immersion in and reliance upon Scripture. He quotes Scripture (the book of Deuteronomy) three different times. It behooves Christians to engage in similar scriptural immersion.

We are invited to engage in spiritual disciplines. Not in a legalistic sense, but because classic spiritual disciplines nourish the spirit the way a physical workout nourishes the body. Spiritual disciplines prepare us for the encounter with evil we will all face. Jesus fasted and prayed;

---

3. Levenson, "The Devil in the Details," 56.

experienced solitude and silence; studied and served. It was this focus on God that gave him strength and stamina to resist the wiles of the devil.

The story of Jesus in the wilderness with the devil is an extended baptism story. It is a commentary on what baptism is and is not. We are not called to hide from evil or pretend that it doesn't exist. We are sent into the struggle to confront the demons of our day. In baptism, we are called into conflict.

For further reflection:

1. Try to define the ancient reality known as "Devil."
2. Is the idea of baptism leading to struggle new for you? How might this understanding shape how your congregation prepares children, parents, and adults for baptism?

3. Nocturnal Midwifery

Nicodemus came to Jesus by night and said to him . . . "How can anyone be born after having grown old? Can one enter a second time into the mother's womb and be born?"(John 3:2, 4)

A WELL-KNOWN RELIGIOUS LEADER sets out after dark and furtively knocks at the door of Jesus. I imagine him creeping down alleyways, peeking around corners, throwing a glance over his shoulder, making sure he remains unseen. Why is this man so careful? Why not look for Jesus during the day? Well, you know why. Jesus was a suspect guy. It would not have looked good to be seen with Jesus out in the open, in the light.

This covert encounter with Jesus reminds me of how I often approach the man. After all, didn't Jesus say that we should do our fasting, giving, and praying in secret? (Matt 6:1–6, 16–18). "Go into a closet," he said. I like that advice. It easily transfers to *everything* about my faith— keep it secret, clandestine, safe, reserved for Sunday mornings with other like-minded people.

So Nicodemus comes at night and I think we really know why. He knocks on the door and maybe Jesus invites him in for tea. It doesn't really say that, but it was some sort of private place—a kitchen, a café; please picture the place in your mind. We are eavesdropping on a private conversation, if you think about it. Ever done that?

Notice how Nicodemus begins the conversation: with flattery. "Gosh, rabbi, you're one whale of a teacher and you've gotta be sent from God. Nobody can do what you've been doing apart from God. Man, you're the real McCoy." But also notice, contrary to the popular maxim, that flattery got Nicodemus precisely nowhere. In Dante's version of hell, the lowest ring of hell (the seventh ring, I think) is reserved for flatterers. Maybe that's why Jesus doesn't even bother to say "thank you" to Nicodemus that night; won't even acknowledge the compliment.

We're under the porch with a hand cupped to one ear. We're in the next room, leaning towards the dividing wall. We overhear this conversation down through the centuries and this is what our Lord and Savior, Mr. Manners, said that night from the shadows: "Let me tell you the truth, sir. Listen to this closely, Nick. You will never see the kingdom of God without dying to who you are now, and being born again from above."

*

A man bursts into a crowded movie theatre in Colorado wearing a Batman outfit. No time to figure out what's happening, little time to get out of the way. He opens fire and we count the carnage.

A man kisses his children goodbye and places them on the school bus. He then drives a couple miles to an Amish schoolhouse and lines other children up in a row before executing them and killing himself.

A couple years ago I spoke at Virginia Tech for a campus lecture coinciding with the anniversary of the tragedy there. I accepted the lecture invitation, and immediately wished I hadn't. Don't be too hard on Nicodemus today. There is a certain appeal to speaking with and about Jesus under the cover of darkness.

We pick up the newspaper, turn on the TV, and it just seems to be such a bizarre and strange world. In the movie *No Country for Old Men*, the sheriff, played masterfully by Tommy Lee Jones, asks the questions we've all been asking. He's at a coffee shop in one scene, reflecting upon his work and a string of strange local crimes, and says, "My God, what's *wrong* with people? Why in the hell are people acting this way? What's happening these days?"

This old sheriff who's about to retire ponders what feels like a seismic change in morality and the presence of evil; a horrible shift in human behavior the likes of which the world has never seen. The sheriff pays a visit to an old cousin of his who lives alone out in the wide Texas landscape. They talk about this world; how people behave. But the sheriff's cousin won't buy into the assumption that the world is changing. I cannot remember the exact line, but they're both in the kitchen, drinking coffee, and this man in the wheelchair looks at his cousin and offers perspective that somehow reminded me of Jesus' words to Nicodemus that night: "No, sheriff, I don't buy it. This is how people have always been. How we've always treated one another." He looks at his younger cousin as if to say, "What you gonna do about that, sheriff?"

*

I suppose we all have our private ideas about how to respond to violence—toughen gun control laws or (conversely) make it easier to carry a concealed gun to defend ourselves against those who might harm us. Hasten executions maybe. Increase money available for mental health services. Increase security (not a few churches have decided to hire armed security personnel on Sunday mornings). There are many responses to the problem of violence in our culture and church is a good place to debate and reflect upon such responses.

But that debate, for Christians anyway, can sometimes be diversionary, no matter your political stripe. It's an important debate—don't get me wrong—but it also (potentially) leaves Jesus out of the equation entirely. With Nicodemus, we can tip our hats to the man ("Gee, you're such a swell teacher, Jesus") but maybe never take our Lord out of the closet, kept safely hidden. Jesus really doesn't want accolades from Nicodemus (or from us, for that matter). He goes directly for the theological jugular: "You must be born from above."

And what does that mean? "Well," he said, "it's about as joyful and painful as childbirth. It's about as unpredictable as the wind. It's about looking at this life not in fear but with anticipation that the Spirit will blow you into places where you will make a difference. It's about offering your life for the sake of this broken world, not retreating into the shadows where it's safe."

Towards the end of this story, Jesus describes "eternal life" in the present tense. We usually talk about such a life as some future reality, a post-death reward for keeping our noses clean. But twice Jesus refers to eternal life in *the present tense* (John 3:15 and 3:16). "Everyone who believes in him may not perish but *may have* eternal life."

Not "will have." May have—now. If eternal life begins now, in this life, and the whole idea of "perishing" (as Jesus puts it) is not the threat we thought it was, how then shall we live?

In a world of campus shootings and terrorist plots and city bombings, how shall we relate to one another? One response (I won't deny the appeal) is retreat, suspicion, and the shelving of the teachings of Jesus as rather impractical and even foolhardy. But, please ponder this: what if you've died and been born again in Christ? What if eternal life begins now?

Our family has a good friend in Virginia, Marty, who is a midwife. She's delivered thousands of babies in a variety of circumstances—most joyful, some unbearably painful. I like to think of Jesus as a midwife sometimes: cheering us on, giving us instruction, birthing us into the church. This can be a process full of both joy and pain.

It's precisely this truthful exchange about conversion and new birth at Jesus' kitchen table that sends Nicodemus off on a whole new life. He appears two other times in John's gospel. Not long after this encounter, Nicodemus rises to defend Jesus in the middle of an emergency meeting of the Sanhedrin as they discuss how to get rid of Jesus, the troublemaker. Nicodemus stands in the middle of that meeting and wonders out loud: "Our law does not judge people without first giving them a hearing, does it?" (John 7:50–52). It must have taken guts to say that out in the open. And then, at the foot of the cross, two people step forward to bury Jesus. One of them, at considerable expense, offers a hundred pounds of spices to anoint the body of Jesus (John 19:39–42). With this lavish gift, Nicodemus has fully emerged from the shadows. His faith is now fully public, out in the light of a new day.

For further reflection:

1. The phrase "to be born again" has often been used as something of a threat to delineate who's "in or out" of God's good graces. How does this story reshape your understanding of this popular theological phrase?

2. If eternal life begins now for the Christian believer, does the way you engage your neighborhood, the stranger, and this gift of life now change? Name a few examples.

4. Coercion Aversion

"If any want to become my followers..." (Mark 8:34).

EVERY OCTOBER IN ABOUT the sixth or seventh game of the World Series a sign appears behind home plate (usually on a 3–2 count) held by an eager fan. The sign says, "READ JOHN 3:16." Listen closely and you can hear Bibles rustling across America as viewers at home locate perhaps the most famous verse in either testament.

I somehow doubt the efficacy of such signs at sporting events, but if you find yourself in some stadium and feel inclined to promote the Bible from the bleachers, I have an alternate suggestion for your sign. Take a Magic Marker and write "READ MARK 8:34." This will accomplish two things. You'll be doing your part to fight biblical illiteracy (for Americans will now know two verses from the Bible). *And* you'll let enamored readers of John 3:16 alone run while there's still time. For the first text says God gave Jesus for the sake of the world. And the second says God also gives us.

Jesus once told a crowd that included his disciples, "If any want to become my followers, let them deny themselves and take up their cross and follow me." If somebody really wanted to sum up Christian discipleship on a sign, that's the verse I'd choose. Deny self. Take up a cross. And get in line behind Jesus. "When Jesus calls a person," said Dietrich Bonhoeffer, "he bids them come and die." Die to self-determination; die to calling the shots for one's own life; die to being in charge of my destiny and purpose. A disciple relinquishes those things and gets in line behind the one who will show us how to truly live. This is not easy; an extremely difficult process of relinquishment, in fact, living where we do in a land that reveres "doing your own thing" with individual zest.

But these words of Jesus are the basic marching orders for the church in this or any era. "Deny self. Take up a cross. Follow me." Here Jesus describes the very essence of what it means to be the church. Without these core elements, this essence, church becomes "club" or social organization or religious dabbling or even "museum." Success in the modern church has normally been gauged on the basis of two numbers—average worship attendance and whether the budget is met. Do well in those categories (say many) and we're on the way. The way I read Jesus, however, those aren't the best criteria for faithful discipleship.

Have you ever noticed that Jesus doesn't seem too concerned about the number of people who are actually lining up to live life the way he's prescribed? He's convinced the way of sacrifice, self-denial, and obedience *is* the way to find life and live it abundantly, but he doesn't seem to sweat about the number of people doing so. A huge task facing the modern church in a still-new millennium is to help church members (and others who seek affiliation with Christ's church) to thoroughly understand what it means to be a disciple. Neil Postman (1931–2003), a communications theorist, wrote: "I believe I am not mistaken in saying that Christianity is a demanding and serious religion. When it is delivered as easy and amusing, it is another kind of religion altogether."[4]

I heard a story several years ago about an unusual congregation in North Carolina. The congregation is incredibly active in the local community, fully integrated across racial lines in a small town setting, and biblically literate in every sense of that phrase. An interviewer from a city paper visited the small town and was amazed at the vitality and commitment of the membership in such an out-of-the-way place. The inevitable question was finally posed to the pastor: "What happened here? How'd you do this?" And the response came quickly. "Well, it wasn't me, you understand. The Spirit was leading us all. But when I first got here, we were a church of about 800 members, many of them inactive. After the first year, I preached 'em down to about 400. Then, after three years, I preached 'em down to about 200. After four years, I preached 'em down to about 75. And then we began."

Jesus is not concerned about numbers. He's concerned about faithfulness. Numbers will take care of themselves if a congregation looks closely at these core values of what it means to be church, this *essence* of life in the church. I'll say it again: a central part of the church's mission is

---

4. Postman, *Amusing Ourselves to Death*, 121.

to be as clear as possible about this essence. When the church does this well, however, expect resistance.

Notice that just before Jesus makes this honest declaration, Peter "took him aside" and began to correct Jesus (Mark 8:31–33). Can't you see Peter putting his arm around Jesus' shoulder, a little patronizingly, pulling him off to the side, and saying in a soothing voice, "Now look Big Guy, we're here for you and all. But you're talking a little nutty all of a sudden. Don't you know you've got the ear of the crowds here and a lot of people are thinking about following you? Let me help you rethink what you're saying, old buddy, old friend."

Notice also the name that Jesus calls Peter at this very point, right in front of his pals. He calls Peter "Satan." Pretty strong stuff. Earlier in Lent, we left Jesus with Satan in the wilderness and maybe thought we were done with the old tempter. Evil, according to Mark's gospel, can raise its head at surprising moments and in surprising ways. So Jesus "rebukes" Peter. Throughout this Gospel, the exact same word is used when Jesus quiets demons and exorcises evil spirits. He "rebukes" these spirits. By using the same word here with Peter, Mark is suggesting that a ministry other than one based on self-denial, cross-bearing, and obedience borders on the demonic. Evil in this Gospel is rather insidious, subtle, and not at all obvious. It can attack the Christian community in ways we do not fully notice.

It's not easy to be a Christian. And we should never suggest ease in the name of evangelism or adding people to a roll. Jesus never says, "Take up your pillow and follow me." Maybe that's why nobody ever holds up Mark 8:34 on television at sporting events. The teachings of Jesus, for starters, will regularly rub very hard against the way we spend money, the type of people we include as friends, and how we think about war and the use of violence, towards whatever end.

*

Jesus has a crowd[5] in front of him as he offers this teaching on discipleship. If he ever had a chance to add to his movement, this was it. He says something very important to this crowd, just before he outlines what I'm calling the essence of church. He says, "*If any* want to *become my followers* . . . ." If anybody here *desires* to become my disciple.

---

5. Mark 8:34 reports an address for both disciples and a crowd.

There is absolutely no arm-twisting here. There is not a hint of coercion or an inkling of judgment from Jesus; no threat of hell for those who turn sadly away. Jesus seems to go out of his way to make sure no one is bullied, manipulated, or coerced into discipleship. *If any want . . .* to be a disciple. Churches simply cannot be in the business of religious coercion because Jesus wasn't.

The flip-side of this, of course, is that we must be crystal clear about what discipleship *does* mean for the church and for newcomers who are looking for Jesus, those who desire to be disciples. Discipleship doesn't happen by osmosis or chance or even by joining a church.

Our mission is to be a welcoming but not a diluted, watered-down church. That, frankly, can be a challenge these days. Perhaps it might help clarify our mission if we focused on three little words:

If any want . . .

*

Long ago they strung him up and killed him on a Friday. Think of the sign above his head. Most testimonies say it reads one way. But look harder. Right above the crown of thorns. Look closely.

I think it says, "READ MARK 8:34."

For further reflection:

1. If your tradition does not include making the sign of the cross as a reminder of one's baptism, consider initiating this old liturgical gesture into your own devotional life.

2. Discover how your congregation welcomes new members and others seeking baptism. Is this process of welcome adequate in describing what it means to follow Jesus? Why or why not?

5. Bad News, Front Page

"No, I tell you; but unless you repent, you will all perish as they did"
(Luke 13:5).

OKAY, LET'S GET THIS right out of the way, first thing. The exchange between Jesus and his pals in Luke 13:1–5 (a story traditionally assigned in Lent) is rather weird. I hear you: *extremely and bizarrely* weird. Maybe the "Odd Top Ten" of weirdness in the entire New Testament.

Some friends are concerned about the latest bad news, two tragedies that have rocked the community in recent days. Maybe these events were reported on the front page of the *Galilean Daily Globe*. Maybe there's just a general buzz in the streets. But the two tragedies pretty much cover the waterfront of human woe.

The first is a tragedy of planned malice. We're familiar with these. An evil despot hatches a sordid crime and carries out the plot in grisly detail. Our news feed is full of such atrocities—planned havoc on scales large and small. This time it's Pilate, a madman who murders innocents. But let's bring it a bit closer to home. I'll try to paraphrase Jesus here: "Those innocent people who were murdered the other day in San Bernardino. Do you think they deserved what happened because of something they did wrong? No way; bad theology. But unless you repent and get *your* act together, your future will also feel like some terrorist breaking down the front door of your home." Jesus didn't say that, of course. But isn't this just about the gist of it?

Another headline sweeping the local community and appearing that week on the front page of *The Capernaum Post* describes the second broad category of suffering and woe. Nobody's to blame; nobody planned it; innocent people just accidentally got in the way of a crumbling tower.

Again, here's an attempt to paraphrase Jesus: "I know you're wondering about the poor Virginians just south of Richmond affected by last week's weather; horrible tragedy, that tornado. And no, they didn't do anything to deserve that storm. Would you please get such shoddy theological thinking out of your head? There's no cause-and-effect correlation here, no matter what Pat Robertson says. But let me tell you something and I hope you're listening. You better clean up your act and do some fast changing or some twister's gonna roar into your own life, and you and your little dog Toto sure as heck won't be destined for any Munchkinland." And no, Jesus didn't say exactly that either. But isn't that about the upshot of what he did say?

We're drawn to tragedies, drawn to the headlines and the morning news; horrified by acts of planned malice and heartbroken by innocents who just get in the way; in the wrong place at the wrong time. We're people who care. We want to know why these things happen. It's human nature, right? To wonder about such things? This is political gravy for anybody running for office. To address our fears about stuff out there that might also get us. But Jesus does not linger with the questions that all of us ask upon picking up a newspaper in any city, any locale. He suddenly shifts the theological ground under our feet. And you have to wonder what in the heck this man of compassion, our Lord and Savior, is thinking. In Isaiah, God says: "For my thoughts are not your thoughts, nor are your ways my ways" (Isa 55:8). No argument from me there.

*

If there's anybody who says they've never wondered why tragedies happen in our world—why God seems to allow tragedy—then I'd say they're either lying or vacationing on some other planet, not this one. Tragedies and human suffering grab human attention like few other things.

Many years ago I received a Saturday morning phone call from our pediatrician at the time; a caring man, Dr. Schiavone. He wasn't calling about any of our three children, but another child in our parish—a little boy named Eric, a child three years old who'd had a tough time of it since birth with severe respiratory problems. "Frank," said Dr. Schiavone, "please come to the hospital, please come now." I was led to a back room in the ER and there found two parents who were completely inconsolable, crying between gasps of breath, almost in a low wail, holding their little boy who was no longer breathing. Eric, a beautiful child of God, had just died. We all held each other, we prayed together, and we all walked out of that hospital, limp with grief.

Many hours later, at the end of that very dark day, Eric's dad asked the inevitable question that hovered unspoken in his heart back at the hospital. "Why, Pastor Frank? *Why Eric?*" I don't even remember what I said. Is there any real answer to such a question that makes any sense?

But I do remember what I *didn't* say, would never say—the very thing that Jesus said that day long ago when he heard about two horrible tragedies. And so I return to my question. What was our Lord thinking? Did he ever say anything more strange or befuddling?

*

Jesus' track record for compassion and care for others is matchless. It's important to state that Jesus is not on trial for this odd exchange, even though our ponderous minds may go there. He wasn't just moved by tragedy from a distance; he entered tragedy and shared it. He wept over the death of a friend (John 11:28–37) and asked the "why" question himself while hanging from a cross (Luke 11:42–44). He railed at injustice and warned the privileged about their neglect of poor people.

Something else is going on here that brings forth these odd words from Jesus. Sometimes a tragedy prods us to action—compassion for another; inspiration to change an injustice. We reach out with tangible assistance.

But sometimes tragedy (especially a headline) can divert us from looking hard at our own shortcomings. What do I mean by this? Sometimes our obsession with the bad guys—ISIS, terrorists, drug dealers on the front page, child molesters on page two—have a diverting effect. And maybe you've never said this out loud, but I suspect you've thought it: "Gosh, I may have several character flaws. I make a few mistakes here and there. *But at least I'm not as messed up as those guys.*" The bad news of the day—the daily headline of woe and concern—can sometimes divert us from the hard work of personal repentance because there's nothing wrong *with me*, you see; it's somebody or something else that's the problem. "I'm not that bad," I rationalize. "Not compared to so many others."

A recent example of this? In our local newspaper (three days running) was a story about a memorial monument that included a cross in the masonry work. A national group called The Association of Freedom from Religion wanted the cross removed posthaste, raising a lot of local ire. People called our church wondering what we might do about such a travesty. "There are evil people out there who want to remove the cross of our Lord. And I'm mad about that. Isn't that awful?"

For the record, I think it's fine that a cross exists in a public monument. But I also think the whole argument is a diversion. This is often the default response from a salacious headline. The more we say "it's those people" who are evil, wrong, and misguided, the less we're able to see our own flaws.

It's easy to point out the wrongdoings of others. It's a much more difficult enterprise to confess our own shortcomings and make changes. The Bible uses an old word to describe our dilemma: the need for personal *repentance*. In this odd exchange about the news of the day, Jesus readjusts my vision. He cares about villains and their warped plans. He cares about tragedy and those who accidentally get in the way. But at the end of the day he also wants to know about me—how *I* stand before God. How Frank Honeycutt stands before God. Not others; me.

*

Did Jesus come to fix everything, the divine puppeteer? Or did he primarily come to fix me and you? We are drawn to atrocity stories. We are drawn to mishap and tragedy and wrongdoing. But sometimes we're drawn to such things from motives that are rather dark and complicated.

Lent is a season that confronts this darkness. Lent invites us to hone in *not on the headlines* but rather on our own sin and complicity. The parable of the fig tree attached to these seemingly weird words of Jesus begins to make a little more sense. "I've been looking for fruit from this tree for three years. Cut it down!"

Lent is a season where God offers us time to change and even throws manure-like death into our lives, the odd fertilizer of the cross, to get your attention and mine.

Jesus feels the pain of others. He died for this world and weeps over headlines. But he will not linger there with the daily news—where my attention often gets stuck. He's got even bigger fish to fry. The repentance of people like me.

For further reflection:

1. Take an inventory of how much time you spend listening to or watching the news during a given day. Share with a friend what this might honestly reveal.

2. The previous essay ("Coercion Aversion") claimed that Jesus refuses to be threatening in describing the life of a disciple. Is he coercive in Luke 13:1–5?

6. Snakebitten

"Make a poisonous serpent, and set it on a pole; and everyone who is bitten shall look at it and live" (Num 21:8).

Around eight thousand people in the United States are bitten each year by poisonous snakes. Of this number, only a dozen or so die. Experts advise that the best first aid is to keep the patient calm and get him to the hospital as quickly as possible.... To date, at least seventy-one people have been killed by poisonous snakes during religious services in the United States, including the man said to have started the whole thing, George Went Hensley, who died vomiting blood in a shed in North Florida in 1955. Hensley had started handling around 1910 and had been bitten more than four hundred times before the fatal blow.[6]

This quote is from a fascinating book on snake-handling congregations in southern Appalachia, a fairly minor religious tradition in the region that traces its biblical reasoning back to a single verse (Mark 16:18)[7] where followers of the resurrected Christ are told they can handle serpents and drink poison without ill effect. Maybe George Went Hensley would have emerged from that North Florida shed in 1955 had he also remembered the wisdom of Numbers 21:8.

There one finds the rather bizarre remedy for a poisonous snakebite. Bronze a serpent. Put the snake on a stick. Stare directly into the pupils of the metallic asp. Do not look away. And you'll live to tell your

---

6. Covington, *Salvation on Sand Mountain*, 147–48.

7. It's worth noting that Mark 16:18 is thought by most scholars to be a biblical "add-on" and not part of the original version of Mark's gospel.

grandchildren the story. You'd think someone as biblically informed as George Went Hensley would have known about this serpentine escape clause, but it's tough to catechize the dead in these matters.

*

Please forgive my rather sarcastic tone. I don't mean to judge anyone else's religion; Lutherans have our own share of flaws. But a careful reader runs into this strange stuff fairly regularly in the Bible and if one takes it all literally, well, the result can be rather problematic.

For example, this old story from the book of Numbers (Num 21:4–9) is not a *voluntary* handling of serpents. No, these snakes were sent from God who was pushed over the edge because the people grumbled about the wilderness menu one too many times. *Manna in the morning; manna at the noon day; manna when the sun goes down.* Three squares of the same thing for days on end. "We detest this miserable food," say the faithful. And then whammo. This story might make you think twice before grumbling about a fly in the soup on your next trip to Cracker Barrel.

It must have been hellish for Moses to lead such an impudent bunch day in and day out. The man's patience had limits and I suspect he enjoyed (in a rather warped way) the sight of his flock being reminded who was in charge out there. Did Moses smile just a bit as he said to God, "Lord Almighty One, let's now loose the puff adders to bite a few of these complainers right on the shins. You want names, Lord? Got a pencil? Oh yes, I have just the very people in mind."

The response from the congregation, of course, is immediate. Catastrophe (in any century) tends to awaken religious sensibility. "Moses, we have sinned! We were wrong and we'll do better! We promise to change our behavior, just get rid of these snakes!" *Yeah, right,* Moses must have thought.

It's tough to reason with a rattlesnake. Get a sense of a poisonous serpent in the wild and get out of its way. You might be able to cajole your dog or pet cockatoo, but there's something ancient and symbolic and unmanageable about a snake. You might recall the sly "talking snake" in early Genesis in the long-ago garden. Keep that garden in mind, by the way, as this old story from Numbers unfolds.

"We'll do better!" they all say. "We promise." And so Moses (instructed by the Lord) does a very strange thing. He fashions a serpent, attaches it to a pole, and anybody snake-bitten could look at the bronzed biter and be well.

*

I'm sure you will agree that this is a very strange story, perhaps not told to children at night just before tucking them into bed or as a negative incentive to eat all their green vegetables or else. Is it easier to agree with certain friends who sometimes say, "This is why I don't read the Bible anymore"?

To get at the truth embedded in this old story about snakes, consider one of my favorite movies, *The Boy in the Striped Pajamas* (2008). The central characters are two eight-year-old boys who become unlikely friends. They secretly meet on opposite sides of a fence that surrounds a work camp in Poland in World War II.

One of the boys can run and play; come and go through a path in the woods. His father (a commander) has moved the family to a nearby house. The other little boy, at all times behind the fence, wears a uniform with stripes. They meet at the same secret place for days in a row and share hopes and dreams as Jew and German. Part of the power of the movie is that the children are the ones who dare to really look at the realities of their situation and will not turn away. Their friendship is forged because they dare to look hard at what separates them. Somehow that honest looking also liberates them to act and love and speak.

In a digital age, many cultural observers have noted that our greatest challenge is not hedonism, but rather distraction. We get a sense of something askew and often turn away. Television (and Internet) news invites us to gaze upon the suffering of others without getting overly involved. Wincing, maybe, but really looking and entering—usually not. As one employed in a so-called caring profession, I sometimes create a "boundary" because I've been taught to do that in order to protect my fragile self and survive over the long haul. But I wonder if I really do this because going further would require just too much effort and focus. Relatedly, I might consider my own shortcomings and want to change, but finally recognize that change is just exhausting. It's often easier (at least in the short run) to stay the course.

6. SNAKEBITTEN

*

This old story from Numbers is a reminder that all human beings have been snake-bitten by the power of sin, a reality as old as a talking serpent who invited the first human couple to be their own gods (Gen 3:1–7). (What fun!) It's not necessary to believe the literal details of either story in order to grasp that something very ancient and primordial is afoot.[8]

Part of the lasting power of the church year is that our histories and our faces are rubbed in death so regularly that this fearful reality somehow ceases to have the paralyzing hold on us that it once did. "Remember that you are dust," opens the Lenten season. Why in the world would a person consciously recall such a thing? Because *looking directly at our sin and disobedience*, directly at our mortality (that which has bitten us all) somehow paradoxically liberates us to live this life without fear. Looking honestly at that which ails us (cyclically and repeatedly via the church year) gives God room to heal us.

Is there anything worse than death? Well, yes; our great fear of it just might be worse. Church is where we're invited to stare death down. Here's a rather strange truth: we're all dying (2 Cor 6:8–10), and God invites us to look at death directly and not turn away.

*

Concerned about numerical growth and the "happy, joy-joy" side of Christianity, some congregations are removing the cross entirely from sanctuaries because of its perception as a worship downer. A response to such foolhardiness: please recall that one of the church's favorite Bible verses, John 3:16,[9] is directly preceded by a reference to these snakes in the book of Numbers and their squirming, slithering reality in all lives. This old observation from Saint Augustine (354–430) describes well the centrality of the cross: "The deformity of Christ forms you." Some advice: never settle for plain Christianity—the vanilla version.

"You were dead," wrote Saint Paul to the church in Ephesus.[10] "We were dead," he claims a few verses later; dead in our trespasses. Now,

---

8. See 1 John 1:8–10.
9. Martin Luther called this verse "the gospel in miniature."
10. See Eph 2:1–10.

offers the gospel, look upon a man *sacrificially* dead who gives his life for the world. Take a good long gander and do not turn away. Look and live.

For further reflection:

1. Revisit the disobedience of the world's first humans (Gen 3:1–9) in tandem with this snaky story. Why are these old narratives necessary in helping to understand the origins of human sin and its consequences?

2. Do you agree that distraction is one of the church's greatest challenges in a new century? Why or why not?

7. Baptism in Seven Scenes

"Then he went and washed and came back able to see" (John 9:7).

EVERY THIRD YEAR, DURING the season of Lent, the church's lectionary cycle includes long stories with multiple layers from John's gospel. The next two essays focus upon "the man born blind" (John 9:1–41) and the raising of Jesus' family friend, Lazarus (John 11:1–44). These stories were favorites in the early church to prepare adult catechumens for baptism at the Easter Vigil. Even if you're already familiar with these stories, it will be beneficial to spend some unhurried time with each before dipping into the accompanying essay. If possible, assigning speaking parts within a study group will bring further understanding and insight to these old classics. With that caveat, here are some thoughts on the first story, a tale of literal and figurative blindness.

*

Scene One—If somebody came at me with a gooey glob of mud, I couldn't sit still even if I was blind. Jesus hocks and spits and makes mud, almost like a little child playing around in the backyard. My mother tells me I used to eat mud in Chattanooga as a little boy; she'd catch me scooping it from the high bank on the other side of the back alley. Maybe I was searching for some missing and needed mineral in my youthful diet; some element from the periodic table.

There's something about Jesus bending down in the dirt that reminds me of that tender scene in Genesis where God stoops down in the primordial dust, scoops up a handful of earth and breathes life into the first human (Gen 2:7). Something new is happening here. *Creation* is occurring. "Go wash in the pool," says Jesus. The blind man with the less than hygienic mud in his eyes obeys. He washes and suddenly sees. "I once was blind but now I see," wrote John Newton (1725–1807), who trafficked in slaves before writing a famous hymn. Washing and seeing. This is the language of baptism, although the word is never used in this long forty-one-verse story.

But that's John's metaphorical way in this old and layered Gospel. Anytime you come across a reference to water or food in John, think sacraments. John is arguably the most sacramental of all the Gospels, but not overtly. He drops lots of subtle hints in this regard. This first scene has been discovered at least seven times in early catacomb art in conjunction with baptism. Something new is happening here. A new creation with dust and spit and water—elemental building blocks of life.

Scene Two—It doesn't take long for the news to get around town and, of course, nobody believes it. Isn't this the guy who used to shake his tin cup and beg for coins down on the corner? "Look, people," said the once-blind man, "we've been neighbors all our lives, right? You see me every day. I couldn't see you, of course, until now—and you're coming more into focus all the time. But come on. It's me, it's really me. How? Well, this guy (you're not going to believe this) put mud on my eyes and I went and washed. Where is he? Well, come to think of it, I don't really know."

Those who now see with the eyes of Jesus have a similar problem to this man who used to shake a tin cup and beg down on the corner. When questioned by others about our new sight in Christ—*Well, where is he? Where'd he go? When's he gonna show up again?*—we recognize in some ways that we're in similar skeptical cross hairs, between the coming of Jesus and his coming again. Most of the action in this old story occurs without the presence of Jesus. He heals the blind man and exits stage left until the very ending of the story. This mirrors our own experience in this in-between time.

We have his word, of course. We have the promise of his presence in the sacraments. But an exact and precise explanation of our life in Christ (and a confident pinpointing of the location of Jesus at all times) is going to elude us here in the meantime in-between. And it will make the task of evangelism all the more challenging in our skeptical world. "Then where is he with Charleston, Darfur, Syria, fill-in-the-blank?" "Well, I'm not really sure," said the once-blind Christian. There are responses to these old questions even in new settings. But they will always be partial and in-between.

Scene Three—Please don't dump on the Pharisees in this next scene. They're only defending tradition. You could probably insert here the word "Lutherans" or "Lutheran pastors" or even the name "Frank Honeycutt" for the word "Pharisees." They/I/we call the man downtown to synod headquarters for a friendly interrogation. We don't buy his story for a minute. He may as well have seen the Virgin Mary singing "Ave Maria" at the top of her lungs halfway up an oak tree in Conyers, Georgia. We are dubious because that is our nature and so we ask the poor guy to repeat his story (yet *again* with the mud and the water and the washing) but the hint of my smirk is discernible even as I try to listen politely.

Sometimes it's a challenge for Christians to know what an authentically real and new movement of the Holy Spirit actually looks like because we (I) often want to closely guard and honor the tradition. The Pharisees are agitated and worked up. But don't dump on them too hard. Their reservations reflect those of any of us who distrust new directions in church life, even the new sight that baptism brings.

Scene Four—This scene is perhaps the most tragic and sad of all in this old story of tragedy and sadness. No one thus far has rejoiced with this once-blind man. No alleluia, no back slap, no prayer of thanksgiving from a neighbor or old friend or religious leader. Not even a word of gladness from his mother and father! And if the man was "born blind" then that means his parents had lived with this challenge since they held their son in their arms as an infant. "We have no idea how he sees," they answer when questioned. "Go ask him. He's over twenty-one now."

I think the parents here are afraid. It's possible to underestimate the division that Jesus can bring to family life. This is all through the Gospels. Baptism shifts allegiance. I am no longer (primarily) child of Bob and Ruth Honeycutt. In baptism, I am child of *God*. This primary allegiance to God does not mean that I will abandon family commitments, but it does put those commitments in perspective within the context of God's family, the church. I sometimes think we should celebrate baptisms with an accompanying warning label. The child or adult is signing on with a brand new family.

Scene Five—Back downtown, the once-blind man undergoes interrogation number two. I see a dark room illumined with a single light; inquisitors in the shadows: "What did he do to you? How did he open your eyes? Where does he come from?" All these rapid-fire questions that begin to test the patience of our hero. He's becoming a little uppity. Good for him. "Look, I've told you people my story about seven times. Why in the world do you want to hear it again? Are you interested in signing on as one of his disciples?" And with this last question, something snaps in those who thought they were in control. "Look, you little whippersnapper, who do you think you're talking to here? We know more about God than you do. So we'll make the rules around here." And they drove him out.

Scene Six—The isolation is now complete. And still no hallelujah, no congratulations, no party, and not even a greeting card to celebrate the good fortune of this man blind from birth. And top off that reality with this: neighbors, friends, parents, and even his religious guides have all let him down; no one comes to his defense.

It's at the height of this isolation that Jesus re-enters the story, as if to underscore what the man has lost and finally help him celebrate the movement he's entering. "Lord, I believe." And his vision becomes fully clear.

*

I've preached on this long story many times in thirty years of parish ministry. But I've only recently noticed that the story has six very distinct scenes and then ends. I thought about that number, the imperfect number six in the Bible, and smiled.

I smiled because I really wouldn't put it past the author of the Gospel of John to be sending a little message from his vantage point to ours, even with all the centuries in between. We are living out Scene Seven: the church in every age. And even though the history and context might change, the issues are similar: spiritual blindness, baptismal washing, resistance to change, the absence and presence of Jesus, and the new family that is the church.

"Surely we are not blind, are we?" It's not a bad question to ask during Lent. In baptism, Jesus washes his children and brings new sight. The church celebrates this watery welcome and the living of a seventh, open-ended scene.

For further reflection:

1. In your life as a follower of Jesus (or as someone contemplating discipleship), have you experienced any isolation and pushback from family or friends who may not be all that excited about your Christian identity? If so, describe this a bit.

2. Sometimes Jesus feels absent to believers even though we simultaneously confess his presence. How might you go about explaining this tension to someone you know who is not a Christian?

8. Bound in the Boneyard

"Could not he who opened the eyes of the blind man have kept this man from dying?" (John 11:37)

THIS QUESTION POSED BY neighbors of two grieving sisters not long after the death of their brother, Lazarus, is also asked by honest Christians of any time or place. If Jesus is *capable* of preventing suffering and woe, why doesn't he protect his followers from such? Jesus pulls off all sorts of miracles in the Gospels, ranging from the feeding of thousands to walking on water. Why not perform a little favor for a family friend? *"Could not he who opened the eyes of the blind man have kept this man from dying?"* A perfectly reasonable question, if you ask me. Watch for the questions in the Bible. This neighborhood chorus is speaking for all of us, twenty centuries removed.

If Jesus does indeed *have it in him* to shield us from suffering and grief, what's stopping him? As a close friend of mine, a non-believer, once put it, "If God has the power to change things and either can't or won't, then I choose not to respect him." It's the same point made by these neighbors. "Why couldn't he keep our friend from dying?" And indeed, it's our question: *Why can't Jesus keep us from dying?*

And if Jesus cannot do that, a great many people just go ahead and ask another question rarely asked in church. *If he cannot protect us, then what real good is he?* Jesus may become a nice, well-intentioned teacher from the past who, even for a great many Christians, has nothing much to do with our present sufferings.

Lazarus and his sisters lived in the little town of Bethany. A lot of places in the Bible begin with the prefix "Beth-," which means "House of . . ." something or other. So, for example, Bethlehem means "House of Bread" and Bethel means "House of God." Bethany means "House of Affliction." Can you imagine growing up in such a place? "Where'd you say you were from, son?" "Well, I was raised over in the next valley in the little town of House of Affliction, South Carolina."

A case could be made that all of us grow up in a place called "House of Affliction." We certainly don't have to go searching very far for the afflicted. Keep your eyes open and they'll make their sad march before your door. Suffering will barge right in uninvited sooner or later and take a seat in our lives. To the cynic, the world is one big cemetery, a virtual valley of bones once described by the prophet Ezekiel (Ezek 37:1–14). So have a seat in this old boneyard. A body is bound to come by before long, some who've hardly had a chance to live.

This is when we usually ask that question. The one asked by the friends of Lazarus. Why couldn't Jesus have prevented this? Kept our friend from dying? And while you're at it, go ahead and ask the one that didn't get printed in your Bible: *what is Jesus good for anyway?*

*

I'm sure it's not news to you that many have concluded that Jesus is good for nothing. Even for many church members, Sunday becomes just another Saturday and the Bible just another book.

So Jesus arrives in Bethany, the "House of Affliction." The sisters are rather irked with him. Jesus is oddly late for this funeral.[11] "If you'd been here, my brother would not have died." Twice that's thrown in the face of Jesus (John 11:21 and 32). I love these two sisters, so uppity and honest in their grief. *If you'd been here, pal.* The neighbors join the chorus. If he did a good thing one town over, why not here? Pay close attention when people sass Jesus in the Gospels. They're usually speaking for all of us.

"Jesus wept," says the old King James Version. If you cannot remember any other Bible passages when appearing on *Jeopardy* one day, this is the verse most easily summoned. But here's a seemingly dumb question: Why is Jesus crying here? I used to think that Jesus was indeed sad for his old pal and on this sad day tears are appropriate. But I don't think that anymore.

Look closely at the story. Twice (John 11:33 and 38), on either side of the tears in verse 35, the text describes Jesus as "greatly disturbed." In

---

11. Add up the days in John 11:6 and 11:17 and Jesus has some explaining to do.

the Greek, the word is "angry." Jesus is very upset, ticked. Anger brackets the tears. Then in verse 40, Jesus is somewhat impatient with Martha who tries to warn him that it's going to stink to high heaven when they take the stone away. "Didn't I already tell you about this, Martha?" Jesus asks rather curtly.

And finally, at the tomb, in the graveyard surrounded by bones, Jesus offers a prayer where he seems more than a little put out with those gathered for the funeral service. I love this: "Dear God, I know that you always hear me, but I'm praying this prayer *for the sake of these thick-headed people who are listening to me right now.*"[12] Have you ever heard a preacher deliver a sermon and then continue the sermon in a later prayer? Jesus is sort of doing that here. He's praying, but he knows who's listening right behind him. He's using the prayer to take aim.

So no, I really don't think Jesus is crying because he's sad. I think Jesus loses it here because he's completely misunderstood. People are expecting him to snap off a miracle. And when he doesn't they ask, "So, what's he good for?" The actual raising of Lazarus, coming at the very end of the story, almost seems to be an afterthought from Jesus—a bone (pun intended) he throws to the sisters and neighbors who have misunderstood his purpose in a valley of dry bones. "Unbind him; let him go." But a question begs to be asked here: *Who's really bound in this old story? The dead guy or those gathered at the cemetery?*

*

Before the days of embalming in England, it was somewhat common to bury people in a casket rigged with a string. The string was run through a narrow tube and connected to a bell above ground. If you were buried but somehow not quite dead, you could pull the string and sound the bell. Apparently, this happened occasionally. People were exhumed and found breathing. I've seen pictures of elaborate caskets from this period fully equipped with food, beverage, and other amenities besides the popular string and bell. I think I'd like a nice supply of Guinness Stout in my casket, just in case.

We sometimes believe we'll never die. There's always a string to pull, a bell to sound. We were getting ready for work the other day, all the morning bodily preparations, and I asked my wife, Cindy, out of the blue:

---

12. See John 11:41–42.

"Which one of us do you think will die first?" There was a pause. "I don't know," she said, "but I hope it's you." "Why would you say that?" I asked. "Because women tend to handle it better than men." I thought about that a second and concluded she was probably right.

*

"Could not he who opened the eyes of the blind man have kept this man from dying?" That's our question. We're the ancient chorus. If Jesus does not prevent death, what then does he do? What good is he? Jesus can't (or maybe won't) keep us from dying. But if we watch him closely, and learn to live his story, he will keep us from *the fear of dying*. And according to the Bible, the fear of death (which leads us to live in so many harmful ways) can be worse than death itself.

So we bring old bones to our congregation's altar, where so many have knelt before. We hold out open hands for the bread and wine, a taste of death reframed. Jesus is a trustworthy guide in our shared house of affliction—into the tomb and beyond.

That, among other things, is exactly what he's good for.

For further reflection:

1. As stated in the essay, Jesus is late (unfashionably late) for this funeral and even seems to misread the health situation of his good friend. What do you make of the unusual details revealed in John 11:1–6? How do these details function in the story's overall interpretation?

2. Recall a recent funeral service you attended. What did you hear there (from pastor or congregants) that was helpful? And perhaps not so helpful?

9. Save Now

"Hosanna in the highest heaven!" (Mark 11:10).

PALM SUNDAY IS ONE of those days in the church year that seems fairly cut and dried. Hoist a palm branch, shout for Jesus, and go home. But here are a few things I find strange about this day.

For most of Jesus' public ministry, unplanned, spontaneous events seemed to fill his days. He was teaching in a house and a paralyzed man was lowered through the roof and interrupted his lecture. He was walking along a road and a little man in a sycamore tree interrupted a hike that was heading elsewhere. He was once in a crowd and a woman who had a strange blood disease reached out to touch him. He was teaching on a deserted beach and spontaneously threw one of the biggest unplanned picnics ever recorded.

What these and many other events have in common is that they all seem to happen without forethought or planning, no real reflection or deliberation beforehand. Our Lord's ministry seems utterly unscheduled and spontaneous. He healed those he bumped into. There is no evidence that Jesus ever observed office hours, made a to-do list, or kept a calendar.

The events of Mark's version of Palm Sunday (Mark 11:1–11), however, could just as easily have been arranged by a travel agent. Our Lord gives precise, painstaking instructions to two disciples: A) Go to a certain village; B) Borrow a special colt, not just any colt mind you but one on which no posterior has ever sat—a colt tied up at a particular door, a specific address; and C) If anyone asks any questions about this suspicious behavior which looks an awful lot like horse rustling, just tell them we're borrowing their pony and will bring it back later. Is this precision strange to you after all these stories of spontaneity? The details here are so specific that I wonder why Jesus didn't just go ahead and include the donkey's eye color and shoe size.

Why does Jesus seem to orchestrate and plan his own parade? Why couldn't he have just *walked* into town without the added hoopla? His arrest would've occurred either way. Here's a guy who seems to avoid much attention. Indeed, all through Mark's gospel he told people to remain quiet, *shhh*, "don't say anything about me."[13] Now it seems like he's agreed to emcee the Macy's Thanksgiving Day Parade. Do you find this a little strange?

Equally baffling to me is the vegetation the crowd seems to be waving. Mark calls them "leafy branches" and only John comes right out and calls them "palms." Let's assume that they are indeed palm branches. What do the palms mean anyway? If Jesus had walked through my little town of Walhalla long ago in the spring, would followers observing this day centuries later be waving redbud or forsythia? Would pussy willows work just as well? Happy Pussy Willow Sunday! Just doesn't have the same ring, does it?

Any significance to the palms? As it turns out, the palms have plenty of religious significance. And the parade itself, planned down to the last detail by the normally spontaneous Jesus, is also jammed with symbolism.

*

In the year 167 BC, almost 200 years prior to Jesus' ride into Jerusalem, one of the notorious bad men of the Bible began to raise havoc with God's people. His name was Antiochus IV Epiphanes. His last name suggests his own conviction that he fathomed himself a Greek god.[14] Old Antiochus did some pretty raunchy things. For example, he desecrated the temple by tossing out the holy things of Judaism and erecting an altar to Zeus. He brazenly sacrificed the flesh of pigs in the holy of holies, a huge no-no for Jews. He even turned the outer courts of the temple into brothels.

Antiochus was a brutal, genocidal maniac, not unlike some of the madmen roaming Syria and Iraq these days, but with more power.

---

13. See Mark 8:30 for a single example of Jesus' many commands to keep silent.

14. Antiochus's heinous deeds are found in First Maccabees, an apocryphal book between the Testaments.

"According to the emperor's decree, they put to death the [Jewish] women who had their children circumcised … and they hung the infants from their mothers' necks."[15]

Many Jews lived in dire fear of Antiochus, under his royal thumb. Others were "mad as hell and weren't going to take it anymore." One of the latter bunch was Judas Maccabeus, the son of a priest, and one of five brothers who plotted a successful overthrow of the tyrant who had no regard for God or Jewish tradition. Most of the balance of First Maccabees describes a violent and bloody resistance movement where the rebels finally prevail. Jerusalem is liberated, temple worship is restored, and Antiochus is roundly defeated. Jewish people still recount this marvelous victory every year. You've heard of it—the festival of Hanukkah and the lighting of the menorah.[16]

Here's the description of the celebration as God's people enter the city of Jerusalem on that great day of joy and liberation: "On the 23rd day of the second month, in the 171st year [which was 141 BC], the Jews entered the city *with praise and palm branches*, and with harps and cymbals and stringed instruments, and with hymns and songs, because a great enemy had been crushed and removed from Israel."[17]

This old story, undoubtedly one of the top five in defining Jewish identity then and now, was not lost on Jesus. And no, pussy willows will not do. Jesus planned this parade down to the last detail and people *waved their palms* because they all saw Jesus for what he truly was: a liberator, a messiah, who would free them once again from foreign domination—this time the Romans. "Hosanna!" they shout. "Blessed is the One who comes in the name of the Lord."

"Hosanna" literally means, "Save us—*now*!" This crowd saw in Jesus an immediate answer to all their problems. They likened him to a messiah from 200 years before who liberated them from a violent madman. They waved palms. They knew that old story. Jesus, they were convinced, was riding into town to proverbially kick some Roman behind and remove the new tyrants.

Later in the week, the same crowd discovers that Jesus is not this type of messiah after all; that he won't take up arms and fight the way that Judas Maccabeus once fought. They become disappointed, even furious,

---

15. 1 Maccabees 1:60–61.

16. For a catchy (and educational) musical rendition of this old story, see the YouTube video by The Maccabeats titled "Candlelight."

17. 1 Maccabees 13:51.

with Jesus and want someone named Barabbas released instead. "And among the rebels in prison, who had committed murder in the insurrection, there was a man called Barabbas" (Mark 15:7). Barabbas wasn't in jail for petty larceny. He was the Jewish leader of a rebel movement, an insurrectionist, willing to resort to violence to get his way. When the crowd begs for Barabbas's release later on, this is what they're really saying: "Give us Barabbas instead of Jesus; maybe he'll get the job done a little faster."

*

Centuries later, we wave palms in the middle of a parade dripping with irony. For Jesus still refuses to conform to our expectations of how we think he ought to liberate us. "Hosanna! Save us now!" We often want immediate answers and quick shortcuts to the truth using whatever means a God of his stature might muster.

But the donkey he rides into town is essentially his hearse. Some liberator he's turned out to be. Perhaps many Christians will up and choose some other messiah given a choice. This one just hangs there and chooses to die rather than resort to violence. A hard lesson that his followers are still coming to terms with.

For further reflection:

1. I have a friend who once confided: "Jesus is my Lord, but I'd never vote for him for President." What do you think he meant by that?
2. Do a bit of close reading in First Maccabees (available online if not included in your Bible). Discuss the emotional turn in the Palm Sunday crowd upon learning that Jesus was not the liberator they expected.

10. Giving Tree

"They put him to death by hanging him on a tree" (Acts 10:39).

I ONCE TOOK A slow hike with an old friend into the gorge just below lower Whitewater Falls, not far from my home The trees were coming alive; massive oaks, stately spruce. Bluets and wild iris were just beginning to poke through the early spring soil. All the water rushing through the narrow canyon from recent rain created clear pools in the river, eight to ten feet deep in spots.

It's always good to be reminded of a natural order that keeps humming along without our notice or assistance; a seasonal rhythm set in place by a gracious and inventive hand. A huge oak served as a temporary backrest that Friday. I read somewhere that adult trees of this size, in summer, sponge up *a ton of water* every day from the earth. One could almost hear this ancient granddaddy slurping a long, slow sip, its branches silhouetted against the dim light of a late afternoon. Down the trail, from a distance, the boughs of the tree appeared as if they could hold a whole town.

*

Down through the centuries of Christian history, the cross of Christ came to be known as "a tree." Several times in the book of Acts, the author doesn't use the common word "cross," but instead says something like, "They took him down from the tree and laid him in a tomb" (Acts 13:29). Clarence Jordan, in his *Cottonpatch Gospels*, must have had this image in mind, in addition to a civil rights statement, when he refers to Jesus' crucifixion as a "lynching." In this country still quite new, I wonder if those who thought they could squelch a movement with violence knew that their chosen vehicle of death was actually connected to a very old and powerful metaphor, rooted in a truth exceeding any earthly power—the cross as *tree*. Saint Peter's correspondence puts it most graphically: "Christ carried up our sins in his body *to the tree*, so that we might live" (1 Pet 2:24).

In early Christian tradition, the cross was understood to be planted in the exact same place where the Tree of Life once grew in the garden of Eden. This tree will now have a new garden growing outward from its roots of grace. There is a great and mysterious paradox at work here. Jesus gives his life on a tree, but this tree in turn gives life to others.

*

If you've read Shel Silverstein's classic children's book, *The Giving Tree*, you know that the author is tapping into powerful Christian themes that find their roots in the cross. In turn, the tree offers a boy branches for play, apples for snacks, shade for romance, wood for a house, a trunk for a boat, and finally a stump for the boy (now an old man) to sit upon. The tree was always happy to give whatever it had, without complaint. The tree is a sacrificial symbol suggesting that we are offered life as sheer, unconditional gift. The cross of Christ is the church's "Giving Tree." Jesus holds nothing back.

In John's version of the trial, passion, and death, Jesus is never an unwilling victim. He doesn't complain or cry out to God in John's account. He talks back to the authorities and even carries his own cross; totes the lumber himself to the high hill (John 19:17). "My kingdom is not from this world," he says. "If my kingdom were from this world, my followers would be fighting. But as it is, my kingdom is not from here" (John 18:36). *Jesus is never afraid in this version of the story.* Those who are in charge, those who seem to have all the power, are the ones who (strangely) seem the most afraid and nervous.

I recall an odd story at the height of El Salvador's long and violent Civil War, the story of a massacre in the small village of El Mozote, not far from where my daughter, Marta, was born. I quote here from the account:

> There was one in particular the soldiers talked about that evening, a girl whom they had raped many times during the course

of the afternoon, and through it all, while the other women of El Mozote had screamed and cried . . . this girl had sung hymns, strange evangelical songs, and she had kept right on singing, even after they had done what had to be done, and shot her in the chest. She had lain there on La Cruz with the blood flowing from her chest, and had kept on singing—a bit weaker than before, but still singing. And the soldiers, stupefied, had watched and pointed. Then they had grown tired of the game and shot her again, and she sang still, and their wonder began to turn to fear—until finally they unsheathed their machetes and hacked through her neck, and at last the singing stopped.[18]

If the tree that is the cross still teems with life, is there any earthly threat that can touch a person marked with its power in baptism? Christians are grafted through baptism into the same family tree as our Lord. As one pastor puts it, "A faith that is well-grounded has an evenness about it. It doesn't rise and fall with the Dow Jones average or the inflection of a physician's voice. Why, in the eyes of faith, would you entertain adding a dimension of panic to your prayers tomorrow when it's not in them today?"[19]

*

Every Lent on Whitetop Mountain in Virginia (near one of my previous parishes), residents bore into the maple trees and out flows the sweet sap. In the passion story, as Jesus hangs there, breathing his last, soldiers pierce his side with a spear. Out comes blood and water (John 19:32–34). Humanity pierces the side of Jesus, bores into the tree of life, and out flows the sweet sacramental love of chalice and font. Even in death, Jesus nourishes the world.

This tree and this flowing inform a powerful vision of the Bible's final chapter: "Then the angel showed me the river of the water of life, bright as crystal, flowing from the throne of God and of the lamb through the middle of the street of the city. On either side of the river is *the tree of life* . . . and the leaves of the tree are for the healing of the nations" (Rev 22:1–2).

---

18. Norris, *The Cloister Walk*, 204.
19. Marty, "Holding Steady," 9.

The leaves of the tree. And who are they? The leaves are surely God's people, rooted in the love of the cross, growing for the sake of the world. We are born in Christ for such healing, the transition from Lent to Easter.

*

There is an old, ancient tree on a hill just outside Jerusalem—much older and stronger than the massive oak I leaned against in Whitewater River Gorge. On it hangs a man, in silence, with arms outstretched—rings of love inside the tree revealing the height and width and depth of the tree's reach. The tree, once planted in sin, now grows in love. And a new garden blossoms forth.

Sometimes, around dusk, I like to look back over the day, back over my life and its many mistakes, and see the long branches of this tree silhouetted against the afternoon's last light. From a distance, the tree looks like it could hold the whole world in its sturdy boughs. Here's the good news.

It can.

For further reflection:

1. Reflect upon the enviable calm exhibited by Jesus before his captors in John's gospel. How might living in an authentic and faithful Christian community form such a trusting calm in its people over time?

2. Take a forest walk this Holy Week and find an old tree to lean against in prayer. Discuss with a friend any images that came to mind.

IV. EASTER

Introduction to the Season

I'VE ALWAYS BEEN RATHER suspicious of Christians who are eternally upbeat. Nothing seems to faze them. Tragedy, job loss, hair loss, and routine constipation are all greeted with the same positive, sanctimonious spin. "Jesus loves you!" they report gleefully in any circumstance. Saint Paul in Philippians does indeed encourage believers to rejoice in the Lord always (Phil 4:4), but whenever I see someone with a "smiley face" faith persona coming my way and wanting to share their perpetual joy, always with a hug, I tend to run the other way—fast.

Part of this, I realize, is due to my Lutheran upbringing. A large part of our heritage came to life in sections of the world where light was scarce and times were tough. Luther wrote much more about the cross than he did about heaven, so I suppose I come by this reserved faith penchant rather honestly. It's hard for me to raise my arms and sway rapturously in a worship service. When I used to work at camp and spirit-filled youth would jump up and down for Jesus, I always held back a bit. Theological exuberance is not in my genes. It's hard for me to cheerlead for Jesus.

*

Saint Paul once described an interesting and rather strange trip into a "third heaven"[1] taken by someone who seems to be a close friend. I love his personal take on this celestial up and back. "Whether in the body or

---

1. See 2 Cor 12:1–10.

out of the body I do not know, God knows." He says this twice—*Hey, I don't know, God knows*. I've decided this is a reasonable and reflective posture to adopt upon experiencing something that's theologically weird. Rather than basing one's entire witness and faith stance on an oddity such as a weeping statue of the Virgin Mary, we step back. In a recent episode of *Orange is the New Black*, I was amused when silent Norma (a longtime sufferer of stuttering) developed a large flock of followers when her visage was discovered on a piece of breakfast toast. Taking Saint Paul's lead, we pause. We ponder. We say, "I don't know, God knows," and perhaps leave it at that.

My wife recently influenced several of our church members who were trying to sell previous residences in various locales. When we moved from Columbia, South Carolina, a few years ago, Cindy buried a small Saint Joseph statue in the front yard, upside down, facing the house—a fairly common practice but one that I'm sure would leave Martin Luther spinning in his grave. I asked why she didn't just go straight to the top and bury Jesus himself in the front yard.

I suppose there's a tug toward supernatural ecstasy even among the most skeptical. I'm reminded of a character named Carolyn in David Guterson's wonderful novel, *Our Lady of the Forest*. Even though Carolyn becomes a devotee of a young woman who reportedly receives several revelations from the Virgin, she retains her reflective skepticism.

> How ironic, thought Carolyn. But I'm committed already. A secular humanist. A material girl. All I wanna do is have some fun. And I definitely can't be one of those Christians with their myriad insanities: God's *son*, of all things, ridiculous! So what does that leave? Nothing, I guess. All I can say at Saint Peter's Gate is, I'm sorry, I went with Mexico and science. Darwin and margaritas.[2]

Most scholars of Second Corinthians believe that Paul is describing his own past personal event. Why does he describe this strange journey as if it happened to somebody else? Perhaps to curb the natural inclination of boasting that seems to have afflicted the early church and its leaders, and is still with us today. "It is necessary to boast," says Paul, but "nothing is to be gained by it" (12:1). A rather odd confession that gets to the heart of the elation of personal ecstasy, but also the resulting confusion that often emerges upon sharing anything out of the ordinary.

---

2. Guterson, *Our Lady of the Forest*, 296.

I'm not saying that all religious ecstasy should be disregarded entirely. My pastoral ministry has occurred in Virginia and South Carolina, mostly in the mountains of those states. Not long out of seminary, I discovered Dennis Covington's amazing book, *Salvation on Sand Mountain: Snake Handling and Redemption in Southern Appalachia*. Covington was a reporter for the *New York Times* who was assigned to cover the bizarre trial of an Alabama pastor accused of poisoning his wife with strychnine. Covington got caught up in the snake-handling churches of the region and offers many interesting insights into the nature of religious ecstasy:

> The entrance into ecstasy is surrender. Handlers talk about *receiving* the Holy Ghost. But when the Holy Ghost is fully upon someone like Gracie McAllister, the expression on her face reads exactly the opposite—as though someone, or something, were being violently taken away from her. The paradox of Christianity, one of many of which Jesus speaks, is that only in losing ourselves do we find ourselves, and perhaps that's why photos of the handlers so often seem to be portraits of loss.[3]

I've never attended a snake-handling service[4] and certainly do not endorse the practice, but I think Covington is on to something here concerning authentic religious ecstasy. In contrast, watch religious television for very long and there's often a theological litmus test that has nothing to do with loss; a badge of faith worn on the believer's sleeve that designates having "made it" to a special level of divine favor; a "near death" story, a miraculous recovery from cancer; an escape from a plane crash, a car crash, a close call at sea. A "third heaven" story, if you will, that certifies God's clear and unmistakable presence. Or, here lately, the story of a little boy who gets sick, goes to heaven, and comes back to sell millions of books.

I occasionally wish I had such a story that could be disclosed at just the right time. I've had cancer twice now and gotten out of some rather tough jams (including diving off a dam, stupidly), but nothing that would make the news. It's just as well. Often when people are thanking God for their escape during some headline-grabbing tragedy, they fail to explain the theological curiosity offered by the presence of other (now lifeless) bodies gathered at their feet. It's a good thing to remember to say: *"I don't*

---

3. Covington, *Salvation on Sand Mountain*, 99.
4. See Mark 16:17–18 for the biblical origins of the practice.

know, God knows." God does not require certainty from us, but rather faith.

*

After describing this obviously strange and wonderful trip into heaven, Paul refuses to overly boast about it or go on *Larry King Live* to gush about specifics. He turns abruptly from this paranormal tale and says, "Therefore, a thorn was given me in the flesh." The reason for this thorn? "To keep me from being too elated," says Paul. He reports this twice in the same sentence (2 Cor 12:7) to perhaps underscore the dangers of religious ecstasy. After trying to pray the thorn away three times (12:8), Paul comes to realize that *it's the thorn* (and not the trip to heaven) that will define his walk with the Lord.

We have no idea, by the way, what this "thorn" might have been for Paul. Historians have surmised everything from depression to hemorrhoids. And it really doesn't matter what the affliction was. What's clear is that Paul trumpets *this weakness* as strength. He quotes God's strange reply: "My grace is sufficient for you, Paul, for power is made perfect in weakness" (12:9).

This comment will not be taken seriously in the halls of power where national decisions are made on our behalf. And it doesn't seem to make much sense in cancer wards or divorce courts or refugee camps. It's a curious and baffling thing to say in a world where might and the mighty seem to call the shots. And yet this claim is at the very center of the Christian story: "Power is made perfect in weakness." We've recently witnessed how one congregation in Charleston (after the shootings there) movingly revealed how apparent weakness absolutely trumped human perceptions of power and force.

Robert Farrar Capon was fond of saying "resurrection only works on dead people." People who are literally dead and no longer breathing and people (or groups of people) who have reached what looks like a dead end in their lives and whose own personal power has been depleted, used up. Another way of saying this is that grace can only appear where there is weakness. I'm agnostic about whether God intentionally sends us thorns in this life to knock us off a high horse, even though I'll admit that the Bible sometimes suggests such.[5] I am convinced that God's power is

---

5. See 2 Pet 2:4–16; Isa 45:5–7.

most real not in trips to some "third heaven," but rather in places we tend to turn away from—places where suffering and hopelessness and shame and embarrassment seem to hold sway. Places that look much like a cross.

"A thorn was given me in the flesh," says Paul. Jesus wore a crown of them on that Friday afternoon long ago, mockingly affixed to his head.

I've seen the truth of Paul's unusual claim enough in my own life (and in the lives of others) to mistrust religious elation as the litmus test for true faithfulness. We are handed body and blood each Sunday morning, after all, not sunshine and cookies. God meets us in our messes more than in our personal accomplishments. This is the truth and power of Easter. It's not certainty that God requires of us, but rather faith, a kind of thorny strength that God intends to form in us over time.

The man wore thorns. He enters our thorny places.

1. Scar Show

"After he said this, he showed them his hands and his side"
(John 20:20).

AN EARLY EASTER STORY (John 20:19-20) focuses on a man known as "Doubting Thomas." Christians sometimes use that title rather derisively, almost hissing out his name. He often has a "bad guy" image among the disciples, second only to Judas. And both unfairly, if you ask me—the disciples in these old stories also reflect our own flawed and halting attempts at following Jesus. There's lots of Judas and Thomas in any of us, including pastors, if we're honest.

In spite of his doubts, Thomas, towards the end of the story, offers what's been called the most mature theological confession about Jesus from anyone in any Gospel. He shouts there at the end, "My Lord and my God!" Now think about that statement. Thomas is not just offering a belief that Jesus is back; he's not just claiming that Jesus is God's Son. Thomas is yelling that Jesus and God are *one and the same*. "My Lord *and* my God!"

But I'm getting ahead of the story. It's important to notice how Thomas got from "Point A" to "Point B"—how he moved from being so very full of skepticism and doubt, to so very full of excitement for Jesus. I hope you have a few skeptics in your life as close friends. They can oddly be your theological allies, pushing you a bit to state what you believe and why.

On that first day of the week, Easter evening, the doors were locked. Please recall how dangerous it was (and is) to be a Christian. The disciples had seen what became of Jesus. They knew what people were capable of.

Crucifixions do not instill much gospel bravado. So lock the doors. Don't you lock yours?

Jesus can move through locked doors—the locked doors of our lives, the locked doors of our hearts. He stands among the disciples and says, "Peace be with you." Do you reckon those words filled those first disciples with peace that night? I'm not sure.

What really strikes me here is what Jesus does next. "Peace be with you," he says. And then he shows them his wounds; his hands where the nails were driven in, his side where the spear entered his body. There is no break in the text between the sharing of the peace, and the showing of the scars. Jesus does not say, a la Schwarzenegger, "I'm back." No high fives. No singing of Kum-ba-Yah. *He shares the peace and shows his wounds.*

I've decided there's a profound connection between these two actions—his peace and his wounds. We are a wounded people. It's the nature of being alive. All of us carry around wounds in our bodies—emotional wounds, physical wounds; scars that often go pretty deep. And yet sometimes we pretend, even with those we know fairly well, that everything's okay, nothing's wrong. We live in a culture where it's still often considered bad form to confess our weaknesses. And so, when asked, we so often say, "Fine, everything's just fine," lying, of course, through our teeth. But here on this first Easter evening, Jesus refuses to pretend. He refuses to pretend that nothing happened.

Jesus shows his wounds, points out the scars, hikes up his shirt, and says, "Take a look; take a gander. Take a good hard look." His past will always be part of his present; Easter always connected to the cross. If we're smart, we will also come to terms with our wounds. It's tempting to hide everything, push it all down. But our past will always be part of our present. Corporate health in a Christian community involves how church members choose to share their scars with one another.

*

I once had a very revealing conversation with a church member in a former parish, someone very involved in the life of that community. She said, "Frank, I love our church. I love serving Christ in my various involvements. And I love the worship services and the music. But I've been here several years and something's troubling to me." The person paused a second. "I don't know exactly how to say this," she said, "but I don't really feel like anyone knows me here. I mean, they know my name and everything, but no one really *knows* me—who I am, what's important to me, what I believe or why. No one really knows the real me."

I was so grateful for her honesty. I was grateful because it reveals a very large gap in many congregations. If things *look* right, if the committees are up and running, if the money is flowing in, if the attendance remains respectable, we can fool ourselves sometimes into believing that we are doing okay. But that conversation with that very active parishioner reminded me that church, its essence, is not primarily about any of these so-called gauges of success. Church is about relationships: our relationship with Christ and our relationships with each other as followers of Christ. All else springs out of this—worship, learning, service, true community.

In the Facebook-Twitter-i Phone era, many people are almost desperately seeking others to acknowledge and listen to their stories. The key for a church worth its salt is to somehow find intersection between our stories and the overarching narrative of God. Everything else in church life follows from this core.

*

Notice that Thomas wasn't around when all of this happened. It was a full week later that Jesus appeared a second time (John 20:26). I like to think that Thomas was allowed to voice his doubts all through that week with no arm twisting. It's an excellent metaphor for community life. Do we allow newcomers plenty of unhurried time to voice their doubts and questions, without pressure to move them towards some orthodox confession they're unable to make?

Thomas says, "I won't believe until I see the wounds." If you ask me, it's a legitimate request. Perhaps any test of authenticity in a church community involves *seeing wounds* in the body of Christ—that is, *in us*. Do we hide them, or do we bring them to Christ's body for healing?

When he shows up the second time, Jesus again says, "Peace be with you." And watch: *again*, the first thing he does is show Thomas the wounds. Jesus doesn't try to talk Thomas into anything. He doesn't hand Thomas an evangelism tract or tell sweet Easter stories about "the by and by." There is no dramatic "believe or else" here, as we often see in misguided attempts at evangelism. Thomas's doubts are not overcome by any proof.

Sometimes I hear people say, "Well, you know, *I'd* believe the story if I saw the wounds of Jesus." And that's just the point. We'll be effective in sharing the gospel to the extent that we're willing to show one another our wounds, our past, our present struggles, and how Jesus transforms crucifying situations. We need to recover the ancient art of testimony—telling people precisely *how* Jesus has entered our wounds and transformed them. The Thomases of this world are not looking for assurances about heaven. They are trying to make sense of the present, and find the peace of Christ in a world of scars. Only then can the "Thomas" in any of us confess, "My Lord and my God!"

Once in our church's Wednesday preschool chapel service, I talked about Jesus and Easter with the three- and four-year-olds. "He came back!" shouted a little girl before I'd gotten ten seconds into my little homily. I told them that yes indeed, he came back. But I also took a red marker and drew a line on each of my palms. And we talked a bit about where and how Jesus had gotten hurt. Usually, when the chapel service is over, the kids exit in a line and we shake hands or hug; some of the boys give me a high five. But on that Wednesday, almost all of them wanted to see the red places in my palms. Many traced the line with a finger. Early on, we want to touch people where they hurt.

Jesus showed them his wounds. The disciples rejoiced. They could not see him, the real Jesus, until then. Maybe Thomas, in particular, needed to see Jesus' wounds before he could make any sense at all of Easter.

*

So what does this story say about the modern church? What does it say about all of us who carry around scars and old wounds? It means that we are to find ways to safely show our scars to one another. Perhaps the true test of any authentic church is to follow Jesus' lead. "He showed them his hands and his side." His wounds and his peace forever connected.

Call this what you will. I think it's theologically safe to call it Easter.

For further reflection:

1. Try to discover how your congregation encounters people who arrive with a definite stance of theological skepticism, but are also curious about church life. Is yours an adequate welcome? Why or why not?
2. How are wounds and peace related in your own life?

2. Elliptical Easter

"... and they said nothing to anyone, for they were afraid"
(Mark 16:8).

IF YOU'RE UNCOMFORTABLE WITH ambiguity, then the Easter narrative from the Gospel According to Mark might frustrate you (Mark 16:1–8). If you prefer "Happily Ever After" endings, this story may disappoint you because Mark tells the Easter story from a decidedly odd angle. I'll get to this strange ending (which isn't really an ending at all) momentarily, but first want to share a hunch.

On any given Easter Sunday morning, I suspect there are more than a few people in church pews who are not totally convinced that Jesus rose from the dead. *Something* surely happened on a Sunday morning close to 2,000 years ago, to be sure. (That much cannot be denied even by a certified skeptic.) But of all the varied people assembled in congregations across the land, I suspect there are not a few who have a couple questions about how a completely dead guy gets up and begins to walk around. I suspect this is also true for the variety of people reading this book.

Many people are absolutely sure of the resurrection, the questions settled long ago; others don't believe a word of it and maybe never will. These latter folk are the ones, according to one writer, who think the sacraments are "as silly as a séance."[6] Still others are open to Easter, but have a lot of questions—not quite ready to pin their whole lives on such outlandish possibility, but open nonetheless. If you happen to fall in this latter category, then welcome; the church is just the place for you.

---

6. Kaminer, *Sleeping with Extra-Terrestrials*, 25.

And it's especially the place for you in Mark's version of the story[7] because there we are handed an Easter story that's really not an Easter story at all; at least not the usual telling. In three of the Gospels—Matthew, Luke, and John—Jesus is crucified on a Friday and then on Sunday he's up and about and, well, *viewable*. One time he's mistaken for the gardener (John 20:15). Another time he hikes (incognito) along a road several miles with two guys who don't recognize him until Jesus cracks open a loaf of fresh pumpernickel (Luke 24:28–31). And still another time Jesus is frying fish on the beach and calls the disciples out of their boats and in to a big breakfast (John 21:9–14). I love these stories. Jesus, once dead, now walks, talks, and moves around.

But Mark's gospel records none of these encounters. Please note: in Mark's gospel, the resurrected Jesus *never once appears*. The most reliable versions of this Gospel end rather oddly at verse 8: "The women said nothing to anyone, for they were afraid." The early church was clearly uncomfortable with this ending. Consult a Bible and you'll notice another ending or two tacked on to the original, but for the lion's share of scholars of this Gospel, Mark ends rather abruptly. It's almost like ending a story with an ellipsis.[8] Remember those from freshman English? An ellipsis is a "dot-dot-dot"—something to be continued.

For Mark, for the record, these are the basic Easter details: an empty tomb, a young man offering vague instructions, and three women filled with pure and holy terror—end of story; hardly the Hallelujah Chorus. We want more. There is no more. The credits roll, the curtain falls, and Mark's version of the Easter saga is done.

Now what kind of Easter is this? Well, it's the *earliest and oldest* Easter on record. That is to say, it's the first. It's intriguing that at least some early Christians did not depend on actual Easter sightings of Jesus at all. So here I want to return to my original hunch that there are quite a few people populating Sunday morning pews who are open to Easter, but perhaps dubious about how a completely dead guy gets up and walks around. Don't get me wrong. I'm perfectly comfortable with a once dead Jesus walking around. In fact, I confess such things regularly in our creeds. But here's the curious thing: *for Mark*, these visual sightings of Jesus did not an Easter make. What, then, was Easter for Mark?

---

7. Considered by most scholars to be the oldest of the four New Testament Gospels.

8. In the original Greek, verse 8 ends so abruptly that it feels like a conclusion in mid-sentence.

2. ELLIPTICAL EASTER

*

The women in Mark's version of the story grab my attention. You've got to give them credit because the men are nowhere to be found, not a single guy out this early. But it's the progression of emotion from these three that really impresses me. On the way to the tomb, Mary Magdalene, Mary (James's mom), and Salome all seem fearless and only concerned with the weight of the stone. Even when they see a young man wearing a white robe they're only "alarmed." Being alarmed is different from being afraid.

They are filled with terror, say nothing to nobody, and run for the hills *only* when they hear the words of this young man: "He's not here. He's going ahead of you to Galilee, there you will see him. He told you about this," says the young man. And off the gals go, "for they were afraid." End of story, curtain falls.

That little geographical hint (just a bit of bread dropped on the path) is the key to understanding Mark's Easter. "He's going ahead of you to Galilee." And where is Galilee? Galilee is the very place where Jesus originally called those first fishermen and invited them to follow.[9] In other words, the women are told that they will find Jesus, *the resurrected Jesus*, exactly where the sick, poor, leprous, and despised happen to live. *That's* Galilee—then and now.

"You really want to see Jesus?" the young man seems to ask. "Well, you just missed him. He's not here. *You're looking in the wrong place.* You'll find him from now on in the Galilee of a thousand different towns, wherever people are thirsty for the good news." The story has come full circle; it's starting over again and baptized people of any century are now characters in the plot, each and all now marked with the cross of Christ. There's a clear way to experience resurrection in this Gospel and Mark paints the path subtly, but clearly. One can follow, or run in fear. There are a hundred ways to run.

*

If you're reading these words and wondering how you might possibly square personal doubt with the ancient claims of the church, know that at least one storyteller, the very first to describe Easter, wasn't all

---

9. See Mark 1:14–20.

that interested in your intellectual doubts in the first place—how in the world it could have possibly happened according to the laws of science. Mark seems to be more interested in your willingness to give life away for others in the name of Jesus. That, apparently, is what Mark meant by the word *Easter*.

When my children wre very small, my oldest daughter Hannah ran through the hallway one morning, ratting on her little sister: "Momma, Marta says she's never going to die. Tell her she will!" And we will, of course, but there are lots of ways to live and die. Mark's version of the Easter story invites the church to experience resurrection on this side of the grave wherever we serve the lost and the least.

So the Gospel ends. The curtain falls on Mark's Easter. Or does it? From Mark's perspective, that's up to the followers of Jesus as we're drawn back into the story. Jesus clearly told us where we can find him.

This story does not end with a period.

It ends with an ellipsis. To be continued in your life and mine.

For further reflection:

1. Compare and contrast a couple of Easter stories in the various Gospels. Discuss the merits of Mark's version of the Easter events. Do you know someone on the fringes of church life for whom this version might have special appeal?

2. Name some limits of intellectual persuasion and "proof" concerning Jesus' resurrection (for example, the Shroud of Turin).

3. Trapper of Air Revisited

". . . but their eyes were kept from recognizing him" (Luke 24:16).

EVERY MONTH OF MAY, my loving wife bestows on her husband a rather derisive and playful title that has its genesis from at least fifteen springs ago. I'm known, seasonally, as "The Trapper of Air" on Woodland Way. And why does she call me this?

Well, because I'm obsessed with luring and capturing and containing the cool air God has given us each spring night in order to stave off the actual use of air conditioning until the latest possible day. The Apostles' Creed says that Jesus "descended into hell," which may have meant he spent a summer in South Carolina. I'm just trying to delay the inevitable *ascent* of my energy bill as a steward of limited resources. I tell my children (now with homes of their own) that refusing to trap air is like seeing a bundle of cash on the front lawn each morning and refusing to pick it up. But there is no limit to the hoots and guffaws of my loved ones as The Trapper of Air engages in the frenetic science and art of the raising and lowering of windows at the proper time coordinates; positioning screens, checking forecasts, monitoring movement of cumulus and cirrus. *All for them. All for the benefit of these snide ingrates!* Yes, go ahead and laugh, suckers. God sees; God knows. God appreciates these efforts of natural thermostat manipulation, even if Duke Energy does not.

*

Here's something you may have noticed: the Easter Jesus is a pretty slippery and elusive sort of guy, post-tomb. He's a lot like air moving around, hard to trap and pin down. Here he is in the garden with Mary

Magdalene, right in front of her. They're old friends and she mistakes him for the gardener (John 20:15). Here he is on the beach, frying up fish for the disciples. They don't recognize him at first (John 21:4). It's like not recognizing someone as familiar as your mother cooking breakfast on the beach! Here he is disguised in hungry, thirsty, sick, and imprisoned people with disciples rather baffled that they've missed him (Matt 25:35–36). And here he is in the middle of a seven-mile hike (in other words, two or three hours) and the pair with whom Jesus travels has no idea it's him (Luke 24:13–35). In fact, please notice this curious verse: "Their eyes were *kept* from recognizing him"—a clear case of intentional obfuscation, not a pitch for new eyeglasses.

Even The Trapper of Air (used to wispy thermal paradox) is confused by all this. Why is the resurrected Jesus always so elusive and sly? You'd think God would want widespread clarity about Easter; overwhelming proof that would surely lead to belief. When I was a summer camp counselor at Lutheridge, we used to sing a song: "Have you seen Jesus, my Lord? He's here in plain view." I used to love that song, but let's be honest: he's really *not* in plain view. In fact, he seems to be intentionally hidden after his ordeal on the cross, blinking here and there like a firefly in the forest. That's no way to get the attention of the masses. Why doesn't God stick Jesus on *American Idol* and have him sing "How Great Thou Art" until a nation weeps and kneels? Wouldn't that be a good and savvy thing for God to arrange? This old story on an old road to Emmaus makes me wonder: *How do people who've never seen Jesus come to believe and follow him now that he seems as wispy as air?*

*

Two people are walking away from Jerusalem. In other words, two people are walking away from the community that would become the early church. Others have stayed to wait and see. Not these two. People leave the church for lots of reasons, but how about Cleopas and his unnamed companion? The most telling detail is verse 21: "We had hoped that Jesus was the one to redeem Israel." Their hope is decidedly in the past tense. *"Had hoped."* Maybe those other suckers back in Jerusalem still had a bit; these two did not. They were on the road out of town. Jesus is not who they thought he was.

Well, Jesus comes near. Jesus always comes near. He enters their conversation, but chooses not to identify himself and actually plays rather dumb. It's hard to interpret tenor in these old stories, but I think Cleopas is a little irked here. "Are you the only bozo in town who doesn't know the things that have taken place over the weekend?"

Jesus replies coyly (I love him for this), "Uh, what things?" Jesus could have responded in a lot of different ways to the irksome question of Cleopas. He could have said: *Do you know who I am, buster?* He could have said: *Hey, it's me. It's really me.* He could have said: *Bring down fire on the head of Mr. Impertinence, O God.* But Jesus says, *What things?* We often think of Jesus as rather dour and serious, but here he's rather playful and you can almost see the twinkle in his eye. It's only a two-word question, but on these two words rests a key hinge to understanding Jesus and understanding Easter.

*

I'm sure you've had teachers in your past who expected the class to memorize and regurgitate long lists of facts. Who was the fifteenth President of the United States? What is 7 x 7? Name all the countries of Central America. What are the twenty-seven books of the New Testament? You memorize a list and pass a test. You memorize another list. And maybe you appear on *Jeopardy!* one day, knowing a lot of disconnected facts.

Memorization and regurgitation have their place in educational pedagogy. But this is not the way Jesus taught, not even close. In most instances, Jesus tried to draw truths about God *out* of his followers rather than pound facts about God *into* them. The question he asked on the road that day with two ex-followers moving away from Jerusalem, away from church, is classic Jesus: *What things?*

The incognito Jesus still teaches on that road. He draws people back into the story, back into the community they were intent upon leaving.

*

They arrive in Emmaus. Jesus stays with the two travelers. He took, blessed, broke, and gave the bread. In those four verbs, we hear echoes of the Lord's Supper. Their eyes fly open in recognition. And even after dark, these two get back on the road and walk the seven miles back to the community they'd just abandoned. (Try to think of even one thing you'd walk seven miles after dark to report.) Even though Cleopas and his companion report the sighting of Jesus to the others, it's not the actual sighting that brings them back to the community. Look again. "Were not our hearts burning while he was talking to us on the road, while he was *opening the scriptures* to us?"

A very important detail: it was not a sighting of Jesus that got those two moving back to the community, but rather the breaking open of Scripture. Twenty centuries removed, the church often wonders how to be relevant in a culture of diminishing interest; wonders what an authentic experience of Jesus might look like; wonders how to reactivate members of the community who are no longer active.

A large siren temptation exists—to be snazzy and culturally entertaining; to market Jesus compellingly in order to make him palatable and accessible for the masses; to create an encounter with the risen Christ that might remove all doubt all the time. But that's not how these two doubters became believers so long ago, right? Entertainment and marketing are not part of this old story on an old road. These two believe not upon viewing a risen Jesus, but when the Scriptures are broken open in such a way that they see their lives there, and feel their hearts burn again.

The church, more than anything else, does not need reinvention, but rather rediscovery of this word; to see our central identity as a people of the word who portably take our cues from the pages of Scripture out onto the road. Jesus is not altogether obvious to us at times for a reason: because he travels *in us* now; his people, his body.

We do not need to trap him like air.

He takes on flesh and blood as we assimilate his story into our lives.

For further reflection:

1. It's been said that Jesus will never return as a guest contestant on *Hollywood Squares* to make the resurrection completely obvious and undeniable. Why not?

2. This old Emmaus Road story offers several cues for congregations serious about ministry with skeptics. Name a few.

4. The Gotcha God

"Come and have breakfast" (John 21:12).

MY DAUGHTER MARTA RECENTLY installed a diagnostic device in her car to help lower the monthly insurance premium. Plug it in just below the steering wheel and for six months the device gathers information about your driving habits. Brake too hard and the device beeps and suggests you might want to stop more gradually next time. At the end of six months, Marta will unplug the device, mail it away to the Progressive Insurance Company, and Flo will diagnose if she qualifies for a lower rate. Pretty neat, huh? Marta's not so sure about this.

"Just look at it this way," I said the other day. "Think of it as God watching your every move. Only this way you'll learn how you're doing after six months instead of waiting until the end of your life."

"Oh, thanks Dad," she said. "That's very helpful."

Human beings behave differently when watched. I once saw a sign in a hospital that mentioned the high percentage of both men and women who fail to wash their hands after using the bathroom. The sign mainly caused me to wonder how in the world anyone knew these percentages, and if there was some sort of camera monitoring even these private moments.

We're all capable of various behaviors when no one is watching, when the chances of getting caught are slim to none. I'm sure you can think of several instances where this maxim may ring true, ranging from helicopter police who monitor interstate highway speeds in a growing number of states, to various evasive income tax practices people get away with every April. Very often, human beings behave one way when watched and another way entirely when the chances of getting caught are rather low.

Take this a step further and bring God into the picture. Do we behave a certain way in life because we have a hunch that God may be watching our every move? Do we refrain from certain behaviors because Jesus may be snooping around even the fringes of our lives, ready to swoop in and lower the boom? Gotcha!

There's a line occasionally used in the church's weekly confession that describes God as a deity "from whom no secrets are hid." Yikes. Is God like the Cosmic Santa Claus who "knows when we've been sleeping, knows when we're awake, knows if we've been bad or good, so be good for goodness sake"? In confirmation class not long ago we came across a verse in Luke's gospel that mentioned Jesus' awareness of "the inner thoughts" of the disciples (Luke 9:47). *The inner thoughts.* Double yikes. That sort of ratchets up the theological stakes, right? The middle-schoolers in my class weren't all that thrilled about this discovery—God's awareness of not only our behaviors, but also our thoughts. If that's true and you're like me (someone with a grab-bag of odd thoughts), that's quite a bit of weirdness to keep track of.

*

As briefly mentioned in the previous essay, I've always loved the Easter story involving breakfast on the beach (John 21:1–14). Jesus has risen from the dead. He's up and about. He's given crystal clear instructions for the disciples to leave nets and "fish for people." And here we find some disciples back at their old jobs, out on the sea trying their luck in the middle of the night. Their return to this former way of life seems to be in direct disobedience to the marching orders given by Jesus.

Peter and friends are sitting around one evening. Jesus has made two Easter appearances (in John's gospel, heretofore), and that was nice, but it's time to get practical. Following Jesus around for three years was wonderful and instructive and they had all undeniably grown from doing so. But it was time to get a job, or go back to graduate school, or start a family—you know, back to the real world. If I'm counting heads correctly, there are seven guys[10] sitting around the den that night. Given Judas's fate, that still leaves four absentees, suggesting that it was just difficult for

---

10. See John 21:2.

these early disciples to hold things together. People started missing meetings and doing other things. And with Jesus absent, their leader missing, well, who could blame them? We all behave differently when no one's watching.

So Simon Peter says that night, "I am going fishing." It's impossible to detect the voice inflection Peter may have used here, but I think he said that with some resignation and maybe a bit of boredom. "We will go with you," say the other six. Peter knew he was supposed to be "fishing for people," but he returns to his old job—the old familiar nets.

Dawn breaks. A man on the beach is grilling fish and bread. We know exactly who this man is, but please note that these seven guys (at first) do not. From their perspective, it's just some picnicker out early. Is Jesus messing with them, is it a loaded question, when he says, "Children, you have no fish, have you?" I'll let you decide.

It's the point of recognition that interests me. Peter is naked, by the way, as he fishes (John 21:7). Make of that what you will (maybe he was just hot), but I think it might be fun to psychologically parse Peter's lack of clothing. When Peter realizes who's really there on the beach; when he's suddenly aware of the divine eye of "the hidden camera"; when Peter realizes he's been caught with his pants down at work he supposedly left—ignoring the clear marching orders of the voice he now recognizes over the waves—then his lack of clothing perhaps becomes a symbol for what we've all felt from time to time: Jesus can see right through him. He's been caught, busted, nailed. Think of Adam back in Eden, also naked when caught. The story says, "Peter put on some clothes and jumped into the sea." It sounds rather irrational, but maybe not given the circumstances.[11]

I don't know if you've been caught doing something rather forbidden. Maybe you've felt powerless to break old habits, old routines. Maybe you've felt that religion was largely a theological setup where some divine authority was waiting for you to slip-up, to catch you in some indiscretion with a divine diagnostic device that makes the Progressive Insurance beeper look rather lame. Maybe there's something in your past for which you feel Jesus (the divine Cop in the Sky) is standing in judgment—the Gotcha God.

Peter was naked in the boat and Jesus could see right through him. As he swam to shore, I'm sure that many of the feelings I just mentioned

---

11. I've somewhere read that the clothing and moisture combination is an allusion to the new garment donned by a newly baptized catechumen.

must have raced through his mind. Was he excited to see Jesus? Absolutely. Was he apprehensive to see Jesus? Undoubtedly.

What Peter found on shore that morning perhaps shaped his understanding of Easter more than any empty tomb. With soggy clothes, he walks towards a man tending a charcoal fire. This was a man who knew everything about Peter, who could see right through the man. A Lord from whom no secrets were hid who could've had a fairly honest and straightforward conversation with our erstwhile fisherman. The first "Come to Jesus" meeting, so to speak.

It's curious to me, given what *could have been said*, that this man tending the fire only offers four words: "Come and have breakfast." I suspect that Peter truly understood Easter for the first time on that beach. Peter may have been caught red-handed, but Jesus offers him some red snapper.

*

We're all very dark and complicated people, pastors included. We behave certain ways when others are looking. Differently, quite often, when they are not. Like Peter, God has given us very specific Easter marching orders. But we have a hard time maintaining the excitement of Easter, falling into routine and old, familiar behaviors.

Jesus can see right through us—our failures, our bad habits. Even though our sin and rebellion disappoint him, he waits for us on a new shore, the dawn of a new Easter day. He points to a fire, to an altar,[12] towards heavenly food of bread and wine.

And he offers four little words. The best possible words:

"Come and have breakfast."

For further reflection:

1. Describe an early memory of a feeling that God was keeping track of your mistakes in order to pounce with punishment or correction.
2. Revisit the connection between Adam's nakedness in the garden of Eden and Peter's return to fishing, without clothing. How do the stories intersect theologically?

---

12. See Isa 6:6–8.

5. Get Up, Gazelles

"Tabitha, get up" (Acts 9:40).

I'VE PRESIDED OVER HUNDREDS of funerals since graduating from seminary. One of the most memorable was for a close friend—a part-time pastor and National Park Service naturalist in Virginia who died in his early forties of brain cancer. Funerals are always hard, but it was very hard to be a pastoral leader that day for that very close friend, Bill. In the congregation were about 600 people—many clergy in their red stoles and robes; a whole cadre of Park Service employees in their tan and green uniforms; and a large representation of Mennonite women (dressed in traditional garments) who had a connection to my friend's spouse, Marty, a local midwife. I looked out over the crowd from the vantage point of the chancel and was reminded of the day of Pentecost—such a colorful, diverse gathering under one roof.

We worshiped that day at Muhlenberg Lutheran Church in the city of Harrisonburg, Virginia. Peter Muhlenberg (1746–1807), at the dawn of the Revolutionary War, once thundered from a nearby Virginia pulpit: *"There's a time to pray and a time to fight!"* Pastor Muhlenberg tore off his robe to reveal a military uniform underneath and walked out of the church to war. This dramatic scene is depicted on everything from police cars to stained-glass windows throughout the Shenandoah Valley.

Bill's brother—also a good friend who teaches theology at the Lutheran seminary in Philadelphia—rose that afternoon and entered the pulpit. As he spoke about Jesus and recalled a variety of incidents about his dead brother, I noticed that John was slowly taking off his outer robe, completely stepping out of it. What was he doing? Underneath the robe were hiking clothes, a shirt, shorts, and boots that his brother had worn on their many walks in the woods. At the end of the sermon, now out of the robe entirely (recalling Muhlenberg), John grabbed a water bottle the two brothers had often used "to honor a view with ample libation," ran down the long center aisle of the church and paused at the baptismal font. He filled the font with water. "Praise be to God," John said, "whose baptismal life was poured into my brother." There was not a dry eye in the whole church.

*

If the funeral from that day in Harrisonburg makes you a little nervous about liturgical decorum, then you would've also felt some discomfort, I'm guessing, at the funeral of a woman named Dorcas, who also went by the name of Tabitha in the Book of Acts (Acts 9:36–43). Both names,[13] curiously, mean the same thing: *gazelle*. When Dorcas died, they laid her out in a room upstairs. Should we also think of that other "upper room"? Maybe. They bathed her body according to the tradition of Jewish custom.

Teary-eyed and weeping, her companions received friends. The body was present; people filed by. I don't know whether they signed a guest book, but it's possible to detect the early origins of our funeral customs in this passage. This was in somebody's house. Visitation at an actual "funeral home" is a fairly modern practice. Visiting my grandparents in North Carolina as a little boy, I remember seeing bodies and grieving families in neighborhood residences.

We aren't told whether Dorcas, their beloved "gazelle," resembled her name. But I think it's safe to read between the lines. She was probably a woman, fleet of foot, who ran all over town caring for the needs of others—doing lots of little things for so many, scampering here and there with the love of the Lord. Dorcas reminds me of a lot of wonderful older women I've met in various churches who see their entire lives through the loving lens of Jesus; running here and there to serve the Lord wherever they're needed, generations of gazelles.

Notice the clothing these women pull out for this funeral—the tunics, sweaters, shawls, and wraps. It's possible that these widows received their livelihood from a sewing cooperative organized by Dorcas. The funeral resembled a state fair showing, recalling the handiwork of

---

13. The first is Greek, the other Aramaic.

this woman who meant so much to them. I suspect these garments were draped over and around Dorcas's body.

After a person dies, sometimes the clothing is the last thing we can bear to part with. A man told me once that for months after his wife's death he would walk into her closet and just linger there in silence. He could catch her scent and the memories would all flood back.

*

The setting for this funeral is very important. *Four times* in the story we're told the name of the town where this all takes place. Joppa is where Jonah boarded a boat so many years before in direct defiance of the Lord's instructions (Jonah 1:1–3). Upon hearing that name (Joppa), the whole story of the big fish, the radical boundary-breaking love of God, and Jonah's reluctant resurrection come to mind. To underscore this wider biblical context and new directions for mission, the story later reports that Peter stays "for some time" with a tanner (Acts 9:43), a vocation deemed off-limits for an orthodox Jew since it required contact with animal carcasses. All sorts of boundaries are stretched here in Joppa in death and life.

Up and down the Carolina coast are seaport towns with museums and historical exhibits depicting famous events at sea. Maybe in Joppa's town square, outside Dorcas's funeral service, there was a statue of Jonah being swallowed by that famous fish. At any rate, the nautical setting of this town should prepare us for what's coming with Dorcas, the beloved gazelle—resurrection against all odds, perhaps foreshadowing our own watery baptismal rebirth; our own past encounters with being swallowed; and how God triumphs over death.

*

It's very important to recall people like Dorcas who've helped bring you along in this life—a Sunday school teacher, a grandparent, a mentor or counselor; somebody who seemed always to be running on your behalf, running by your side, running to you like a gazelle with the love of God even when you (like Jonah) didn't even want to hear it. Those who love Dorcas in this story honor her life by draping their woven treasures, their entire livelihood, over her body and into that room of great sadness. They are overcome with gratitude and thanksgiving.

When Peter arrives in that upper room, he sends everyone outside. He kneels down to pray, turns to the body and says, "Get up" (Acts 9:40). In the original Greek, these resurrection words are only one word and, curiously, it's the exact same word from a verse prior where Peter is summoned from a nearby town: "So Peter *got up* and went with them." When Peter "gets up" to serve and when Dorcas "gets up" to start a new life, it's the exact same word.

Resurrection, the Easter life, is not solely some shadowy reality out in the distant future. Resurrection can also happen with individuals (even entire churches) whose lives seem all but over. Resurrection occurs in relationships and in marriages that seem stagnant and in friendships that have soured. Jesus does this. He reminds us of the many gazelles who have run this race before us and calls us forth from the tombs of the whale's jaws. In this old story from Acts, there is not a great deal of distinction made between getting up to serve Jesus and getting up from the grave.

For further reflection:

1. Think of someone like Dorcas who tirelessly ran on your behalf. What difference has this person made in your life?

2. Is the possibility of resurrection and new life on this side of the grave new to you? How does the sacrament of baptism connect to this invitation of "getting up" to serve Christ in boundary-breaking ways? See Romans 6:3–11.

6. You Know the Way

"And you know the way to the place where I am going" (John 14:4).

METHODIST BISHOP AND FORMER Duke University chaplain Will Willimon describes his failed attempt to read the Koran from cover to cover. He worked at a school with an increasing number of Muslim students and thought it would be a good idea to add the Koran to his summer reading list as a way to better understand a religion that was new to him. Halfway through, he gave up reading.

> For one thing, Mohammed got on my nerves. [He] has an opinion on everything: how to weigh grain, how to cut meat . . . . I bogged down in the eight pages or so on women and their menstrual cycles. It really is amazing how many issues there are in which Jesus appears to have had absolutely no interest. And we can all be thankful for that. For another thing, Mohammed never tells stories. Ask him a question, he gives you a straight answer. "I have three things I want to say about how to run a government," he will say. Quite a contrast with Jesus telling Peter to go get tax money out of the mouth of a fish. Mohammed always answers every question. Jesus, almost never. The Koran has a low tolerance for ambiguity, narrative, enigma; the Bible wallows in it.[14]

A prediction: if you happen to possess a low tolerance for mystery and paradox, reading the Bible will be rough sledding. If you like your message all laid out, crystal clear, and with a single "sitcom" sort of point, the gospels will constantly confound you. If you admire a leader who

---

14. Willimon, "Postmodern Preaching," 108.

"says what she means and means what she says," then you will be regularly frustrated with Jesus.

Please ponder this: *Jesus befuddled and bewildered his followers as much as he enlightened them.* He told stories with no single point that were difficult to summarize, inviting the listener ever more deeply into ambiguity and enigma. His stories are open-ended and we find meaning in them long after they're first heard—which is why it's important to keep reading the Bible. If you think you've exhausted a story's riches, thinking "Oh yeah, I know that one," there's a very good chance that you don't; even if you've got the story memorized.

The New Testament was inspired and written in such a way that it's endlessly revealing. The Bible "wallows" in enigma and double entendre. I used to think modern people gave up reading the Bible with any sort of regular frequency because we are busy people and have other things to do. I've stopped believing that. We honestly have more leisure time than any era of our country's history.

The truth: modern people are often uncomfortable with ambiguity. We like divine truth neatly packaged and quickly accessed like everything else: billboard-obvious, wrapped in a bow. Witness how many books in the religion section of your local bookstore begin with the word *Little*. Church growth experts now advise congregations to remove any and all hindrances to a newcomer's instant assimilation and understanding. With so much information at our fingertips, why muddle over something that's not crystal clear and to the point?

*

The story of Jesus' pending departure (traditionally assigned during the Easter season) may seem sequentially misplaced (John 14:1–14). He's only got a day or so to live and takes time to say goodbye[15] to these men he loves, the very men who will play a key role in the birth of the Christian church. You know Jesus must have been worried about that—how things would go; how they would carry on in a hostile world. Doesn't this story seem to be a better fit with Lent? It's found here in the church year, thematically, to prepare the church for Jesus' ascension,[16] the post-Easter farewell preceding Pentecost.

---

15. This passage in John actually kicks off a lengthy three-chapter goodbye.
16. See Acts 1:1–11.

In John 14, Jesus offers the disciples reassurance about three things: 1) A "dwelling place" where he will wait for them; 2) A road map showing the way there; and 3) A promise of power that will allow his disciples to do the same deeds that he did, even greater works. (This latter promise is a central theme of the Pentecost season, which we'll address in the next section of the book.)

One might think that in his last will and testament Jesus would be especially clear and compelling, absolutely certain that these disciples "got it" and were on board with the game plan. He would stay after school with them to make sure.

Their initial reaction, however, is not comfort or certainty at all. The disciples are completely baffled and befuddled by his words. Two of them get a little sassy with Jesus. I think we should always pay special attention when the disciples sass our Lord, because they are usually speaking for us all. Thomas, never one to nod his head at something he doesn't understand, speaks for the group and says, "Lord, wait a minute, we don't have a clue where you're going or what in the world you're talking about this fine day. How can you expect us to make heads or tails of what you're saying?" Thomas, in short, is pleading for clarity, not ambiguity. Jesus seems to talk in riddles while Thomas just wants straight speech.

A little later, I sense that Philip gets weary of listening to The Riddler and says, "Lord, enough of this. Just *show* us the Father. That will satisfy our curiosity. Make it plain for us, please!"

The comments of these two disciples reveal more than a hint of separation anxiety. They want to know where the road ahead leads. Can you really blame them? They need a clear map and reliable directions—assurance that someone, somebody, will have the light on, waiting for them at the other end.

Each June for the last quarter century, the extended Honeycutt family gathers at the beach from Washington state, Idaho, both Carolinas, and Tennessee. Like all families, we tell stories about the past. The one my mother invariably trots out is the time we all went to the coast in the mid-1960s *without reservations*. My parents didn't have a lot of money and Dad wanted to hunt for a bargain upon arrival. Bad move, reports Mom. We wandered up and down the coast searching for a room that summer, finally landing at Kure Beach in a tight, hot, loud room with antsy children and dangerous waves at the end of a long walk. Fifty years later, my mother still loves to rub that story in my father's face.

We want clarity. We desire specific directions. Don't you love MapQuest? Such precision. Turn right after six-tenths of a mile. Excellent. We like that security—precise and foolproof guidance with no surprises or strange turns in the road.

But over and again in the Gospels, that's the very thing Jesus seems unwilling to provide. He will not serve up the mystery of the kingdom on a silver platter and make it all plain. He refuses to Map Quest our lives, telling us exactly where to turn between points A and B. With his death only hours away, Jesus seems quite content to leave the disciples scratching their heads and muttering. He leaves a last will and testament that is almost intentionally enigmatic, baffling, and ambiguous.

So here's a question you perhaps knew was coming: *Why?* Why was Jesus prone to use such a challenging teaching style? Why weren't his stories easier to understand? Why do we sometimes leave church shaking our heads, frustrated with the open-ended nature of Jesus' way in a world crying out for absolutes?

Flannery O'Connor, the late fiction writer, once said: "The purpose of art is not to explain the mystery of life, but to deepen it."[17] When a teacher tries to explain mystery and make everything all clear with a common denominator of meaning, that teacher robs mystery of its power to shape us. The best Jesus would do in his stories was point at mystery. "The kingdom of God is like this . . . or like that over there."[18] But he never would nail it all down. (Interesting, come to think of it, that people tried to nail *him* down.) Mystery, if nourishing, will not be boxed in. The search to discover Noah's Ark and "prove" the Shroud of Turin seem silly to me for this very reason. Jesus, the divine mystery, ever before us, will give us peeks and glimpses, bits of bread along the path. But he will not be fully revealed. He will not completely remove our bewilderment.

We must learn to love, then, the ambiguity we find in the Bible; love the strangeness of many of Jesus' stories and not be so eager to explain their "sole" meaning. In reading the Bible faithfully, we come to better appreciate how mysterious life is; how mysterious *we* are.

---

17. Quoted in Srigley, *Flannery O'Connor's Sacramental Art,* 49.
18. See Mark 4:26–32.

6. YOU KNOW THE WAY

*

Many years ago, Thomas said, "Lord, listen. We have *absolutely no idea* where you're going. How are we supposed to know? Can't you make all of this a bit more plain?"

"Just show us, Lord," said an impatient Philip. "Show us God the Father and then we'll all be satisfied." Some days I wish Jesus was indeed a little more straightforward and clear. But I suppose if he were, we'd make a theme park out of the revelation.

There is a mysterious distance between us and God. "You have not come to something that can be touched, a blazing fire, . . . and a voice whose words made the hearers beg that not another word be spoken to them" (Heb 12:18–19). Preachers can try to describe the distance. Theologians can point at it. But we dare not try to cozily remove it. We are all on the way to God. "You know the way," says Jesus. To be honest, the way of this man is often filled with marvelous and mysterious ambiguity and paradox.

Learn to love the Bible in all its puzzling perplexity. For such was Jesus' way. A way that leads to both truth and life.

For further reflection:

1. Why are we often uncomfortable as a culture with ambiguity, preferring quick clarity and unhindered insight?
2. Revisit the objections of Thomas and Philip in this passage. Centuries later, how are their concerns our own?

7. A Life Laid Down[19]

"We know love by this, that he laid down his life for us—and we ought to lay down our lives for one another" 1 John 3:16.

FRANCIS SPUFFORD, A TEACHER and writer, lives in the United Kingdom. He's among the 6 percent of citizens there who still worship regularly on Sundays. The Church of England may trot out clergy and bishops for royal coronations, but the overwhelming majority across the pond largely ignores the church. In Spufford's book *Unapologetic*, he mentions his daughter: "Some time over the next year or so, she will discover that her parents are *weird*. We're weird because we go to church."[20]

How weird are they? To contrast, in the United States the equivalent figure of regular Sunday churchgoers is 26 percent of the population. But here's what I find doubly interesting from Spufford's book: "Some surveys, tellingly, reveal that a further 16 percent of Americans *claim to be* regular churchgoers. From the British perspective this second statistic is even more startling and alien than the first one. The idea of people pretending to be regular churchgoers because it will make them look virtuous—or respectable, or serious, or community-minded—is completely bizarre to us. Here in Britain, it is more likely that people would deny they went to church even if they actually did, on the grounds of embarrassment."[21]

We are living in challenging times for the church. I once had lunch with an employee of the American Bible Society. He told me of the society's ministry and its translation work in many countries. Our

---

19. This essay first appeared (in slightly different form) in Honeycutt, "A Life Laid Down."

20. Spufford, *Unapologetic*, 1 (italics in original).

21. Ibid., vii (italics added).

conversation turned toward Europe and England, in particular. He had just toured many of the beautiful gothic churches dotting the countryside, which were largely empty on Sundays. He said, "You know, Frank, this reality in Europe is coming your way in America. Not as quickly, but it's coming."

What are we to do about such realities? If the current trends continue, what will our congregations look like in twenty-five, fifty, or one hundred years?

Look closely at 1 John 3:16 sometime. Two 3:16s should come to mind. We tend to recall the more famous one from John's gospel: "For God so loved the world that he gave his only Son." But 1 John 3:16 suggests that if this amazing gift really soaks in, our lives in return will resemble his: "We know love by this, that he laid down his life for us—and we ought to lay down our lives for one another." This echoes a phrase that says a Christian is a person who should be prepared to look good on wood—someone who's willing to love in the shape of a cross.

Recently I was home for lunch during three waves of rain and hail. I stood at the kitchen window and watched a small hummingbird nonchalantly sip nectar as ice chunks fell from the sky. Somehow he dodged all of them. I expected the little guy to hightail it for cover, but no—it was a serene scene of nourishment in a context that could clock the bird's brains out at any second. I was envious of such peace and security, and I concluded that the hummingbird's behavior involved more than simple survival. It had everything to do with sacrifice—for family, even for a species. It was some built-in inclination to love.

We live in a land that has kidnapped what love might look like: love is a many-splendored thing; love is never having to say you're sorry. Ask most people to draw a picture of love and many will produce a Valentine heart with an arrow through the center. But for Christians, love is concentrated in the gift of the cross.

We are dunked into the sacrificial life of Christ at baptism and marked with the cross of Christ forever. Martin Luther signed his body with the cross before his feet hit the floor in the morning and again at night before dropping off to sleep, bracketing the day. This was a reminder of his core identity in baptism—a reminder that the shape of our lives is meant to look like a cross, love poured out for others.

"A life laid down" was a core message in the early Christian church. John's community was definitely in the minority—a small band of people trying to remain faithful to Jesus. Perhaps the dwindling percentages of Christians in Europe and North America can learn something here. Maybe others will be drawn to Jesus not through threatening pamphlets or door-to-door sound bites but instead when they actually see a different sort of love in his people—love that resembles a cross.

Rodney Clapp tells a story[22] of a church's renovation project that required new sanctuary carpet. The new carpet was beautiful, but there was a problem: it held a rather wicked static electricity charge that packed quite a jolt. This was especially true when coming forward for communion to sip from the metal chalice. The dry air of the building built up a charge on the carpet and taking a sip of wine was enough to knock you on your duff. The pastor started sending young acolytes in the first wave to absorb the brunt of the chalice's electric charge.

Maybe the metaphor works for any celebration of communion in our congregations—we come forward for peace and tranquility, green pastures and the status quo, and Christ chooses instead to knock our socks off with the radical forgiveness offered in his body and blood.

He laid his life down for us. In the strength of this meal, we go and do likewise.

For further reflection;

1. John 3:16 is a traditional Lenten text while First John 3:16 is usually found in the Easter season. Discuss how the theology of these two church-year seasons might naturally lead a disciple from one 3:16 to the other.

2. Describe the celebration and frequency of Holy Communion in your home congregation in light of the communion chalice mentioned in the essay.

---

22. Clapp, *A Peculiar People*, 112.

8. Holy Detour

"Come over to Macedonia and help us"(Acts 16:9).

CHECK CLOSELY TO SEE if I get the details from this next story (Acts 16:6–15) fairly straight. On a missionary journey, Paul and his companions are forbidden by the Holy Spirit to speak the word in Asia. Even though churches will eventually appear in Asia, there's a big divine stop sign at the regional line so they bop over towards Bithynia and try to share the gospel there, but nothing doing. "Keep on heading west," says the Spirit who seems to be providing their road map.

Averted in Asia and barred from Bithynia, Paul tacks over to Troas (named for ancient Troy). Troas is on the edge of the Aegean Sea, a coastal town. Paul has never been farther away from home in his life. Maybe they breathe some ocean air. Maybe they grab some seafood at a local diner or check in to some bargain beach motel. Maybe they begin to wonder a bit about all these unusual directional signposts from the Holy Spirit. Here at the edge of their known world, there's a pause in the journey.

So Paul beds down for the night, water lapping in his dreams; more bits of bread dropped along his missionary path. A man from Macedonia speaks in a night vision. "Get over here please and help us." (I've no idea how Paul recognizes this man *as* a Macedonian; he's never been to Macedonia in his life. Maybe the guy is wearing a university t-shirt.)

Paul awakens and boards a boat—sea breeze in his hair; lots of time to think. The first day they travel about eighty miles[23] over to Samothrace, an island eight miles long with tall mountains. Tempting to stick around and explore, but they were back on the boat the next day: seventy nautical

---

23. Roughly, according to handy maps in the back of most Bibles.

miles to Neapolis (literally "Newtown"), aptly named; for all this is brand spanking new for Paul.

But there's more. They disembark the boat in Neapolis and hike about ten miles inland to Philippi. (A curious little cuss, I also looked up this distance.) They look around the city a few days. On the Sabbath, Paul and Company are led to a river and a particular spot that looks like a place of prayer. A woman shows up; a fairly wealthy woman, a cloth merchant with a penchant for purple. Her name is Lydia. She likes what she hears and her entire household is dunked into the mercy and grace of God.

This river encounter—born from a series of stop signs, sea crossings, and dreams in the night—is how the church in Philippi came to be. It's why we have the book of Philippians in the New Testament, the very first Christian congregation in Europe. For some holding this book, this church fans out over the centuries into your genealogy (perhaps) and mine.

*

Okay, catch your breath a second. Disembark the boat and think with me. I have close friends who have no idea how I can base my entire life on stories such as these. I suspect you also have a few friends in this category. "Really, Frank? Really? Do you really believe it all happened just like that? Come on. So you also believe the Spirit of God directs *your* every single move? Will the Spirit instruct you to brush your teeth tonight at 9:37 p.m. and tell you to take out the trash Tuesday morning at seven? If that's true, it sounds like you're more a puppet than a person." I love my skeptical friends. Everybody needs a few. They keep me theologically grounded.

I too am suspicious upon hearing spiritual anecdotes like this one: "You know, I was driving all over that mall parking lot and just prayed to the Lord, *just prayed to the Spirit*, that a parking space would come open and right then, *right then*, a spot opened that wasn't there earlier and I just have to think that was God. Don't you?"

This is a real dilemma for any thinking Christian: What part of our lives is directed by the Spirit? And what parts are just random instances? For Paul's entourage crossing the Aegean, everything seems so purposeful and linear: *yes, no, proceed*. Go here, not there, with pleading

Macedonians in the mist of night. Clear detours directed by a higher power. I would love for God to just stop me sometimes from being boneheaded and stupid: "You're about to mess up big time, Franklin. I really would not do that if I were you." A dream, a sign, making the path ahead all clear.

These thoughts I'm planting in your head have been a source of consternation for people of faith for centuries. Can God direct my life? Well, how do I tap into that direction? The questions become especially tricky looking back upon your own life. Fiddle with just two or three seemingly insignificant details and you'd probably be in an entirely different state, living an entirely different life, with an entirely different set of friends and personal biographical details. Two or three small changes thirty or forty or fifty years ago and presto, it's a different life. You know it would be. What is the relationship, then, between *destiny* (God's leading in those details) and *freedom* (my personal decision-making ability to say "yes" or "no" to a certain decision waiting at multiple crossroads)?

This story from Acts seems so clear cut. They were not allowed to go certain places; other locales got the green light. Certain boats were boarded. Visions in the night gave the travelers their map, details that led from here to there to Lydia—a crazy series of connected dots. We wonder about such stories. (And I suspect Paul and company, because they were human, did their own share of prayerful head-scratching the farther they got from home.)

*

Just before his death, Jesus tried to reassure his disciples: "Do not let your hearts be troubled, and do not let them be afraid" (John 14:27). That's still our dilemma, right? Trouble and fear. It sometimes seems like Jesus is absent and getting his ear for decisions is often challenging; nothing like the direct line Saint Paul and the boys in the boat once had on their way to Lydia.

These beautiful words are found in the vicinity of the same reassurance: "Those who love me will keep my word, and my Father will love them, and we will come to them and make our home with them" (John 14:23).

The purpose of the church is mightily connected to these words. The purpose of the church is to form people whose lives become a home, a portable container, for the words of Jesus. It behooves us to know these words. The words provide our map.

*

They came to a place called Troas, poised at the edge of the sea. We too were once right at the edge and, with God's coaxing, dove in. The church calls this baptism: the start of a new life spent listening for the directional nudges of the Spirit.

There is a delicate balance between God's guidance and our freedom. We are not robots or puppets. God will allow us to choose our own way if we insist upon it.

At the edge of the sea, with the words of Jesus, we listen. We listen for what's next.

For further reflection:

1. Spend a bit of time with the challenge issued in the essay. Reflect upon one or two details from your past, at the time perhaps seemingly minor encounters or decisions. How might you now see these details as important crossroads actually authored by the Holy Spirit instead of random chance?

2. Look up the definition of a word that has largely vanished from modern theological parlance: *providence*. Why do you think this word is rarely used in church circles these days?

9. Step by Step[24]

Then Peter began to explain it to them, step by step, saying, "I was in the city of Joppa praying, and in a trance I saw a vision" (Acts 11:4–5).

IN OCTOBER OF 1908 a sixteen-year-old white girl was assaulted in a cotton field just off South Spring Street in Concord, North Carolina. A black man was arrested for the crime and jailed in Raleigh at the state penitentiary to protect him from a lynch mob. Justice (or what was called that) was rather swift in those days. By mid-December a strong wooden scaffold was erected and on the eighteenth day of that month, just two months after the arrest, the young thirty-six-year-old sheriff of Cabarrus County presided over the last legal hanging in the state of North Carolina.

The sheriff was a towering man, six feet, seven inches, a Lutheran, as were 90 percent of all county residents in 1908. The sheriff, widely respected in Concord, was personally opposed to the death penalty. Maybe something he heard in his Lutheran Church or read in the Bible shaped his thinking. His wife, Agnes, had the unhappy task of making the hood used at the hanging. December eighteenth arrived, a chilly day on the cusp of winter. Upwards of 2,000 people filled the public square in the vicinity of the jail to see justice served (or some version of it); vengeance meted out; the streets now made safe—something. Crowds have always gathered at such events like vultures circling carrion.

The Cabarrus County sheriff who presided over the hanging that day was Frank Honeycutt, my great-grandfather, for whom I am named. I do not know the name of the black man, which is telling. I do know

---

24. This essay first appeared (in slightly different form) in Honeycutt, "Step by Step."

(according to my mother who has researched details of the trial) that there is almost a 100 percent chance that this man was innocent.

*

"Why were you eating with *them*?" ask the elders at First Jerusalem Church when Peter returns from his little junket to Joppa by the sea,[25] mentioned in the Book of Jonah,[26] largely about a prophet of God who slowly learns that God's love is much wider than he once thought. We tend to remember the incident of the whale and the prophet's time in the belly of that beast, but those three days in the dark amidst digestive juices and carcasses of various sea creatures were just props to get the prophet's attention: God wanted Jonah to go into a city, Nineveh, and tell those Ninevites that God loved *them* as much as God loved Jonah's relatives. That mission was a huge stretch of the prophet's theological imagination. The love of God was much wider than Jonah desired, so he didn't do handstands on the way to the city. He went slowly step by step; slowly waking up to the love of God, its breadth and depth.

Peter's vision in Acts of a heavenly bedsheet laden with a variety of animals occurs in Joppa, thus conjuring Jonah's historic, halting insight. I think of William Faulkner's famous quote here: "The past is not dead. In fact, it's not even past." Peter's revelation in Joppa mirrors Jonah's, centuries earlier. People of faith spend a lot of time breathlessly trying to keep up with God who is out ahead of us, far out ahead of us, beckoning us to places we should go, to people we should include. But something gets in the way.

"So why were you eating with *them*?" ask the church elders. A Gentile outsider, the soldier Cornelius,[27] had been baptized. Highly irregular—not one of them; Peter knew he would have some explaining to do. His colleagues in Jerusalem were rather irked and critical of his actions. Peter was in hot water to say the least.

---

25. See Acts 11:1–18.

26. See also the previous essay in the Easter section of the book, "Get Up, Gazelles," where I make a case for the book of Jonah as theological backdrop for the raising of Dorcas.

27. See Acts 10:1–8.

9. STEP BY STEP

Here's a truth: when you're doing the work of Christ, sharing the radical love of God, loving "as" Jesus loved,[28] count on receiving a fair amount of criticism for it. Does that also mean that if you never receive *any* criticism in your life as a Christian, you might be playing it a little safe? Well, possibly. Maybe that's what Jesus meant when he said, "Woe to those of whom all speak well" (Luke 6:26). Jesus constantly angered folk. He was not afraid of conflict, divisive sometimes; confrontational for the sake of the kingdom. Congregational leaders need to move beyond the fallacy that the church exists to make everyone happy. When we radically extend the love of God to all people, that's going to inevitably make some angry.

*

"So why'd you have to go and eat with *them*? They're not our kind. Don't look like us. What are you doing, Peter?" Oh, they were hot.

So, "step by step" says the story, Peter begins. "I was in the city of Joppa praying." If you have no interest at all in change, please avoid prayer. Fill your day with busy tasks and television. If you like things the way they are, I advise you to leave prayer out of your life entirely. Prayer is one way God changes the world. Peter's vision occurred in the middle of his prayers.

I recall a visit to a dear woman, Nola (ninety-nine at the time), several years ago at a nursing facility. (She died in November of 2014 at age 103.) Even though her memory was not what it once was, she named several members of the church, sending her love. In our conversation, I was reminded that Nola still spent an hour each day on her knees (at ninety-nine!) in prayer to her Lord. This is a practice she observed for decades since her days as a nurse at the State Psychiatric Hospital in Columbia, South Carolina, and through the illness of her husband whom she cared for at home until he died. What a laugh this woman had, rising and falling like a flute. What joy. "You know, sometimes people today don't want to talk about Jesus," she said. "And that's okay. So we talk about other things. But I can still pray. And I do."

Prayer is one way God gets at us. Again, if you have no interest in change, avoid prayer intentionally. All the great religious movements of change in our world began with a vision that was born in prayer. And

---

28. See John 13:34; 15:12.

step by step, at lunch counters, in public schools, in voting booths, in courts of law, (and even in churches!) that vision became reality.

*

Why'd you have to go and eat with them? "I was praying. I was in a trance. I saw a vision. The Spirit told me." These are not words that comfort most Lutherans, even though Martin Luther employed them all as he went about helping to change the world. Peter sees an incredible variety of animals in that sheet (something that contradicted his kosher biblical viewpoint) and even though the command was initially dietary in nature, the vision would come to embody the very gospel for him.

He looked at those angry churchgoers, his friends, and said, "The Holy Spirit fell upon them just as it had upon us at the beginning . . . . Who was I that I could hinder God?"

There is a huge tug for human beings to categorize and separate and codify. Human history is full of this. Black and white, gay and straight, North and South, Protestant and Catholic, public and private, Republican and Democrat, contemporary and traditional, homeless and employed. And that's just a beginning list.

But sometimes we're given a vision as Christians where labels vanish and a whole roiling ark of creation rubs shoulders in the same heavenly bedsheet called baptism.[29] Note the variety in that sheet. And note the possibility of tension and locking of horns between the different types descending from heaven. It took three separate sightings of this odd vision, but the message is clear to Peter as he explains, step by step, to his astonished partners in the Gospel: "The Spirit told me to go with them and not to make distinctions between them and us." It was the end of "them" and "us."

*

A lot has changed in Cabarrus County, North Carolina, since 1908. Over a hundred years have passed. Racism (and all the other ugly –isms) are still part of our world, but a lot has changed. Step by step.

Remember these three words that connect you to a mission that strives to eliminate old divisions between people: *Joppa. Prayer. Baptism.*

---

29. See Gal 3:23–29.

Words that form God's people, and invite the church to take that next step.

For further reflection:

1. Prayer is one of those commonly encouraged habits in church life: unquestioningly touted, but difficult to maintain with consistency. Consider seeking out a "prayer partner" where part of the expectation in the relationship is holding each other accountable to this important spiritual discipline.

2. Find Joppa on a Bible map and read through the short (and sometimes amusing) book of Jonah this Easter season in the Old Testament.

10. Keeper of the Keys

". . . he put them in the innermost cell and fastened their feet in the stocks. About midnight Paul and Silas were praying and singing hymns to God" (Acts 16:24–25).

IN THE NEXT STORY, Saint Paul is trying to give a series of sermons to new and potential Christian converts down by the river[30] and a strange girl keeps interrupting. She reads palms and tells the future—crystal ball sort of stuff. People lined up to see her and she told the curious what was about to befall them, good or bad. She was a strange girl. The money rolled in. Uneasy with the present, people were desperate to know the future; not so different than today. She was worth quite a bit to her handlers; their bread and butter.

The girl kept calling out when Paul tried to preach. He'd get to the very pinnacle of his sermon and she'd bellow out, "These guys are slaves of God!" I have it on good authority that preachers do not enjoy having their sermons interrupted. Paul was a patient man and could understand if somebody needed to go to the bathroom or care for a squirming child, but this yelling out from the girl went on for *several days*. The preacher would go to make his point and the girl would yell out like she was at a ball game.

His patience razor thin, Paul finally loses it. Right in the middle of the sermon, he turns to the girl and says with a great deal of annoyance, "For Christ's sake, shut up and come out of her!" And whatever *had* hold of her hit the road. All of this happened right in the middle of worship.

---

30. See Acts 16:16–39.

I've never had to perform an exorcism partway through a sermon, but I'd never rule it out.

I suspect the girl was pretty happy about all this. And perhaps she had a mom and dad who were quite pleased. But her handlers? Were they happy? You know they weren't. You don't fool around with a person's money. People jump out of windows over money, use money as a weapon in acrimonious divorces. Church members sometimes withhold money when things don't go their way. Money is power—then, now.

When these guys see that their dog and pony show has vanished, they get hot. They're furious. Paul is dragged downtown, snatched out of his riverside pulpit and brought before the authorities.

Things go from bad to worse for poor Paul and Silas. Preaching was dangerous business back then (and sermons, let me tell you, have their own hazards now). It's a lynch mob down there at the town hall. This wasn't about theology. A time-tested political adage is that people vote with their pocketbooks and citizens turned out in force that day to vote. These preachers had the power to disrupt an entire economy; they had to be stopped.

I really wish the Bible offered access to the minds of Paul and Silas at this point in the story. They'd done a good thing and helped that poor girl. The thanks they receive involves stripping, a beating with rods, flogging, and jail time. These two dangerous threats to the local economy, these two river preachers, are tossed into the brig completely naked, without a stitch of clothing or even a penny to their names. The story takes special pains to mention that the jailer securely places these two pastors "in the innermost cell and fastened their feet in the stocks." There's a saying in legal circles when a person really messes up: "They put him *under* the jail." That's the basic location for Paul and Silas—under the jail, no hope of escape, basically Alcatraz.

This is exactly where I wish we had some access to the innermost thoughts of these two in that innermost cell. I know what *I* would be thinking. "Note to self: *time to look for another line of work.*" But please notice what these two guys are doing there in jail, naked and bleeding in the middle of the night: they're singing. *Singing!* Belting out songs of love and freedom past midnight. Please don't pass over this detail. Given the events of the day, I'm pretty sure I'd be doing something else.

*

One huge theme running through the Bible is that those who think they have all the power actually don't. And those who think they're free often aren't. A recurring message: *Jesus is our key to freedom.* Nobody and nothing else. He's the one who has the audacity to forgive people even as they're killing him (Luke 23:34), invoking a power beyond any earthly force. This is not the sort of power we usually turn to when the going gets tough.

The jailer in this story (the one holding the keys) is full of fear and worry and even considers suicide as a result of this fear. In contrast, those bound in the "innermost cell" (those supposedly lacking freedom, absolutely under the jail) are singing songs.

How can a person come to know the freedom of Paul and Silas, singing even in prison? The Philippian jailer knew the right question: *What must I do to be saved?* And please understand that his question had less to do with the next life and everything to do with this one. He could've put it another way to Paul and Silas: "How in the world can I get in my life what you seem to have in yours?"

*

Most churches share prayer concerns in congregational life, but a lot also goes unspoken when we gather, unannounced—fears about illness or family or money or security; the future. These fears can bind a person, tie us in knots; make us feel like we've been bound in the "innermost cell" of the prison, powerless and depressed.

Maybe this will help. In this old story from Acts, which concludes the Easter section of the book, remember that the people who *seem* to be free actually are not free at all. They are jerked around by money and fear. And those stuck in prison, the ones bound and bleeding, are utterly liberated beyond their external shackles, even before the earthquake liberating them comes along. They were already free. They knew the real keeper of the keys.

The jailer, the guy on the verge of a fear that almost ends his life, also comes to know the liberation of Paul and Silas. And so does his household. The jailer bathes the wounded backs of Paul and Silas, who in turn bathe the jailer and his family with the gift of baptism.

It's at least one o'clock in the morning and they share food and new life. The jailer, for the first time in his life, is free, out of jail. "His entire household rejoiced that he had become a believer." I like to think that this celebration and rejoicing went long into the night. And I like to think they were singing.

Singing songs of freedom. Such is the gift of Easter.

For further reflection:

1. Discuss the power of corporate hymn-singing in congregational life.
2. What binds you in fear these days? How does the present promise of Easter resurrection temper and bring perspective to such fears?

V. PENTECOST

Introduction to the Season

I'M SITTING IN MY bare church office on a Thursday morning, the last week before retirement, looking out a window towards our old cemetery that dates back to the dawn of the Civil War. All my books are gone, donated to a nearby Wesleyan college. The stones outside are silent but speak stories, especially the graves of Confederate soldiers, old ghosts who still somehow raise local emotion and tempestuous argument whenever the topic of honor and proper remembrance arises in congregational life. I'm thinking about my thirty-one years as a pastor. But mostly I'm thinking about the power of Pentecost and the Spirit's ability to effect change.

Just a few weeks ago I led a procession from the sanctuary into the graveyard for the interment of a woman whose family was from out of state. On the way to the burial site at the far end of the cemetery, we silently walked by at least twenty-five small flags flapping in the breeze. "Damn it," I muttered to myself. "The Sons of Confederate Veterans are at it again." The flags keep appearing in our cemetery on days I cannot predict. I wondered what these particular sons from faraway were thinking as we walked through the sunshine to bury their mom.

"Can these bones live?" asked the Lord of his servant, Ezekiel (Ezek 37:3). In my little town of Walhalla, they most certainly can and do. In an amusing short story by my friend Ron Rash, a regional fiction writer and poet, an enterprising pair of grave robbers sneak into cemeteries late at night to dig up dead Confederates for the lucrative memorabilia. But here in South Carolina, there's no need for that. The dead practically shout already.

Our church cemetery policy has undergone various revisions during my five-year tenure. Small "heritage flags" are allowed on veteran graves, despite my objections, each Confederate Memorial Day, observed on May 10 in our state. We've had sometimes heated discussions in church council meetings concerning how this allowance might make our neighbors feel who drive by on a busy street that borders the space and wonder what in the hell is going on.

In some ways, I get all this. I grew up in Chattanooga, went to college at Clemson (just down the road from Walhalla), and spent half of my pastoral career in Virginia. Words like "Appomattox" and "Chickamauga" are as familiar as collard greens and corn bread in my family's conversational diet. My great-grandfather (for whom I'm named) was sheriff of Cabarrus County in 1908 and is remembered for presiding over the last *legal* (emphasis intended) hanging in the state of North Carolina as upwards of 2,000 people turned out in Concord's public square on a chilly December afternoon to witness the execution of a black man accused (falsely, my mother later discovered) of raping a young white girl.[1] His wife, Agnes, had the unhappy task of sewing the hood. Sheriff Frank was personally opposed to capital punishment and over 90 percent of the county residents at the turn of the century were Lutheran, but neither fact stood in the way of whatever "justice" was meted out that dark day. Inescapably, the South (the good and the ugly) is in my blood.

One of our church members, Luther (yes, his real name),[2] is a passionate advocate for allowing the flag in the Saint John's cemetery on this one day. Luther is a brilliant local historian; a calm and respected voice. He tirelessly worked to open a museum a block from the church to honor and recall the memory of the Cherokee people who once populated Oconee County. He is certainly not a fringe reactionary like those who roar up and down Main Street with Confederate flags the size of bedsheets flapping from the beds of their pick-up trucks.

In his book *Confederates in the Attic*, Tony Horwitz interviews the legendary Shelby Foote, who refuses to equate the familiar battle flag and its "stars and bars" with slavery. While acknowledging the flag's modern association with hatred, Foote is adamant that originally "it stood for law,

---

1. See my previous essay, "Step by Step," in the Easter section of this book for a more complete description of this incident.

2. I'm grateful to Luther for helping with the final draft of this essay.

honor, love of country"[3] and was kidnapped in the civil rights struggle by white supremacists. (Luther would agree wholeheartedly with Foote.) Even so, our state has more than its share of odd residents who seem to revere the flag abnormally. Even though I love this land and its people, a famous quote coined in 1860 by native son James Petigru at times still seems accurate to me: "South Carolina is too small for a republic and too large for an insane asylum."

Luther appeared once before our church council the evening we were deliberating our church cemetery guidelines. He brought several scrapbooks of articles depicting Civil War history in our county, spoke passionately (almost tearfully), and showed pictures of young and old people of various races honoring the flag. I asked Luther if he'd drop by the office later that week to talk and tell me more.

We spoke that morning of many things, many historical dates that are important in Luther's life. He's a very good man. I love him and the people of this church. That day I listened for some time, and then somehow had the gumption to ask a question. "Luther, you know so many dates. They shape your life and your work in this county like few people I know. But I'm curious about a particular date in your life. Do you celebrate the date you were baptized?"

The question hung in the air awhile. Luther smiled, perhaps a bit embarrassed, and admitted that he did not know the date. I asked him why not. We talked awhile about baptism's centrality in the Christian life, and how this watery date shaped all others in his life, but also the graves and lives of everyone in our church cemetery. I challenged him as an excellent historian to research his own baptismal date and begin celebrating it with surpassing vigor and gusto compared to any other date he could name. Luther agreed to the challenge. We parted that day with prayer. His mind had not changed concerning the presence of the Confederate flag on that certain day in May in our cemetery, but I could tell he now had a much wider historical (and theological) context for his passion.

Several months passed. June 17, 2015 brought unspeakable tragedy to Charleston, and our entire state. A broken nation wept. One of the slain—pastor and state senator Clementa Pinckney—was a graduate of Lutheran Southern Seminary in Columbia. The murderer, Dylann Roof, grew up Lutheran in a congregation across the city from the campus,

---

3. Horwitz, *Confederates in the Attic*, 153.

served by a friend and seminary classmate, Tony, whose calling suddenly became even more challenging. All of our lives changed overnight.

The Sunday afterwards I preached a sermon that directly addressed the tragedy. There are some sermons where you can hear a pin hit the floor in church and that Sunday was such a time. I talked about violence in our country and the sixty mass shootings since 1982. The Gospel text appointed for the day was the story in Mark 4 where the disciples encounter a stiff wind and take on water as they attempt to cross from the Jewish side of the Sea of Galilee to the Gentile shore on the other side. Jesus sleeps placidly through the mayhem until his friends wake him up. The sermon included these lines: "They killed him on a Friday because he tried to cross over one too many times. They killed him on a Friday because his ideas about love and mercy and inclusion were just too threatening for too many. They killed him on a Friday because he would not stay with his own kind." I shared this story:

> Our family had some friends in town six or seven Sundays ago and we took them to Arby's for lunch after worship. Our daughter, Marta, was up from Anderson for the day. Marta was born in El Salvador. Her ancestors are undoubtedly Mayan. Marta's been with our family, our daughter, since she was eleven months old. Several years ago we learned that her orphanage where she lived as a baby was completely destroyed in an earthquake. Children died as a result. We settled into our turkey sandwiches. An older man walked up, looked at Marta with confusion, looked at us, and then said with some volume, "Now whar's *she* from?" I'm pretty sure this man intended no malice. It came off as rude, for sure, but no intentional malice; at least I don't think so. We told him where she was from; answered him geographically. He went back to his table and his own sandwich. It was a rather awkward moment. Looking back on that encounter, I wish we'd answered another way. I wish we'd said, "She's from God, by water and his word."

I greeted our parishioners afterwards in a long line. At the end of the line was Luther, waiting on me patiently. I thought I knew what he was going to say: another defense of the flag. I tried to avoid him. "I have to tell you something," he said. "Five minutes." We were actually standing beside the baptismal font.

At the time, there were three public monuments in South Carolina that flew the Confederate flag. The most famous is in Columbia on the state house grounds, but a lesser-known monument is in Walhalla on the west end of town. "I've taken down the flag," Luther said. "People don't understand it anymore." I was flabbergasted. "You've taken it down? Do you have the authority to take down the flag? I'm glad to hear this, Luther. But are your friends going to be upset with you?"

"Let them be upset," he said. "I have the only key to the flagpole. The Battle Flag has been taken down and I have replaced it with the Palmetto State Flag." Luther suggested that this act was partly motivated to protect the monument from vandalism in the wake of the tragedy, but there was certainly more emotion revealed in his eyes than a practical act alone. Everyone had cleared out of the sanctuary. We talked for several more minutes. I drove home that afternoon, astounded and surprised.

*

Just out of seminary, very early in my pastoral ministry in a very small congregation in the apple country of Virginia's Shenandoah Valley, I approached a church leader named Oiva, who was born in Finland. He had the most marvelous eyes, always twinkling. I wanted to start a fellowship time after worship—just something to drink and maybe some cookies. "Pastor, why do you want to do something like that?" "Well," I answered. "You know, so that we can get to know each other better." Oiva paused a second, and smiled. "That's just the problem, pastor. We know each other too damn well already."

On the last two All Saints Sundays since the tragedy, our congregation has processed into our cemetery in silence at the conclusion of the liturgy, remembering those who've died in the last year, and reflecting on the importance of baptism for all the saints. I hope this will become an annual tradition after I'm gone. Somewhere in the Midwest, after every baptism, there's a congregation that processes into their cemetery with the newly baptized leading the way. They stop at the family plot and pour the baptismal water directly on the future resting place of the newest member of the flock whose "dying and rising" in Christ just occurred.[4]

*

I'm looking out the window towards the graves in my bare office during my last days as a pastor and thinking about lots of things—events

---

4. See Rom 6:3–11.

that have surprised me over the years with people I thought I knew pretty well. "You have died," says Saint Paul of baptism. "And your life is hidden with Christ in God" (Col 3:3). There is no date more important in the Christian life.

A lot has occurred in this office over the years—lots of prayers, tears, and conversations. The small flags will probably still fly on May 10 next year, adorning the resting places of the Confederate dead just outside my window. But I've rarely been as surprised—and thankful and proud—as the day Luther took his key and bravely took down the flag on the west end of town.

Such small but important steps are the gifts of Pentecost.

1. Something on the Edge

"And suddenly from heaven there came a sound like the rush of a violent wind" (Acts 2:2).

IN ONE OF HER poems,[5] Patricia Hooper describes a chance meeting with a roving evangelist in her neighborhood who wants to talk about the Bible. She's watering the garden and weeding the phlox, busy with chores, and turns down the man's invitation to converse. Hooper concludes that this is probably how it's always been with potential followers of Jesus: some let go of their work and others make excuses. But she also admits that there's more to it with her than simple busyness. She would have been, in the pages of Scripture, one of those requiring miracles, needing proof.

*

Pentecost (think pentagon and pentathlon, related to number five) is one of those paranormal religious festivals the church remembers each year that gave once timid disciples the guts to take the message of Jesus out into the streets. They were all together there in Jerusalem one morning,[6] about 120 of them, inside in one place, when a violent wind whistled up their spines and under their robes, knocked over tables, and rearranged their idea of church. Something so strange happened that it looked like their heads were on fire.

---

5. Hooper, "Where I Was."
6. See Acts 2:1–21.

And Peter, who in this very city and same streets just over fifty days ago was reduced to sniveling denials by a bar maid who sent him running for the shadows,[7] somehow stands up on the corner of Main Street and Vine and delivers a stunning sermon that results in close to 3,000 baptisms before the sun goes down. Absolutely nobody in a million years could have predicted this guy saying those words in that place. Something has gotten into Peter and he swears it isn't wine that's given him this new bravado. It's only nine o'clock in the morning, after all. So no, it's not spirits, but the Holy Spirit. Peter is so changed and different and those disciples are so bold compared to their embarrassing Holy Week behavior that we modern disciples say, "Look, hey, I'm not sure what those people got into that day, but I'd like some of that in my life, too."

Some churches say that if you stay long enough they'll get you an authentic experience of the Holy Spirit. You'll speak oddly and get fire in your pants. And other churches, like mine, claim that we "believe" in the Holy Spirit but this third person of whom our creeds speak is usually more like an unobtrusive sparrow than an eagle with claws that disrupts worship services and knocks over tables. I sense, however, that the faithful of any denominational persuasion long for some sort of meaningful Pentecostal experience, some sort of memorable moment that might once and for all put all doubt and skepticism to rest—something unmistakable; something on the edge.

Several years ago, Peter Jennings hosted an excellent ABC News special titled *In the Name of God*. Various people talked about their faith and initial experience of church. One man recalled coming to church three Sundays in a row and enjoying the services enough to keep coming back. But he also remembered getting frustrated, finally approaching a church deacon. "Well, when do they do it?" he asked. "Do what?" asked the deacon. "You know, the stuff." "What stuff?" "The stuff in the Bible," said the man. "What do you mean?" the deacon wondered. "You know, multiplying loaves and fishes, feeding the hungry, healing the sick, giving sight to the blind—that stuff."

Your expectations may not be quite as pronounced as this man's. But there's a side of anyone (skeptic or true believer) that wonders occasionally if these are anything more than stories. Many would certainly find it easier to believe if the fire and wind would blow into our lives for real just once; a single unmistakable time, something on the edge. The poet

---

7. See Luke 22:54–62.

watering her new trees sees the young man walk towards her with a message. She knows the story and regards it highly from a certain distance. But she confesses to herself that this message has about as much of a radical pull on her life as pulling weeds among the phlox.

How does the church speak of the Spirit's wind and fire on earth these days? Does God still act the way God acted in Jerusalem that morning so long ago? Is it still possible that God can rearrange routine, set people's lives aflame, and bring renewal to congregations satisfied with staying indoors? Does the "stuff" mentioned in the Bible still happen? Well, how? How does it happen? These are reasonable questions.

"There is nothing you can do to make it happen, as far as I know," writes Barbara Brown Taylor, "except to pray 'Come, Holy Spirit' every chance you get. If you don't want anything to change in your life, then for heaven's sake don't pray that. But if you are the type of person who likes to stand out on the porch when there is a storm moving through so you can feel the power that is pushing the trees around, then you are probably a good candidate for the Holy Spirit prayer."[8] The unruly third person of the Trinity means to come into our lives and rearrange the way we look at the world and is not at all mannerly in accomplishing such change. I've always loved the image of the Spirit as a "little old lady who wades in to a barroom brawl, shooting her six guns in the air."[9] For modern people of faith, this does not usually mean that your pants are going to catch on fire some fine Sunday in church, or that the wind will blow so unmistakably one day that you'll have no more doubts. It means instead that the restless, intrusive Spirit, the little old lady with her blazing guns, is not content to have just a part of your life—a "Sunday bone" we toss in appeasement. Slowly but surely, the Spirit's aggressive intent is to stake more and more of a claim on my whole life—my sinful life, my blinded life, the life I thought was my own. So much so that God's holiness is perceived in more and more places until finally you'll perceive something of God everywhere and anywhere. Sang the seraphs during Isaiah's famous call: "Holy, holy, holy is the Lord of hosts; the whole earth is full of his glory" (Isa 6:3).

---

8. Taylor, *Home By Another Way*, 145.
9. Gallagher, *Things Seen and Unseen*, 158.

*

The novelist Henry James (1843–1916) once said: "A writer is a person on whom nothing is lost." That's also not a bad way to describe the identity of a Christian filled with the Holy Spirit. Such a person will begin to see things—holy, marvelous things—that others pass by without notice; fire and wind in nooks and crannies of the kingdom.

A Christian is a person on whom nothing is lost, everything on the edge—the edge of the holy.

For further reflection:

1. Look up Isaiah 6:1–8, the prophet's famous call experience, and notice verse 1 in particular: "the hem of his robe filled the temple." If just the hem filled this old worship space, reflect upon the grandeur of God that spills outside.
2. Three words. Pray the ancient Holy Spirit prayer daily for a month: "Come, Holy Spirit." Take this short prayer into your daily schedule and take note of how you now approach routine tasks differently.

2. God at Rest

"God rested from all the work that he had done in creation"
(Gen 2:3).

THE FESTIVAL OF PENTECOST, recounting the origins of the church, is often followed in the church year calendar by the festival of the Holy Trinity, a celebration of the nature of God. As remarkable as it seems that God created light, darkness, sea monsters, creeping things, galaxies, the whole ball of wax, it seems even more remarkable to me that God rested after all the work was done. I have an artist friend who gave me a picture with the caption, "God on Vacation." God's kicked back at the beach with sunglasses under a wide umbrella. A cooler is nearby as the radio blares "the music of the spheres." Young nymphs frolic in the sand. It's a picture that I chuckle at, but nervously.

The first creation story in Genesis (Gen 1:1—2:3) is a remarkable rhapsody to a God who provides everything we need in stunning variety and abundance. God speaks the world into being. "Let there be porcupines," and it was so. "Let there be supernovas," and bingo. "I believe in God the Father Almighty, creator of heaven and earth," the church confesses in the Apostles' Creed. Ours is such an intricate, beautiful, and complex world. Theists have their own set of theological challenges, but atheists are not off the hook. It's hard to fathom that a world of such lush goodness and peculiarity is an accident.

But what mostly startles me each time I read this old Hebrew account of how the world began is the claim that "God *rested* from all the work." God was worn out and needed a nap. Now come on. It's far easier for me to believe that God created a beluga whale than to swallow the possibility that God was plumb tuckered from working overtime. God is not a fatigued coal miner, after all, who comes dragging home after pulling a double shift. God doesn't get *tired*, right? God is, well, *God*—all those "omnis"—omnipotent, for example. Why would an all-powerful deity need to take a break?

Walter Chalmers Smith (1824–1908), the Scottish writer of the famous hymn "Immortal, Invisible," also expresses similar ambivalence when he describes God as "*unresting*, unhasting, and silent as light" in verse two. But Genesis clearly disagrees. Not only does God take a break in this old story, God also commands all of Israel to knock it off. To take a sabbath one day per week. To cool it. Stop. Quit. Cease.

Why? Two books in the Bible list the Ten Commandments, but with different reasons offered for observing the sabbath. In Exodus 20:8–11, we're reminded that God rested on the seventh day and presumably, the logic goes, if God needed a breather at the dawn of creation then so do you, my mortal friend. The other reason appears in the book of Deuteronomy: "Observe the sabbath day . . . and remember that you were a slave in the land of Egypt" (Deut 5:12–15) God does not want slavery for anyone. A sabbath spells the end of sweat shops. A sabbath from work is not some legalistic way we please God by obeying one of his rules. The benefit is ours. The wise rabbi Abraham Joshua Heschel (1907–1972) once put it this way: "The meaning of the Sabbath is to celebrate time rather than space. Six days a week we live under the tyranny of things of space; on the Sabbath . . . we are called upon to share in what is eternal in time, to turn from the results of creation to the mystery of creation; from the world of creation to the creation of the world."[10]

Those are haunting words. So many of us live under the "tyranny of things of space." It will be hard for compulsive people like me to take a true sabbath. There's always something: a chore to be done, somebody to see, and if I don't do it, who will?

A friend once told me, "I don't have time to take a sabbath. There's too much to do around the house and with the kids, even on my day off." There's truth in that statement. Isn't it true that there's *always* something pressing you could be doing other than to lie back in God's arms and let God run the world for awhile? Are not taking a hike, going for a bike ride, and even prayer to God rather frivolous, time-wasting activities when there's so much to be done? Stuff that won't *get* done without you? "I don't take a sabbath," the person said. "Not enough time." Absolutely

---

10. Heschel, *The Sabbath*, 10.

right. And in truth there will *never* be enough time to get everything done. "Observe the sabbath," says the commandment, "and remember that you were once slaves in Egypt." Moses led slaves out of captivity. So did Lincoln. But slavery is still with us, much closer than you think.

*

In the first creation story, there's a small detail that's easy to miss.[11] After each of the first six days of creation, the narrator weaves a repeating rhythm by announcing: "There was evening and there was morning, the first day. . . . And there was evening and there was morning, the second day. . . . Evening and morning, the third day." And for each of the days the pattern is the same. Evening is mentioned first, then morning. A day is measured and marked by this ongoing pattern.

"Well, so what?" you might ask. The Hebrew notion of measuring a day is quite different from how we measure a typical Tuesday, for example, in much of North America. Our day begins with an alarm clock before dawn and ends well past nightfall, electricity allowing us to stay up as late as we'd like, catching up on chores until we finally fall exhausted into bed.

For the ancient Hebrews, though, a day was measured in a completely different way. Evening didn't end the day; evening *began* the day. Why was this significant? Evening was the time of ceasing and storytelling and sleeping. Evening was marked by a profound lack of productivity. Nobody had any cash value in the evening.

The Hebrew day started by turning it over to God. God was at work, not humans, holding the world together while people ceased and slept. So when one woke up the next morning, it was not to begin the day, but to join the work already in progress. To join the God who was minding the stars in their courses and mysteriously giving life to seeds as people slept. *To lend a hand with what had already been initiated by somebody else.* The day had already started hours earlier without a smidgen of human assistance.

---

11. I'm indebted here to Eugene Peterson and his thoughts on Hebrew notions of measuring time in *Working the Angles*, 48–50.

*

The doctrine of the Holy Trinity is not some bizarre theological gymnastics meant to explain God mathematically. Instead, the wonder of the Trinity becomes a profound invitation to rest in the arms of a God who is creating, redeeming, and enlivening a world that mistakenly believes it can save itself by hard work alone.

Perhaps God gets tired from his own work from time to time and needs to take a break. Perhaps God gets weary of trying to get our attention.

I'm certain of this much. You will never have enough time to do what needs to be done. And if you're bent on trying, call it what you will.

The Bible calls it slavery.

God was so concerned about this that a commandment was drafted for our freedom.

For further reflection:

1. What would happen if you creatively attempted to measure time like the ancient Hebrews, with the day *beginning* at sundown?
2. What do you honestly think about the idea of God resting?

3. Storm Dozing

"And they woke him up and said to him, 'Teacher, do you not care that we are perishing?'" (Mark 4:38)

THIS NEXT STORY MAY seem to take the previous idea of "resting" in God's arms to a theological extreme.

*

In the early days of television when only three channels existed, my parents watched Edward R. Murrow and Walter Cronkite. When it was our turn, though, my brothers and I were a little more high brow. We watched *Mighty Mouse*. I thought it was so cool that such a little guy could swoop in and take care of sinister criminals ten times his size. It was impressive to watch a mouse lift a car or stop a moving train. I was sort of small for my age so Mighty Mouse was my hero. I'd swoop around the den or front yard wearing a cape, singing his famous theme song. *Heeere I come to save the day!* I cannot ever recall a time when that little but mighty mouse failed to save the day. He was strong and courageous and always victorious.

Who knows how or when theological sensibilities begin to form in children? For me, as a boy, it wasn't so hard to make some sort of hazy connection between Mighty Mouse and Jesus. They were both mighty and powerful even though they sometimes appeared to be weak. They both were on the side of good and used their powers in admirable ways. They swooped in to make a difference. Jesus did not wear a cape, of course, but my Bible always showed him in a robe. Close enough. Jesus didn't have a theme song, but there were enough miraculous stories in

Scripture to warrant him swiping the mouse jingle: *Heeere I come to save the day!* And he usually would. Save the day, that is.

But if you've read much of the New Testament, or experienced much of life, then you know that such a cartoon depiction of Jesus is hardly accurate. Read, for example, a fascinating book about Jim Jones and the 1978 Jonestown massacre in the Guyana jungle where almost 1,000 church people lost their lives by suicide.[12] The book is based on interviews, videotapes, and journals only recently released by the FBI. I could not put the book down. The community was aggressively interracial, attracted and included the down and out, and was supported in San Francisco (before their move to South America) by upstanding folk like Harvey Milk. What interested me most was how people got involved in the church and gave themselves over to a pastor's rather warped vision of Jesus. If you had enough faith, Jesus could cure any malady; still any storm. Miracles were regularly staged to increase offerings. Jesus would indeed swoop in and fix everything, like Mighty Mouse, if you had enough faith and unquestioned allegiance.

When I was in high school, just after confirmation, I gave up Jesus and church for a few years. It's an old story. Mighty Mouse, Jesus with the Cape, and early intellectual observation of how the world seemed to work (with lots of unexplained suffering) just did not add up. I gave up cartoons. And I also gave up Jesus. "Here I come to save the day," I once sang. There were lots of days, I noticed, where nobody got saved.

*

And then I noticed something else. With help from a caring Lutheran campus minister who literally "saved" me from leaving Clemson one afternoon during my freshman year, I began a serious search of the Bible. I came upon a fair number of stories in Scripture where Jesus doesn't just swoop in and make everything instantly okay. The man is many days late, for example, for the funeral of a good friend and has to face the dual ire of sisters (John 11:1–44). Another time he tries to heal a blind man who reports that his vision is still so fuzzy that people "look like trees walking" Mark 8:22–26). He cannot heal in certain towns and places because of the tenor of those who mock him (Matt 13:54–58).

---

12. Scheeres, *A Thousand Lives*.

3. STORM DOZING

And then this story from Mark (Mark 4:35–41). "A great windstorm arose." It's worth noting that the word for *windstorm* here and the word for *whirlwind* in the Greek Septuagint version of Job 38:1[13] is the exact same word. The author of Mark's gospel undoubtedly had Job's doubts and questions in mind as he described this night storm at sea. Questions like: Why is this happening? Why aren't you fixing it, God?

I love the image of Jesus sleeping like a baby while the disciples run around the boat bailing for dear life. The story even describes a little pillow for the head of our Savior as water collects at the feet of his friends. It's almost comical. Can we get you anything else, Jesus? A glass of sherry? Maybe a little green Andes mint for your pillow?

Some people can sleep through anything. Many years ago I had two guys, Peter and Andrew, on one of the youth backpacking trips our church offered each summer. (Names of Jesus' disciples, it suddenly dawns on me.) We were on a section of the Appalachian Trail in Virginia. The boys had a free-standing tent that required no stakes. The next morning I got up early and noticed Peter and Andrew had turned over in such a way that they were sleeping soundly on the roof of the tent; the floor straight up in the air. Some people can indeed sleep through anything.

The waves are crashing over the side of the boat. Mayhem among the crew running around. Early feelings of a first-century *Titanic*. And Jesus sleeps on. His disciples have to wake him up. And here, please note, is the very crux of the matter. The disciples have a question for Jesus when he wipes the sleep out of his eyes. This is also our question, if truth were told: "Teacher, do you not care that we are perishing?"

Do you not care? There are few words that carry more emotional freight than the word "care." The lack of feeling "cared for" is why marriages end, friendships sour, and faith in God wanes. But watch what happens in the story. Jesus is roused. They wake him up. He does indeed care and stills the storm.

Jesus saves the day. Tragedy averted; peace on the water. "A dead calm." But please note: *not in the boat*. There is a great deal of tension suddenly in the boat between Jesus and his disciples.

---

13. This verse begins a long response from God to Job's honest questions about his suffering.

*

In the Bible, Jesus often refuses to provide "instant rescue." In this old story he seems more interested in the faith resources of his disciples in the middle of a storm *more than the storm itself.*

"Why are you afraid? Have you still no faith?"

Sometimes I long for a Jesus from my childhood who will instantly swoop in and make everything better. *"Here he comes to save the day!"*

Jesus actually does consistently save the day. But not in the way we often expect. His teachings and his divine care for us, over time, form disciples who can rest faithfully, even during the worst of storms.

For further reflection:

1. Share with a friend an incident that really shook your faith. What (if anything) helped bring calm during this turbulent period?
2. Try to describe the difference in these phrases: "faith in Jesus" and "faith of Jesus."

4. Trusting in a Lie

"The Lord has not sent you, and you made this people trust in a lie" (Jer 28:15).

CHURCH FIGHT! (WELL, SORT of.) One man of God verbally attacks another. One man of prayer goes after another with all the salacious titillation of a Jerry Springer episode—pushing, shoving, death threats, oh my. This wild scene happened "in the house of the Lord" and "in the presence of all the people."[14] You think attendance would rise if churches offered this kind of entertainment?

Now lest you think this scene from Jeremiah is some sort of strange clergy anomaly, listen to this little tidbit concerning two ninth-century popes:

> In [the year] 897, Pope Formosus stood trial for perjury, covetousness, and unlawful promotion. The unusual aspect of the proceedings was not so much his innocence as the fact that he was nine months dead.... His successor and bitter enemy Stephen VI had him dug up and enthroned in full regalia, then screamed at him to answer the charges. When Formosus exercised his right to silence, he was condemned, stripped, deprived of his fingers of blessing and thrown into the Tiber.[15]

Move ahead a little in church history and you'll find Martin Luther and his detractors going at it with colorful invective. I have in my files a print of a woodcut showing Luther grinning with his pants down, bent over, breaking (and aiming) wind at the Roman church leadership.

---

14. See Jeremiah 28:1–17.
15. Tomkins, *A Short History of Christianity*, 90.

Jonathan Edwards may have been one of the brightest theologians on the American frontier, but he was summarily dismissed from his Massachusetts pulpit in an ugly little church fight in 1750, when followers of his grandfather (who served the same church for fifty-five years) decided his preaching conflicted mightily with granddaddy's style. Some may think Joel Osteen (the popular TV preacher) is a nut. Others deem the man a saint who wants us all to be rich. And who's to say yours truly is not a con artist?

This story about two men of God in conflict raises a very important question about religious (and political) leadership: *How do we know who's telling us the truth?* Two very different voices claim to speak for the same God. Whose voice do we trust?

*

The real issue here between Jeremiah and Hananiah seems to be the difference between instant gratification (the easy short-cut, the religious ditty, the half-truth) and the way of sacrifice and servitude ("the road less traveled by," to recall the words of Robert Frost; "the long way,"[16] to recall the language of the Wilderness Road out of Egypt). These were tough times for the people of God. They were gathered for worship that morning in Jerusalem in the house of the Lord. Foreigners had desecrated the temple and hauled off some of the precious worship furnishings to Babylon. The first deportation of exiles—relatives, brothers, sisters, even their king—were enslaved many miles away.

Two preachers offered two distinct (and conflicting) messages in reaction to this national crisis. "Don't worry," said Hananiah that morning. "This will all be over soon. Two years. God told me this will all be over in two years and we can get back to life as normal." It was a popular sermon. Lots of "amens" and head-nodding all around. Hananiah told the people what they wanted to hear. (That's a huge temptation for preachers, by the way.) I have it on good authority that people were swooning and swaying and dancing in the aisles. "Be patient," says Hananiah, "and this will all soon be over. Just a little divine turbulence here. Trust me. The yoke of Babylon will be broken within twenty-four months. God told me so in a dream." Hananiah preached the good news of the express exile. It would all be over soon. People loved hearing his morning message.

---

16. See Deut 8:2.

But then Jeremiah stood up and interrupted all those "Amens." He was actually wearing a wooden yoke in worship that day. I guess the ushers used to let people in wearing such stuff. Jeremiah really wanted to believe the promise of this brief inconvenience for God's people, but his gut wouldn't let him. The wooden yoke symbolized a much longer exile. Jeremiah suggested that God was using Babylon, a foreign power, to teach the homeboys in Jerusalem a thing or two.

Jeremiah was always doing this sort of thing in the book that bears his name. The guy even once buried his underwear near a river (and then dug it up later on, unlaundered) to symbolize national fickleness in obedience to the living God (Jer 13:1–11). The people were not "clinging" closely enough to God as good underwear should. Says Kathleen Norris of this prophet: "Listening to Jeremiah is one hell of a way to get your blood going in the morning. It puts caffeine to shame."[17] It's tough to be a prophet, having to tell the tough truth all the time. I suspect Jeremiah did not sleep well at night, even though he turned out to be right.

*

It's startling to me how very contemporary this story is for the church, even though the setting is 594 (or so) BC. In almost every day's mail, I receive slick advertising pitches promising to increase attendance, offerings, program effectiveness, and member commitment. Everyone's smiling in the brochures, so glad and happy to have Jesus as their Lord and Savior. "My life was a mess," say the accompanying testimonies, "I was on my eighth marriage, addicted to Almond Joy bars, and suffering from hypertension until Jesus came along and then all my problems were amazingly and instantly solved."

Instantly? Some advice: always be suspicious when somebody claims that Jesus will instantly solve all your problems. The man died on a cross, an inherently sacrificial act, and now invites us to pick up the same. This is not a message that plays well in America, where we are so used to getting things so quickly with the snap of a finger or the push of a button. God help us, we're all addicts of instant gratification, even in church life. Learning how to follow Jesus faithfully *may take a while* because the man is . . . Just. Doggone. Weird. That is, compared to how we're usually invited to live.

---

17. Norris, *The Cloister Walk*, 31.

The church is facing a huge sea change in this new century, 500 years after the dawn of the Reformation. Commitment to basic theological assumptions and practices (including simply showing up on Sunday mornings) have eroded at an alarming rate. Many church members are living out a competing and alternative story (or simply don't know the story to begin with). Those of us who are worried about such things are sometimes prone to the quick and easy fix: Better sermons to get people to give more money! More winsome and bubbly pastors! Entertaining programs! Zesty music! Make it easier to join!

For the life of me, I just don't see Jesus using the exclamation point like these quick-fix brochures I receive. He says instead, "If anybody wants to become my disciple, let them deny themselves, take up their cross, and follow me" (Mark 8:34). Renewal in church life may take awhile. A good long while. It will take unhurried time to "make a disciple" in our culture because we are frankly formed and shaped by so many competing things. A faithful process of conversion usually involves honest "detox," if you want to know the truth—detoxification from the many things that are killing us.

Following Jesus is not a two-year project, not a feel-good Hananiah-type sermon with as little inconvenience as possible. As it turned out, Jeremiah was completely right. This little project of God would not take a couple of years, but instead about seventy. It dawns on me that this is just about the length of a life.

Call me an old pastoral fuddy-duddy, but I do not trust the theological quick-fix for what's ailing us in church life today. Following Jesus, learning to bear *his* yoke, will take some time—a long time to learn the ways of this man and practice living his strange life; especially in this context we live in that so often invites me to worship and adore the self. There *aren't* any shortcuts to faithfully following Jesus. More advice: please stop looking for them.

*

"Listen, Hananiah," said the prophet so long ago. "The Lord has not sent you, and you made this people trust in a lie."

It's often a tough lesson for those who love Jesus and his church. Sometimes we must learn to expose the lies that so captivate us before we can live his truth.

This can be painful. Conversion will take awhile for any of us.

For further reflection;

1. Describe a few shortcuts a congregation may be tempted to make in the name of fast success.
2. Is the image of "detoxification" in the essay too harsh? Why or why not?

5. Delayed Weed-Whacking

"For in gathering the weeds you would uproot the wheat along with them. Let both of them grow together until the harvest" (Matt 13:29–30).

IN THE SIX MONTHS it took me to hike the Appalachian Trail from Maine to Georgia in the early 1980s, I never had a single troubling incident. But maybe something you might file under the heading of a "close call." The A.T. is peppered with a series of small shelters for its 2,100-mile length. Open in the front with three sides and a roof, the shelters usually sleep eight to ten people with a spring nearby.

I normally slept in my tent to avoid the mice, but shelters are great in a thunderstorm. I remember sleeping alone in this one shelter in the southwest corner of Virginia near the town of Pearisburg. A couple weeks later, a young couple was shot and murdered in that very shelter moments after they fed a stranger a meal. Their bodies were buried in the woods.

Crime is very rare on the Appalachian Trail. You're more likely to experience a crime in your own neighborhood than on the trail. But this incident spooked me a bit. I'd left a logbook for hiker entries in the shelter that was confiscated as evidence by Virginia State Police. They caught the guy in Myrtle Beach a few weeks later. Randall Lee Smith, an emotionally troubled man who'd been abused as a child, was sentenced to a very long jail term through a plea bargain arranged with the families of the victims.

Over two decades pass. A friend points me to an article[18] in *The Washington Post*. An attempted murder, a shooting, again had occurred in that same mountainous area very close to that same shelter after two fishermen fed a man a meal. This time, thankfully, the victims lived.

---

18. Haygood, "Blood on the Mountain."

5. DELAYED WEED-WHACKING

Unbelievably, the assailant was Randall Lee Smith, the same man that killed the couple the year I was hiking the Appalachian Trail. A model prisoner, he was paroled and moved back home to Pearisburg, Virginia, to live with his mother.

*

Here's a rather large and glaring challenge in living the Christian life: it's very easy to separate the teachings of Jesus we hear on Sundays from the life we lead and the news we absorb the rest of the week. Many people give up on the Bible (or demote it as quaint, which may be worse), subscribing instead to conventional wisdom for a real world. *Forgive your enemies?* Well, Jesus was special. *Pray for those who persecute you?* Please, they had it coming to them.

I remember a young man with a great personality named Daniel who once came to fix our home air conditioning system. When he discovered I was a pastor, we started talking about the Bible and also church. Daniel said something interesting. "You know, Pastor Honeycutt, I've tried to attend church and read the Bible. I really have. But I just don't understand it. I read a little bit and read it again, but it just doesn't make any sense to me." I appreciated Daniel's candor because the Bible is indeed a strange book.

Christians assemble on Sundays, listen to odd stories, and then walk into a world where all the rules seem different. If discipleship does not seem difficult to you, I'd have to conclude you're reading a different Bible than the one I read each morning. Jesus told vexing parables that often leave us quite confused with their ethical implications.

*

In the parable[19] of the Weeds and the Wheat (Matt 13:24–30), everybody seems to go to bed happy. The farm hands are tired from the day's planting and they all dream of the wheat harvest—warm bread slathered with homemade apple butter. But during the night, a vandal sneaks onto the farm and sows weed seeds among the wheat. This is the worst kind of

---

19. "Parable" comes from a conflation of the Greek words *para* (alongside) and *bolle* (to throw). When Jesus tells stories he often throws disparate ideas and situations alongside one another. Friction occurs; sparks fly.

mischief: a *timed* mischief that will only become apparent later on in the growing season.

When I was a summer camp counselor at Lutheridge near Asheville, North Carolina many years ago, friends pulled a very creative prank of timed mischief in my "Pioneer A" cabin. The pranksters gathered a dozen alarm clocks and hid them throughout my cabin, set to go off at half-hour intervals throughout the night. I was up and down until dawn searching for those blasted clocks and even found one in the cabin commode. I accidentally washed a clock a week later in some hastily done laundry.

This old parable (unique to Matthew's gospel)[20] describes timed mayhem. The victims are completely unsuspecting. Upon discovering the damage, they're way past agitated. They want to take immediate action—call in the crop dusters, break out the machetes, involve the university extension agent. But the master has some strange advice. "No, enough of that," he says. "Let the weeds and the wheat grow together. You might damage the good grain with your angry aggression. Let them both flourish until the harvest and I'll sort it all out then."

Stop a moment and read this parable again, slowly. Heck, read it fifty times. Not only does it make little agricultural sense, it makes even less practical sense when introduced into a world filled with danger, violence, and people like Randall Lee Smith. What is Jesus really advising here? That we abolish the military, the sheriff's department, and home alarm protection devices? Is he advising anarchy? I love Jesus, but does he really want us to live in the world like that Amish community who forgave and prayed for the man who shot and killed their own little school children? Does he really want us to ignore Klansmen who occasionally peddle candy to kids in a neighborhood near where I live? "I've tried to read the Bible," said Daniel, the friendly air conditioning technician. "I really have. But I just don't understand it. It doesn't make any sense."

*

Let this parable stand in all of its oddness. Jesus did not come into the world, after all, to affirm and commend my biases. He often told stories to shake us up. Ponder three thoughts:

---

20. This may tell us something about the theological issues that Matthew's community struggled with.

1) God is judge and we are not. Ultimately, *only God* can make final and absolute judgments about people. We confess this truth in the Apostles' Creed: "He will come again to judge the living and the dead." Confessing God as final judge does not rule out common sense. It does acknowledge that deciding a person's final and absolute destiny is God's business and not our own. The message in this odd parable reveals one reason why I'm opposed to the death penalty. One might argue that executions rid the world of people like Randall Lee Smith and perhaps make the world (or at least Pearisburg, Virginia) a safer place. I hear that argument and clearly lament the nuttiness of early parole in this man's case, but executions also cut off any possibility of repentance, restitution, or change in the offender. Weedy behavior makes us angry. It's tempting to give up on a weed. Jesus says let both weeds and wheat grow together. Whether we like his words or not, he is surely offering the weed *time*; time to change.

2) "For in gathering the weeds you would uproot the wheat along with them." History is full of the truth inherent in this Bible verse. A nation can become so obsessed with global villains that a blind eye is turned towards the collateral damage of innocents who die in the wake of broad weed-whacking. On a smaller scale, I personally can become so obsessed about a certain just cause but fail to see the negative emotions of anger (and even hatred) that begin to consume me in the process of responding "righteously." Efforts to rid the world (or a community) of evil can often reveal our own worst traits. (Think Hawthorne's *The Scarlet Letter* here.) An odd mixture of good and bad seed exists even in very good people. A true "war on evil" in the world would wipe us all out.

3) It's helpful to recall that Jesus' power is most clearly revealed not in might or punishment, but in sacrificial love. He died not just for good people who've never been to jail and not just for people who worship every Sunday. Like it or not, Jesus died for all—the good, the bad, the successful, the reprobate, the kind, the villainous, the gentle, the violent, the law-abiding and the criminal. That doesn't mean he's equally *pleased* with all behaviors.

Earlier in this same Gospel, in a teaching about loving enemies, Jesus says of God: "For he makes his sun rise on the evil and on the good, and sends rain on the righteous and on the unrighteous" (Matt 5:45). Ditto with the saving death of Christ offered for a world "God so loved."[21]

---

21. The Greek word for "world" in John 3:16 is *kosmos*, which suggests a much broader divine enterprise than we can even imagine.

His cruciform grace is sown far and wide, one of the truths expressed in a parable found earlier in this same chapter as seeds are sown in various places where growth is not normally expected: on a hard path, in rocky soil, and even among thorns, a story revealing more about the reckless largesse of the seed-slinger than the foreseen success of the harvest (Matt 13:1–9). A central purpose for the existence of any church is to sow seed into places the world has given up on—even dark, weedy places; perhaps especially there. God does not give up on anybody.

For further reflection:

1. Many people in jail for extended sentences are completely cut off by family who no longer desire contact. Research how you might establish a letter-writing relationship with an inmate. Chaplains of jails and prisons are helpful resources in this regard.
2. Choose one of the three points raised towards the end of the essay and discuss the practical implications of this particular claim in your daily life.

6. Persuasive Love

". . . yet I would rather appeal to you on the basis of love."
(Phlm 1:9)

IN 1959, PHILIP ROTH (born in 1933) published one of my all-time favorite short stories, "The Conversion of the Jews." The story revolves around theological tensions between thirteen-year-old Ozzie Freedman and Rabbi Binder, his Hebrew School teacher. Ozzie embarrasses his mother (she gets phone calls at home) concerning class questions that seem to infuriate the good rabbi.

Ozzie, as a young Jew, specifically wants to know about the virgin birth espoused by Christians. Ozzie wishes to know why God, who made the world in six days with an astonishing variety of inhabitants, isn't capable of doing just about anything—including making a baby without intercourse. This question only serves to make his teacher mad; the rabbi thinks Ozzie is fishing for laughs.

One day in class this all comes to a head as the rabbi loses his temper and smacks Ozzie across the face. Shocked and embarrassed, Ozzie runs out of the classroom, climbs the stairs to the roof, and locks himself on top, threatening to jump. On the ground below, a crowd quickly gathers that includes Rabbi Binder, Ozzie's classmates, several firemen holding a large yellow net, and Mrs. Freedman, who had just shown up at the school for an appointment concerning her young son. With all eyes on the roof, Ozzie finally speaks:

"Everybody kneel." There was the sound of everybody kneeling
. . .
    As for the firemen—it is not as difficult as one might imagine to hold a net taut while you are kneeling.

Ozzie looked around again; and then he called to Rabbi Binder.

"Rabbi?"

"Yes, Oscar?"

"Rabbi Binder, do you believe in God?"

"Yes."

"Do you believe God can do Anything?" Ozzie leaned his head out into the darkness. "Anything?"

"Oscar, I think—"

"Tell me you believe God can do Anything."

There was a second's hesitation. Then: "God can do Anything."

"Tell me you believe God can make a child without intercourse."

"He can."

"Tell me!"

"God," Rabbi Binder admitted, "can make a child without intercourse."[22]

The story ends well and Ozzie jumps to safety as night is falling. But the reader is left wondering about the author's own religious sensibilities. Philip Roth, who grew up Jewish in New Jersey, may be taking a swipe both at his own rigid childhood upbringing but also the tendency of coercion and manipulation potentially present in any religion, including Christianity. Ozzie, whose own questions were deemed out of bounds, turns right around and holds his potential converts hostage from a height.

*

I want to explore in this essay the nature of conversion, specifically the role of persuasion in the Christian life. And I want to examine these rather large topics by looking at a very small letter once written by Saint Paul from jail: the book of Philemon. There's a fairly good chance that you haven't prowled around in Philemon lately, if ever. It's only a chapter long, a mere twenty-five verses; a breath of a book, easy to miss.

The main issue serving as a thread throughout this short book: Saint Paul is trying to persuade Philemon to do the right thing. Saint Paul is in jail for being Saint Paul and he befriends a slave named Onesimus, presumably on the run from Colossae for an infraction that's never named.

---

22. Roth, "The Conversion of the Jews," 112–13.

Philemon, legally, was the owner of Onesimus. (Philemon, incidentally, was a member of the church mentioned in the book of Colossians. It would be profitable to read these two letters—Colossians and Philemon—in tandem).

Paul essentially wants Philemon to take back the runaway Onesimus and treat him "no longer as a slave" (verse 16) but instead as a "beloved brother." Paul knows this will be a stretch for Philemon, part of his ongoing conversion to Christ. Observe how Paul tries to persuade his friend from a distance, from jail. Several times in the letter he tiptoes right up to the edge of strong-arm tactics and religious coercion, but then backs away artfully. He persuades but does not manipulate—mostly. He refuses to climb on the roof of moral superiority (like Ozzie Freedman), fifteen feet above contradiction.

But he comes close. Verses 8–9: "I could *command* you to do your duty, but I'd rather appeal to you on the basis of love." Paul knows that he has a certain authority over Philemon. He could probably make the guy do what he wants, but refuses that option. He does, however, pull out his AARP card, so to speak, and say, "Look, I'm an old man." This is shorthand for: respect your elders, Philemon. Do what I'm telling you.

In verse 14, Paul wants to make sure that Philemon's decision (his potential good deed) is "voluntary and not something forced." There is wisdom here. Few good deeds have lasting effect if they are coerced by a higher authority—when we are made to be good.

Finally, in verse 19, Paul just cannot help himself. "If Onesimus has wronged you, if he owes you, just charge that to my account. I'll pay you back. By the way, I won't even bring up what you owe me—your own self. Won't even mention that." Paul is like the quintessential worried parent here who finally resorts to emotional manipulation: *After all I've done for you.* Paul is not immune from pulling out the big guns of religious coercion in the ongoing conversion of Philemon. But he mostly appeals to his prayer life, the hearts of the saints, the grace of God, his partnership with Philemon in the gospel, and the ultimate triumph of love over the law.

*

Whether you're a parent, the president, a pastor, or Saint Paul himself, we all engage in the art of persuasion. I suppose there's a time for a parent to lay down the law. "I said for you take out the blasted garbage now and I mean now!" "You will too go to school this morning whether you feel like it or not!"

There used to be a leadership style for pastors—called the "Herr Pastor" model of leadership—where it was the pastor's way or the highway. "We'll be doing it this way from now on at this church and I don't care who doesn't like it!" Related, a national president occasionally needs the authority and leeway to make unilateral decisions without available time to reach consensus.

But lasting change, as Saint Paul illustrates in this old letter, does not come through the law. There can never be conversion coercion in the Christian life. Paul dances right up to the line several times with Philemon, but never quite crosses it. His appeal is based on love.

Conversion is always a process rather than a single moment in time. We are all on the way towards becoming more mature and better informed disciples. *On the way.* It's tempting for church leaders to thunder at parishioners from a height fifteen feet above contradiction. I suspect many of my own sermons sound similar to Ozzie Freedman's thundered threats from a rooftop that afternoon. One of our church council members (a local insurance agent) used to take great delight during his early morning walks in dropping off threatening religious pamphlets that he'd gathered that day at the nearby post office, just to get my reaction. The pamphlets never minced words. Failure to comply with Christ's clear commands spelled graphic and very warm consequences for the infidel.

Authentic conversion, however, is never forced. As Saint Paul illustrates with Philemon: more a pull; less a push.

For further reflection:

1. Describe a time in your past when well-meaning Christian persuasion crossed a line that felt more like a threat.
2. Try to locate a copy of Roth's short story and discuss the flaws and strong points of Rabbi Binder and Ozzie Freedman.

7. Hang on Tightly

"O Lord, how long shall I cry for help, and you will not listen?"
(Hab 1:2)

"The doctors do not know how long I have to live, but we do know the cancer has become much more aggressive than ever. In just two weeks' time, my lungs that were clear now have four lesions, and I've had to have surgery to insert a drain because so much fluid has built up, causing me to wheeze, gasp, and cough while breathing. I am paralyzed from the waist down . . . . I've had many nights in the hospital room to reflect upon life and death, and I tell you truly that I am not scared to die. I do feel a sense of guilt that I've let my body betray me, and I will cause other people sadness. My children, my parents, my husband, and my dear friends will cry, and wonder, and question their faith. I wish that I were able to make everyone feel as calm as I do." These are the words of a former parishioner and beloved state judge, Tanya, in a group letter she wrote to colleagues and friends just two days before she died in 2016 at the age of thirty-nine.

*

I sometimes get the feeling from people outside the church that people inside the church seem to have God all figured out. When I talk to my non-Christian friends they seem genuinely surprised that I, a Christian pastor, actually have doubts from time to time about God, quibbles with God about my faith life, as if being a Christian somehow means a believer is always doubt-free. Here's how one friend put it: "Gosh, I just always thought that Christians were pretty settled in their faith and that if you actually came to church you pretty much believed all of it every Sunday and that's why you were there." I told him we have a faith detector at the door that goes off with a loud buzz if you are not fervent enough.

I wonder sometimes if Christians need to be more honest and forthright about doubt and open skepticism in congregational life. I wonder if our invitational efforts sometimes fall flat because those on the outside have this inaccurate perception that we on the inside have it all figured out. How does the church convey to others that they're welcome, doubts and all?

*

The book of Habakkuk is just a little breath of a book wedged between Nahum and Zephaniah, those old family favorites. Habakkuk's name comes from the Hebrew word for "embrace" or "to hang on tightly." Early on in this short book you'll discover that the prophet comes by his name honestly. He "hangs on tightly" to God even as he rails against God. Here's a rough paraphrase of the opening argument from this old sassy God-hugger:

"Now look God, how long do you expect me to pray for help from you, and you seem to be off on vacation? Or point out all these instances of violence and you really don't seem to care? Why do you make me look at this messy world and all its problems? I'm up to my neck with contentious people, and you don't seem to give a rip."[23]

Allow me to point out two obvious truths: a) This prophetic rant is in the Holy Bible; and b) Habakkuk doesn't get killed (or even scolded) for praying this way.

Nor does he leave the faith. He hangs around complete with doubts. He hangs on tightly in spite of what he's feeling.

*

Habbakuk's tenacity reminds me of a novel by Pulitzer Prize-winning writer, Oscar Hijuelos. In his book *Mr. Ives' Christmas*, the main character undergoes an unspeakable tragedy when his young son, who plans to enter seminary, is gunned down and murdered on Christmas Day. This horrible event shakes the father's faith to the core. An every-Sunday

---

23. Compare Hab 1:1–4.

churchgoer, a man who prays daily and observes the church year with great devotion, Mr. Ives feels his faith in God slipping away. But in spite of his growing doubts and a tug to leave his church and abandon God, Ives continues to attend, continues to pray, and continues to observe the church year until his faith returns. He attends a support group in the city where he hears "hundreds of stories of heartache and tragedy, and concluded that the only way to deal with suffering was to trust in God and cling to the path of righteousness: and this he did, despite his doubts, approaching the whole notion of faith as a matter of will and discipline."[24]

Despite his doubts.

"I will keep watch to see what he will say to me, and what he will answer concerning my complaint" (Hab 2:1). Habakkuk waits on God. He waits *with* the community of faith—doubt and all. True to his name, Habakkuk hangs on tightly.

*

This old and honest exchange provides a powerful blueprint for faith in a world like ours where thirty-nine-year-olds like Tanya (and so many others) die prematurely. We bring our misgivings before God, naming them honestly in community. Our faith doesn't have to be colossal or superhuman. It can even resemble the tiny (and almost invisible) mustard seed (Mark 4:30–32). God can work with that.

"I will keep watch to see what he will say to me, and what he will answer concerning my complaint." This from a man with a boatload of doubts.

Remember the meaning of the prophet's name.

Habakkuk: *Hang on tightly.*

For further reflection:

1. How might a congregation serious about ministry with skeptics develop a known reputation in the community that a person is welcome, doubts and all?

2. Take a close look at the following verses, Gospel details after the resurrection of Jesus—Matthew 28:17, Luke 24:11, Luke 24:41, John 20:24–29. The initial response to Easter is hardly the Hallelujah

---

24. Hijuelos, *Mr. Ives' Christmas*, 173.

Chorus. Discuss the inclusion of these verses in the biblical canon when it would have been quite easy to delete them.

8. The Entitled

"I thought that for me he would surely come out . . . and would wave his hand over the spot" (2 Kgs 5:11).

IN OUR CHURCH WHEN I was a young pastor, there was a very wealthy man (now deceased) whom I'll call Rodney—a big, gregarious man known to throw around his considerable weight and influence in town circles where local power resided. Rodney was a kind man in most ways. Our children were fond of him, but he was a man used to getting his way.

Rodney had this not infrequent habit of driving up our parsonage driveway around 7:30 AM in his Cadillac and honking his horn until somebody came out to see what he wanted. This was not well-received by the occupants inside who were busily preparing to meet a school bus or the tasks of a new day. We'd hear the horn blaring and knew Rodney was outside with a message of some urgency (at least to him).

One morning I decided to wait Rodney out—just hunker down inside to see how long he would keep up the noisy summons. We were all giggling behind the window shades, shushing each other. The horn kept sounding. I lost this little battle and finally answered his tempestuous tooting. Rodney was a lovably relentless man.

*

In the book of Second Kings, Naaman the Syrian offers a fascinating character study.[25] Naaman was a decorated general in the Aramean Army, "a great man" and "a mighty warrior." I suspect the proud general's

---

25. See 2 Kgs 5:1–14.

den included numerous honors and awards tacked to the paneling. He was a regular speaker for the Aramean Rotarians and possessed a healthy military pension. But Naaman had this problem (a contagious problem). His leprosy was driving him crazy and a man used to fixing things, or getting things fixed, probably threw a variety of small fits behind closed doors. So one day, his young maid remembers something. She was from Israel (stolen on one of Naaman's military raids) and recalls a man from back home who may be able to help her boss.

So enter Elisha, my favorite character in the Old Testament. He once made an ax-head float that someone dropped into the Jordan (2 Kgs 6:1–7). Another time he instructed a couple of she-bears to maul a band of insolent boys for the impertinence of mocking his lack of hair (2 Kgs 2:23–25). Never call someone "baldy." (I have two friends in Virginia who are incorporating this story into an odd screenplay.) Elisha even once raised a boy from the dead who then proceeded to sneeze, curiously, seven straight times before opening his eyes (2 Kgs 4:32–37). Proud and powerful Naaman, miserable with his skin ailment, hears of this old prophet and thinks, "What the heck, it's worth a shot." And so the mighty general's entourage rolls up to the prophet's driveway and honks.

*

I recently received a poignant email message from a good friend on the west coast. John is used to resolving conflict. He served as head of the water and sewer system in a southern city for much of his working career and appeared on the evening news pretty often when something went haywire with line breaks or flooding. John is a patient and wise man. He does not overreact.

"Dear Frank," he wrote. "I have terminated my Facebook account because I was tired of the political postings. This election has become a blood sport. What has happened to us?"

I tell my wife (usually after the latest electronic misunderstanding) that social media is of the devil, but I'm only kidding. Mostly. Still, my friend's question is a good one. What indeed *has* become of us? We are a nation of people who often feel entitled to so many things—chiefly our historic place in line. We shout at each other a lot. Talk through and over each other. I had to turn off the debates during the last election and could make sense of neither candidate after each interrupted the other so many times. Listening has become a lost art. We want things fixed and fixed now. We desire a return to a golden age in the country that perhaps never was. We stop talking to each other; stop listening. "What has happened to us?" my friend John wanted to know.

"Dear John," I wrote back. "I'm glad you're off Facebook to be honest. Social media has indeed contributed to 'what has happened to us.' It's very easy to say and post things without the filter (and, hopefully, kindness) of face-to-face interaction. We are bombarded with invective, sometimes without our awareness. And the words of Jesus take a quick back seat."

And of course our current challenges and negative national tenor cannot be blamed entirely on technology. Entitlement is an old sin and the gift of humility our elusive cure. Sometimes when things aren't going my way, I'll turn to my wife and children and say, *"Do these people know who I am?"* I mean it to be funny. Mostly.

*

General Naaman rolls up to Elisha's front door with an impressive entourage. He's got gold and silver and new threads with him to sweeten the health care deal for the old prophet. He brings snazzy clothes for a guy who doesn't have much hanging in his closet; a man who's never seen a Land's End catalog in his life. There's a royal racket in his driveway and the prophet refuses to come out. Maybe Naaman's reputation precedes him and Elisha knows the general's real problem is not the obvious health fix of leprosy, but something much deeper.

All the hoopla quiets down, the horns stop blaring, and a messenger approaches His Royal Highness. You can almost see the storm clouds form over this proud man's brow. *Go wash. Go wash seven times in that old river over yonder.*

And proud Naaman hits the roof. Smoke comes out of his ears. His brain has a meltdown. The general says, "I thought that for me—for me, of all people—that the little medicine man might come out and just wave his hand over the spot and cure me *on* the spot. *Does he know who I am?*"

By this point in the story, it's become clear that Naaman's real problem is not leprosy. His real problem is entitlement. Entitlement, in spades.

Sometimes, when I've made a boneheaded mistake, or when things just don't make sense, God gives me the good sense to head into the woods alone.

There's a trail I like to take that heads away from nearby Highway 107 and slowly descends to a campsite on a small peninsula of land that's surrounded by a steady stream. I listen to the water gurgling. I sit in a small clearing and recall youthful voices from past hiking trips. And I'll pray in the silence—prayers of confession, prayers for guidance; prayers for meaning in someone's suffering.

This time alone never fails to bring perspective and a reminder that none of us is here for very long—that others preceded us and others will follow. I head back to the car beside the same stream, listening for the water sounds. At some point, halfway back, the sounds stop and the water disappears into a bank, underground and unseen.

And I wonder: where does grace come from? And where does it go? And another voice from the font of all new beginnings, even beyond time and space, issues the invitation newly for me:

Go wash and be clean. Go wash in that old river and be healed.

"The Word of God is not chained," says Saint Paul to a young pastor (2 Tim 2:9). The Word of God is loose in the world, quieting the loud horns that distract, splitting open stone and leading people like me, often full of pride and bluster, to the healing waters of grace.

For further reflection:

1. Honestly name a few things to which you've felt entitled in the past because of family lineage, education, or national origin.

2. How does the sacrament of baptism bring new perspective to our sense of Naaman-like entitlement?

9. Night Nemesis

". . . and Jacob's hip was put out of joint as he wrestled with him"
(Gen 32:25).

I HAVE A FRIEND named Andy who was once on a long bus trip. He took the last remaining seat in the back of the Greyhound next to a talkative man, just released from prison, who happened to have a glass eye. Andy was dog tired from a long backpacking trip and wanted to sleep and get home. He was worn out from the trail, but the man talked and talked. He showed Andy photos and talked about his girlfriend and his voice was so animated that Andy began to wonder if drugs were involved. There were two young women seated in front of them, and the man with the glass eye talked their ears off too.

At one point the man next to Andy took the glass eye out of his head, put it between his thumb and index finger, leaned over the seat, and said to the women in a high voice, "I can see you! I can see you!" The bus driver stopped the bus and threatened to throw both men off, the guilty and the innocent.

*

The story of Jacob grappling by a river (Gen 32:22–32) is one of the all-time great Old Testament stories. I liked it as a boy because of the wrestling match. My brothers and I wrestled all the time. We almost broke the coffee table once and I recall my mother just pushing us all out the back door in a tightly bundled sibling troika, thrashing on the lawn in an explosion of bravado and hormones.

There's a small detail that's important in the story that needs some context and amplification. Here are the first six words of verse 22: *"The same night Jacob got up . . . ."* Something is bothering Jacob. He'd gone to bed with his family; then he got up. Sometimes this happens when I go to bed with a problem on my mind that's not easily solved. I toss and turn and finally give in to the anxiety and get up and read.

Jacob was an anxious man that night so long ago. It's been twenty years since he's seen his brother Esau; these two did not part on the best of terms. Jacob's name in Hebrew means "cheater" and he came by the name honestly. He cheated his brother out of birthright and blessing. Jacob and his mom came up with a harebrained idea involving hair and they duped a poor old blind man into mixing up the identity of his sons. Esau was ticked. I could use other words. He was hot about the trickery, threatening his brother, so Jacob hightails it into the hills.[26] Twenty years pass.

Perhaps you're thinking of someone with whom you've had a long falling out; something so intense that you didn't speak to the person for twenty years. Two decades have passed and Jacob hears that Esau is heading his way with 400 men. Jacob is exposed and afraid. It's like Esau's all-seeing eye saying, "I can see you! Oh yes, I can see you, brother, *and I'm comin' to get you.*"

In response to this anxiety, Jacob prays one of the most honest foxhole prayers in the Bible: "I am not worthy of the least of your steadfast love, O Lord. [Jacob probably had that right, by the way.] Deliver me, please, from the hand of my brother, from the hand of Esau, for I am afraid of him; he may come and kill us all, the mothers with the children" (Gen 32:10–11).

Thinking this might butter up his approaching brother, Jacob sends Esau a small gift of goats and camels and horses and cows and donkeys—540 animals[27] in all (I c/ounted.) Jacob the Cheater "express mails" a small token from the Heifer Project and wraps it with a nice bow hoping twenty years of enmity will lessen with livestock. The 540 are galloping towards the approaching 400 while Jacob beds down for the night with his family beside the River Jabbok. Gurgling sounds waft over his sleeping bag. But Jacob cannot sleep. And you know why he can't. Jacob is exposed out there. Esau can see him. "I can see you." And so can

---

26. See Gen 27:30–45.
27. See Gen 32:13–15.

God. "Reunions," someone once said, "are the bread and butter for most working therapists."

*

The Bible has staying power over the millennia not because it describes valorous people who have summoned their very best behavior to overcome life's obstacles in admirable ways. Not even close. Saint Paul once wrote to Timothy, a young pastor, about the nature of Scripture. Timothy (maybe in his youthful naïveté) was shocked about the bad behavior people were capable of in his congregation. So Paul writes to his young protégé: "All scripture is inspired by God and is useful for teaching, for reproof, for correction, and for training in righteousness" (2 Tim 3:16). Not that anyone reading this book needs reproving or correcting or even training, right? *Certainly not me.*

But of course that's exactly it for all of us, including pastors, including Paul and Timothy. The Bible is our book not because it tells the story of perfect people and how you better become one or else. The Bible is our book because it tells the story of how God looks at the world and sees a mess and chooses to love us in spite of such. The Bible is our book because we see the details of our fallen lives all over its pages and God works with us anyway.

It's okay to believe that the garden of Eden, for example, was a specific place with a certain starring cast. I would never try to argue anybody out of that. But look closer. Look closer and you'll see your own backyard and a broil of brotherly (or sisterly) mayhem in a tangled wrestling mess. Look hard and you'll find your own flawed history in the pages of Genesis, where wrestling matches that you somehow need to win have gotten out of hand. See yourself there? Now see a God who loves you, searches for you, in spite of all that. Again from Paul to Timothy: "From childhood you have known the sacred writings that are able to instruct you for salvation" (2 Tim 3:15). These are very old stories. We love them because we see ourselves in them. And God sees us. "I see you," he says.

So Jacob tries to sleep beside the river, but can't. He's so discombobulated and worried that he rouses the whole family and sends them across the stream with "everything he had." At night. With no flashlight.

In 1980, when I was heading south through Maine on the Appalachian Trail, there was a long and rather dangerous ford of the Kennebec River. The river (in spots) was posterior high, with the danger of even higher water when the spillway from a dam opened upstream. After several accidents, the Forest Service now ferries hikers over for free in a canoe. I doubt Jacob had access to a boat, and maybe the Jabbok was relatively shallow where he crossed, but my heavens. Can you imagine awakening fifteen groggy people (I counted) and leading them, little sleepy kids, across slippery river stones, on a moonless night let's say, with their sleeping bags and Gummy Bears? Jacob was a worried delirious nut case. *"I can see you. I can see you, Jacob."*

It's not really clear who jumps out of the shadows that night and grabs Jacob. The pronouns and wrestlers are all jumbled in a delightful stew of ambiguity. Verse 24 reports that "a man" wrestles with Jacob. Later we're told Jacob sweated "with God *and* with humans." Some scholars even suggest Esau jumped into the ring that night.

But isn't that the way of it? Our human conflicts with other people eventually involve God. Perhaps conflicts continue for twenty years when we leave God out of it. Jacob was in a deep unwieldy mess. Years before, he dreamed on a stone pillow about a ladder of angels (Gen 28:10–17). A messy life, fitful sleep, strange dreams. Been there?

"Jacob's hip was put out of joint as he wrestled with him." Jacob would limp for the rest of his life as a result of this encounter. Perhaps life leaves us all with a limp. However painful, we sometimes must revisit and *go through* the past rather than pretend it never happened. Jacob had been on the run long enough. It's an intense struggle out there beside the river, but God seems to be saying, "Okay, Jacob. I see you. I really and truly see you. You've been running long enough. Let's wrestle this thing out."

Maybe the cure for insomnia is a divine night nemesis, one who loves us enough to confront and restore. Sometimes the best we can do is limp up to the table for the bread and wine. The sun rises on Jacob the next morning. I get the feeling he was glad the twenty-year ordeal was finally all over. Glad that someone loved him that much, never letting go.

For further reflection:

1. The Genesis river context (like all rivers in the Bible) has shaped the sacramental imagination of many a preacher since the early centuries of the church. How does the church's theology of baptism find intersection with this old story?

2. Sometimes reconciliation takes a long time. Find a trusted friend who is able to listen to a conflict-story that's involved you and another person. Pray about this conflict and the possibility of reconciliation, even after years of estrangement.

10. Man in the Middle

". . . they crucified Jesus there with the criminals, one on his right and one on his left" (Luke 23:33)

THE CHURCH YEAR CONCLUDES with "Christ the King" Sunday, a festival that serves both as a calendar bridge and a theological fulcrum between what's come before in the Easter and Pentecost cycles and what's up ahead in Advent with the beginning of a new church year. The Christian story has come full circle and begins again, drawing followers of Jesus ever more deeply into the challenges and joys of discipleship. The following essay is based upon a sermon for the last Sunday of the church year that was also the last sermon of my pastoral career.

*

One of my favorite magazine articles[28] from 2016 comes from the pen of Andrew Sullivan, one of our best American essayists, who describes an extended stay at a retreat center where he learned to meditate and observe periods of silence. He says this saved his life. On Day One of the retreat, the leader collected all the phones. She "held a basket in front of her, beaming like a priest with a collection plate. I duly surrendered my little device, only to feel a sudden pang of panic on my way back to my seat. If it hadn't been for everyone staring at me, I might have turned around and immediately asked for it back. But I didn't. I knew why I'd come here."

28. Sullivan, "I Used to Be a Human Being."

His work was killing him. Sullivan says he'd become an addict to the avalanche of information. "[I was] publishing blog posts multiple times a day, seven days a week, and ultimately corralling a team that curated the web every 20 minutes during peak hours."

Sullivan's story may sound extreme, but this part of the article really struck me: "Just look around you," he invites. "Look at the people crouched over their phones as they walk the streets, or drive their cars, or walk their dogs, or play with their children. Observe yourself in line for coffee, or in a quick work break, or even just going to the bathroom. Visit an airport and see the sea of craned necks and dead eyes. We have gone from looking up and around to constantly looking down."

The psalmist once offered a piece of advice that's as famous as any counsel found in the entire Old Testament: *"Be still, then, and know that I am God"* (Ps 46:10). If we learned how to do that—how to become still and discover why it's important—I'm convinced that many problems facing the nation and our churches would find quick perspective and solution. Someone has said that the greatest challenge to faith today is not hedonism, but rather distraction. I've worked as a pastor for thirty-one years. And I've met a fair number of frazzled and distracted and fearful people, including myself at times. Learning how to "be still" and "know God" is not some magic formula that inoculates us somehow from worry and suffering. Instead, the stillness and the knowing teach us (over time) how to cope with (and even make sense of) the suffering; and how to accompany others in theirs.

*

A student once dropped by the office of the chaplain at Duke University to complain about his roommate, who happened to be Muslim. "Well, when we moved into together, he asked me what my religion was. I told him I was sort of Christian. A Lutheran. I told him up front that my family only went to church occasionally, and it wasn't a big deal to me. But my roommate has this nasty habit of asking embarrassing questions."

"What sort of questions?" asked the chaplain. "Like after we had roomed together a few weeks, he asked me: 'Why do you Christians never pray?' I told him, 'We pray all the time, we just sort of keep it to ourselves.' This guy, my roommate, prays, like, half a dozen times a day on his prayer rug in our room. The last straw was Saturday morning, when I came in from a date, and he asked me, 'Doesn't your Saint Paul say something about not joining your body with a prostitute?'"

"I told him, 'Look, she is not a prostitute! *She's a Tri-Delt*. I told you I'm not the best Christian in the world. You shouldn't judge the Christian faith by me!'"

To which the chaplain, God bless him, responded: "Well, how should he judge the Christian faith? I ought to write your Muslim roommate a thank-you note. If that Muslim keeps working on you, he may yet make you into a Christian."[29]

*

"We have gone from looking up and around to constantly looking down," says Andrew Sullivan. *Be still*. Old advice: quiet the noise. Christian maturity involves the ear, but also the eye. Where do we look to find health as Christians? What commands the gaze?

In Luke's version of the story, Jesus hangs on a cross at a place called "The Skull" and three sets of people take turns mocking him (Luke 23:33–43). They tack a funny sign over his head with a title, "King of the Jews." But if somebody had replaced the sign with another saying "Loser," I'm sure there would have been no objections.

The mockery heard by Jesus comes from different angles, but the gist of the humiliation is very similar from all three perspectives. The religious leaders say, "He saved others; let him save himself!" The soldiers chide, "If you are the King of the Jews, save yourself! Show us a bit of pizzazz." A crucified criminal mocks, "Aren't you the Messiah? Save yourself and us!" It's a familiar theme: Save me. Save my family. Protect us. Erect a fence of protection around everything I love.

Save yourself. Well, why not? He fed 5,000 people with a few fish and some scraps of bread. He walked on water, even turned it into wine. He healed a blind man with a bit of mud and a promise. He even raised a family friend from the dead! Why did Jesus *just hang there* and allow it to happen? Why didn't he *do* something? Why didn't he show those smarties a thing or two? "Smite them, O God, as you did your enemies of old." That's the prayer I might have prayed. Instead we get this nutty prayer: "Father, forgive them; for they don't know what they're doing." What sort

---

29. Adapted from Willimon, "Arguing with Muslims," 34.

of prayer is that? "Save yourself," say all three. "Show us your power." Why *didn't* he show them?

And the weird, paradoxical truth of our faith (if we look up long enough) is that he has. The cross is not some bizarre legal exchange between God and humans involving a good man. The cross becomes the very shape of the Christian life. We are baptized into this sacrificial life.

"Come down, loser. Show us some *real* power." But one man does look. He senses the mysterious paradox in the death of this innocent man who "has done nothing wrong." He looks at Jesus hanging there—powerless, humiliated; silent before his tormentors. And maybe that man with a shady past looked a long time that long afternoon, glancing sideways. And he saw something in Jesus that the others did not. "Remember me," he said. "Remember me." He did not say, "Save me." He did not say, "Get me out of this, will ya?" He just said he wanted to be remembered. It's interesting. That's what Jesus asks of us, too. To remember him. "Do this in *remembrance* of me. Look at my body, my blood, and do not turn away."

I recently had a very strange dream where my wife, Cindy, says I grabbed her and woke her up. I was on this football field somewhere wearing a helmet that resembled those worn by the players at the University of Georgia—the helmets with the big letter "G" on the side. Many people in our church were also in the dream. Same helmets. I couldn't tell who we were playing that day, but somebody fumbled. Loose ball. It bounced all around but came right towards me and I so much wanted to recover the ball. It was right there and I tried to grab it. And then I woke up. I had grabbed Cindy.

I'm not at all sure what this dream means, but I've been thinking about that fumble and that letter "G." And maybe the "G" is not for Georgia at all. Maybe it means that we're all on *God's* team and that searching for meaning in Christ can be as intense and invigoratingly strange as going after a loose football. We want it. We want it more than anything by placing this odd "man in the middle" in the very middle of our lives. The middle of our marriages. The middle of our jobs. The middle of our politics, our future. The middle of everything.

Many years ago, at a place called "The Skull," loud voices rang out. "Come down from the cross. Are you not the Christ? Show us then! *Save yourself and us!*"

By staying there, he has.

Be still, look. Live.

For further reflection:

1. In the bibliography of this book is a link to Andrew Sullivan's essay. It's long, but well worth your time. Read this essay and talk about the implications it may have for life in your congregation.
2. How might you incorporate the advice of Psalm 46:10 into your daily life?

Bibliography

Albom, Mitch. *Tuesdays with Morrie: An Old Man, a Young Man, and Life's Greatest Lesson.* New York: Doubleday, 1997.
Basch, Rachel. *The Passion of Reverend Nash.* New York: W. W. Norton, 2003.
Clapp, Rodney. *A Peculiar People: The Church as Culture in a Post-Christian Society.* Downers Grove, IL: InterVarsity, 1996.
Covington, Dennis. *Salvation on Sand Mountain: Snake Handling and Redemption in Southern Appalachia.* New York: Addison-Wesley, 1995.
Gallagher, Nora. *Things Seen and Unseen: A Year Lived in Faith.* New York: Alfred A. Knopf, 1998.
Gillespie, Emory. "Emergency and Rescue." *The Christian Century* website, November 26, 2012.
Guterson, David. *Our Lady of the Forest.* New York: Alfred A. Knopf, 2003.
Haygood, Wil. "Blood on the Mountain." *The Washington Post,* July 8, 2008.
Heschel, Abraham Joshua. *The Sabbath: Its Meaning for Modern Man.* New York: Farrar, Straus and Giroux, 1951.
Hijuelos, Oscar. *Mr. Ives' Christmas.* New York: Harper Collins, 1995.
Honeycutt, Frank G. "Herod's Fear." *The Lutheran,* January 2009, 32–33.
———. "Keeping Watch." *Living Lutheran,* December 2016, 32–34.
———. "A Life Laid Down." *The Lutheran,* February 2016, 28–29.
———. *Sanctified Living: More than Grace and Forgiveness.* Minneapolis: Augsburg Fortress, 2008.
———. "Step by Step." *Journal for Preachers,* Pentecost 2012, 58–60.
———. "Upstairs and Down." *Journal for Preachers,* Lent 2012, 42–43.
Hooper, Patricia. "Where I Was." *Image: A Journal of the Arts and Religion,* Winter 2000, 70–71.
Horwitz, Tony. *Confederates in the Attic: Dispatches from the Unfinished Civil War.* New York: Vintage, 1998.
Johnson, Maxwell E. *The Rites of Christian Initiation: Their Evolution and Interpretation.* Collegeville, MN: Liturgical, 1999.
Kaminer, Wendy. *Sleeping with Extra-Terrestrials: The Rise of Irrationalism and Perils of Piety.* New York: Pantheon, 1999.
Kierkegaard, Søren. *Meditations.* Philadelphia: Westminster, 1955.
Levenson, Jon. "The Devil in the Details." *Commentary,* September 1, 1995, 54–56.
Lewis, C. S. *The Lion, the Witch and the Wardrobe.* New York: Collier, 1950.

Lischer, Richard. *Stations of the Heart: Parting with a Son*. New York: Alfred A. Knopf, 2013.
Malone, Michael. *Handling Sin*. New York: Pocket Books, 1986.
Marty, Peter W. "Holding Steady: The Nonanxious Pastor." *The Christian Century*, April 5, 2003, 9.
Merton, Thomas. *Opening the Bible*. Philadelphia: Fortress, 1970.
Norris, Kathleen. *The Cloister Walk*. New York: Riverhead, 1996.
Peters, Ted. *Sin: Radical Evil in Soul and Society*. Grand Rapids: Eerdmans, 1994.
Peterson, Eugene. *Working the Angles: The Shape of Pastoral Integrity*. Grand Rapids: Eerdmans, 1989.
Postman, Neil. *Amusing Ourselves to Death: Public Discourse in the Age of Show Business*. New York: Penguin, 1985.
Roth, Philip. "The Conversion of the Jews." In *Goodbye, Columbus*, 100–114. New York: Bantam, 1959.
Scheeres, Julia. *A Thousand Lives: The Untold Story of Hope, Deception and Survival at Jonestown*. New York: Free Press, 2011.
Spufford, Francis. *Unapologetic: Why, Despite Everything, Christianity Can Still Make Surprising Emotional Sense*. New York: Harper Collins, 2013.
Srigley, Susan. *Flannery O'Connor's Sacramental Art*. Notre Dame, IN: University of Notre Dame Press, 2005.
Sullivan, Andrew. "I Used to Be a Human Being." *New York Magazine*, September 18, 2016. nymag.com/selectall/2016/09/andrew-sullivan-technology-almost-killed-me.html.
Taylor, Barbara Brown. *Home By Another Way*. Boston: Cowley, 1999.
———. *Speaking of Sin: The Lost Language of Salvation*. Boston: Cowley, 2000.
Tomkins, Stephen. *A Short History of Christianity*. Grand Rapids: Eerdmans, 2005.
Wesley, John. *The Works of John Wesley, Volume VI*. Grand Rapids: Zondervan, 1872.
White, E. B. *Charlotte's Web*. New York: Harper and Row, 1952.
Willard, Dallas. *The Divine Conspiracy: Rediscovering Our Hidden Life in God*. San Francisco: Harper SanFrancisco, 1998.
———. *The Great Omission: Reclaiming Jesus' Essential Teachings on Discipleship*. San Francisco: Harper Collins, 2006.
Willimon, William H. "Arguing with Muslims: God-Talk on Campus." *The Christian Century*, November 16, 2004, 34–35.
———. "Postmodern Preaching: Learning to Love the Thickness of the Text." In *Exilic Preaching: Testimony for Christian Exiles in an Increasingly Hostile Culture*, edited by Erskine Clarke, 108–16. Valley Forge, PA: Trinity Press International, 1998.
Yancey, Philip. *Reaching for the Invisible God: What Can We Expect to Find?* Grand Rapids: Zondervan, 2000.

www.ingramcontent.com/pod-product-compliance
Lightning Source LLC
Chambersburg PA
CBHW031809220426
43662CB00007B/580